T

W9-ATI-826

# The RENAISSANCE

## AN ENCYCLOPEDIA FOR STUDENTS

# *The* RENAISSANCE
## AN ENCYCLOPEDIA FOR STUDENTS

Paul F. Grendler, Editor in Chief

PUBLISHED IN ASSOCIATION WITH THE RENAISSANCE SOCIETY OF AMERICA

## *Volume* 2
### DAILY LIFE—JULIUS II

CHARLES SCRIBNER'S SONS®

THOMSON

™

GALE

New York • Detroit • San Diego • San Francisco • Cleveland • New Haven, Conn. • Waterville, Maine • London • Munich

## The Renaissance An Encyclopedia for Students

**Paul F. Grendler, Editor in Chief**
Copyright © 2004 Charles Scribner's Sons.
Developed for Charles Scribner's Sons by
Visual Education Corporation, Princeton, N.J.
*For Scribners*

PUBLISHER:
Frank Menchaca

EDITORS:
John Fitzpatrick, Sharon Malinowski

COVER AND INTERIOR DESIGN:
Jennifer Wahi

IMAGING AND MULTIMEDIA:
Lezlie Light, Robyn Young, Mary Grimes, Dave
Oblender, Leitha Etheridge-Sims, Dan Newell,
Christine O'Bryan

COMPOSITION:
Evi Seoud

MANUFACTURING:
Rhonda Williams

*For Visual Education Corporation*

PROJECT DIRECTORS:
Darryl Kestler, Amy Livingston

WRITERS:
John Haley, Mark Mussari, Charles Roebuck,
Rebecca Stefoff

EDITORS:
Tobey Cloyd, Cindy George, John Kennedy

ASSOCIATE EDITOR:
Sarah Miller

COPYEDITING SUPERVISOR:
Helen Castro

ELECTRONIC PREPARATION:
Fiona Shapiro

For more information, contact
Charles Scribner's Sons
300 Park Avenue South
New York, NY 10010
Or visit our Internet site at
http://www.gale.com/scribners

Since this page cannot legibly accommodate
all copyright notices, the acknowledgments
constitute an extension of the copyright
notice.

For permission to use material from this
product, submit your request via Web at
http://www.gale-edit.com/permissions, or you
may download our Permissions Request form
and submit your request by fax or mail to:

*Permissions Department*
The Gale Group, Inc.
27500 Drake Rd.
Farmington Hills, MI 48331-3535
Permissions Hotline:
248-699-8006 or 800-762-4058

**LIBRARY OF CONGRESS CATALOG-IN-PUBLICATION DATA**

The Renaissance : an encyclopedia for students / Paul F. Grendler.
    p. cm
        Summary: An encyclopedia of the Renaissance with articles on various
    aspects of social, cultural, and political history such as literature, gov-
    ernment, warfare, and technology, plus maps, charts, definitions, and
    chronology.
    Includes bibliographical references and index.
    ISBN 0-684-31281-6 (set hardcover : alk. paper) — ISBN 0-684-31282-4
    (v. 1) — ISBN 0-684-31283-2 (v. 2) — ISBN
    0-684-31284-0 (v. 4) — ISBN 0-684-31424-X (e-book)
    1. Renaissance—Encyclopedias, Juvenile. [1. Renaissance—
    Encyclopedias.] I. Grendler, Paul F. II. Encyclopedia of the Renaissance.
    III. Title.

CB361.R25 2003
940.2'1'03—dc22

This title is also available as an e-book
ISBN 0-684-31424-X (set)

Contact your Gale sale representative for ordering information

Printed in the United States of America
10 9 8 7 6 5 4 3 2 1

# \text{Table of Contents} Table of Contents

**VOLUME 1**

Academies—Cromwell

**VOLUME 2**

Daily Life—Julius II

**VOLUME 3**

Kepler—Princes and Princedoms

**VOLUME 4**

Printing and Publishing—Writing

## Maps

# Genealogical Charts

# Color Plates

The patterns of daily life varied as much during the Renaissance as they do today. A noblewoman in an Italian city, for example, spent her time very differently from a peasant in England. Forces such as class, geography, and gender played a major role in shaping Europeans' daily lives. They affected the food people ate, the clothing they wore, the houses they lived in, and the education they received.

**Geography.** Life in northern Europe fell into different patterns from life in the Mediterranean region. The fertile plains and forests of northern Europe had mild summers and long, rainy or snowy winters. The Mediterranean region was drier and more mountainous, with hot, dry summers and rainy winters. These differences in climate and landscape affected the crops and livestock that people could raise, as well as the foods they ate and the housing they required.

See color plate 1, vol. 2

The Mediterranean region was also a major center of trade and shipping with many major cities. The rest of Europe, by contrast, was thinly populated except for a few urban centers in Germany and the Netherlands. Rural and urban areas developed distinct lifestyles.

**Gender and Class.** Gender and social class affected many aspects of daily life. In general, women had less freedom and independence than men. Upper-class women tended to stay at home, or, if they were members of a royal household, at the COURT. They spent much of their time supervising their household staff and overseeing their children's education. They left home only to visit the market or to attend religious or civic events, and only in the company of others.

See color plate 3, vol. 2

Men of the noble classes spent their time at court or managing their estates. During wartime, military campaigns often kept them away from home for long periods. Those who lived in cities and towns, especially in Italy, sometimes engaged in business activities. Upper-class men also dominated politics and public affairs. However, as Renaissance monarchs and princes centralized their hold over their territories, noblemen had fewer opportunities to have a real impact in politics. In the countryside, men participated in local affairs through village or church councils.

See color plate 2, vol. 2

Middle- and lower-class individuals spent much of their time working. The middle class contained people of various professions, including lawyers, doctors, merchants, artisans*, and shopkeepers. Women played roles in some of these occupations, such as tending shops or performing craft work like sewing and weaving. However, their main responsibilities were caring for the home and children. The poor often worked as farm laborers or as servants, jobs common to both men and women.

* **artisan**   skilled worker or craftsperson

**Households.** Housing improved slowly but steadily during the Renaissance. In the countryside, members of the upper classes lived in wooden or stone castles or manor houses, furnished with comfortable beds, tables, and chairs. Beginning in the 1400s, stone became more common as a building material, and architects remodeled many medieval* structures in new Renaissance styles.

* **medieval**   referring to the Middle Ages, a period that began around A.D. 400 and ended around 1400 in Italy and 1500 in the rest of Europe

Members of the lower classes spent most of their time working. Many of them served as farm laborers, like those shown here in the painting *Autumn—the Grape Harvest.*

Most peasants lived in houses made of wood or earth, with thatched roofs. Dirt floors were common before the development of inexpensive tile flooring, which made a major improvement in the quality of lower-class homes. People used screens to divide rooms or to separate their living space from the areas where they kept their livestock. Fleas and other insects were probably common. Poor families had simple furniture, such as straw mattresses and a few chairs or a table made from barrel halves.

Lifestyles also differed sharply between the rich and the poor in Renaissance cities. Wealthy urban families lived in elegant and com-

fortable homes and dined on varied and elaborately prepared foods. Italy led the way in establishing a high standard of living for the rich. The Italians were the first to build stone houses and to replace metal plates with beautiful ceramic dishes. They also developed refined styles of cooking and polite table manners. After about 1550 these trends spread to France.

The urban poor generally lived in dreadful conditions. Most lower-class people rented crowded, dark rooms on the upper floors of city buildings. They had few household goods and suffered from infestations of fleas and lice. In Venice the very poor lived in small boats near the docks or under the bridges that cross the canals.

**Private Life.** During the Middle Ages, few distinctions separated public and private life. In general, people thought of themselves and others as members of groups, such as families, villages, churches, and GUILDS*, rather than as individuals. However, during the Renaissance new concepts of private life and individuality emerged. The rise of trade contributed to prosperity, giving some individuals the means and the desire to distinguish themselves from others. At the same time, the general level of education and literacy* rose. More people spent time alone reading and studying. Changes in religious attitudes also encouraged people to focus on solitary prayer and reflection. These factors led to the ideas of individuality and privacy that have become part of modern life. (*See also* **Artisans; Châteaus and Villas; Clothing; Economy and Trade; Family and Kinship; Food and Drink; Literacy; Peasantry; Poverty and Charity; Social Status; Women.**)

* **guild**  association of craft and trade owners and workers that set standards for and represented the interests of its members

* **literacy**  ability to read

---

## Dance

* **aristocracy**  privileged upper classes of society; nobles or the nobility

* **choreograph**  to arrange, direct, or stage the movements of dancers

See color plate 7, vol. 2

Although dance has been part of human culture since ancient times, it took on new importance during the Renaissance. Dancing became an important skill for members of both the aristocracy* and the middle classes. Beginning in the early 1400s, books began to record dance steps in print. As publishing became more available, books featuring dances from different countries spread throughout Europe.

**Dance and Society.** Members of the upper and middle classes considered dance an essential social grace, as well as a useful form of physical training. Many of them employed professional dance masters to teach them dance, music, and martial arts such as fencing. These professionals also performed and choreographed* set dances. The invention of printing helped promote the skills of dance masters by spreading dances and the names of their creators throughout Europe. Among the lower classes, most people continued to learn dances by watching and memorizing them. As a result, few written descriptions of their dances survive, although pictures from the period illustrate them.

Many types of social occasions involved dancing. It was the main event at balls and played a significant part in weddings as well. At court, ladies and gentlemen staged dance performances in honor of royal visitors. Such occasions might also include solo performances from dance

Few written records exist of the dances of the lower classes. Most modern knowledge about them comes from pictures such as *The Indoor Wedding Dance,* by Pieter Brueghal the Younger.

* **classical**  in the tradition of ancient Greece and Rome

masters, often featuring mime routines or mock combat. In noble households, most dancing took place after dinner. Household musicians provided the music, although family members or guests might also sing and play instruments.

Dance masters of the 1500s glorified their art form, using classical* references to describe its virtues. During this period dance began to play a role in grand theatrical events such as the English masque and the Italian *mascherata* and *intermedio.* A masque was a series of poems, songs, and dances loosely tied together by a story line, often performed as part of wedding celebrations. The *mascherata,* a formal parade in costume, formed part of the entertainment at state visits. The *intermedio* was a five-act play with music and dance performed between acts, ending with an elaborate dance.

**Types of Dances.** During the 1400s most dances involved long lines of two or three dancers. The most popular French dance was the Burgundian basse dance, which had five basic steps organized into patterns. An Italian dance called the *ballo* had four basic steps, which could also be performed on their own. Italian dances were more complex than French dances and emphasized proportion and order, causing people to compare them to other art forms such as architecture.

In the 1500s dances became more elaborate, with new dances created for multiple couples, single-sex groups, large masses of people, and solo dancers. Notes on the dances of many nations began to appear in print, enabling them to spread across Europe. For example, a French dance called the *branle* (pronounced "brawl" in England) became popular throughout Europe in the 1500s and early 1600s. In the simplest form of this dance, the single *branle,* a group of dancers formed lines or a circle and performed a series of variations on a basic step pattern. A

*branle couppé* added other gestures, such as pawing at the floor for the "horse" *branle.*

The most complex dances of the 1500s were Italian dances such as the *balletto* and *brando.* The *balletto,* performed by two to four individuals, combined at least two different dance types, with at least one change of rhythm and tempo. The French queen CATHERINE DE MÉDICIS helped import this dance form to France, where it eventually developed into ballet. The complex *brando,* often used to end major theater productions, included at least four dance types and several changes of tempo.

Little information survives about Spanish dances of the Renaissance. Most of the material available appears in books printed outside of Spain. The few known sources from Spain do not describe the steps or the accompanying music. English sources are more plentiful, but even less informative. In many cases they simply advise the reader to learn the dance from someone who knows it. However, these sources list the names of many popular dances, including the *pavane,* the *gagliard,* and many dances from other countries. Literary works, such as the poetry and plays of SHAKESPEARE, also contain many references to dancing. (*See also* **Court; Drama; Music, Instrumental.**)

Death

Beginning in the 1300s, European men and women became increasingly fascinated with death. The waves of bubonic PLAGUE and other life-threatening diseases that swept across the continent killed large numbers of people, reminding the survivors that life was fragile. The growing awareness that death might strike at any time led Europeans to develop new funeral customs and methods of preparing for death.

**Causes of Death.** Bubonic plague was the single greatest killer in Renaissance Europe. The first severe outbreak ravaged the region in the 1340s, killing between one-third and one-half of the population in some areas. The plague reappeared in 1363 and then returned every 10 to 12 years until 1661, with some outbreaks more deadly than others. Diseases such as tuberculosis and syphilis also claimed many lives. Children under age two had an extremely high death rate due to various illnesses. Once children survived their early years, however, they had a reasonable chance of reaching adulthood.

Disease was not the only cause of death in the Renaissance. Men died in accidents while traveling or farming, and many women died in childbirth. Infants and young children were sometimes abandoned or even murdered by parents who could not afford to support them. Child killing, or infanticide, became more common during times of economic hardship. Italian legal records show that twice as many baby girls as boys were abandoned or killed. Parents valued girls less because they earned lower wages than boys and because it cost their families money to supply dowries* when they married.

**\* dowry**  money or property that a woman brings to her marriage

**Attitudes Toward Death.** Renaissance Europeans maintained a complete set of views about death. In the 1400s literary works called *ars*

*moriendi* ("art of dying"), which told readers how a good Christian should approach death, became popular. The texts stressed that Christians should welcome death, rather than fear it, and that they should view life as preparation for the afterlife.

The *ars moriendi* emphasized the importance of making a "good death." They advised dying Christians to confess their sins to a priest and to forgive their family and friends, as they gathered around the deathbed, for any wrongs they had done. A good death also involved disposing wisely of possessions, often through donations to charity. Anyone could fall ill suddenly, but accepting and even planning for death was a way of controlling its unpredictability.

People of the Renaissance lived with images of death. The Dutch humanist* Desiderius ERASMUS, for example, kept a human skull on his desk as a reminder of the shortness of life. In France, Holland, and other parts of northern Europe, artists developed a variety of grim, fantastic images of death that expressed both fear and fascination. Scenes portraying the "dance of death" featured prancing skeletons, and some tomb sculptures showed the deceased lying on top of a decaying corpse. Such images reinforced the ideas that death triumphs over everyone and that the body is less enduring than the soul.

**Funerals and Wills.** Funeral rituals developed in two different directions between 1300 and 1600. In some Catholic areas of Europe, funerals became more formal and elaborate. People spent increasing sums on funeral processions, burial outfits, hired mourners, and mourning clothes. In other areas, by contrast, funerals grew simpler and more subdued. Some Renaissance thinkers—drawing on the ideas of ancient philosophers called the Stoics—urged mourners to show self-control and limit their displays of grief. This tendency was strongest in Protestant countries, where preachers advised people to hold simple ceremonies that focused on the afterlife rather than on worldly trappings.

One aspect of the "good death" was arranging to pass one's property on to others. Most Europeans died without leaving a will, the legal document that contains instructions about funeral arrangements and inheritance. In such cases, custom generally called for burial in the local churchyard or cemetery and distribution of property to close relatives. Some people, however, left specific instructions regarding their deaths. From the thousands of wills that survive it appears that, over the course of the Renaissance, people left increasing sums of money to pay for tombs or church services dedicated to their memory. (*See also* **Hospitals and Asylums; Religious Thought; Sickness and Disease.**)

* **humanist** Renaissance expert in the humanities (the languages, literature, history, and speech and writing techniques of ancient Greece and Rome)

## Decorative Arts

The term *decorative arts* refers to works of art that do not fall readily into the categories of painting, sculpture, and architecture. During the Renaissance, such objects were greatly valued because of the high level of skill and costly materials involved in making them. Items such

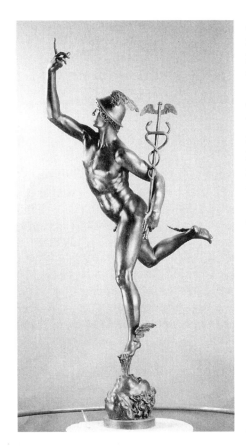

Italian artist Giambologna created this sleek bronze statue of Mercury, the messenger of the gods in Roman mythology, in 1580. In his hand Mercury carries the symbolic staff of a courier, called a caduceus.

---

* **secular**   nonreligious; connected with everyday life

* **relics**   pieces of bone, possessions, or other items belonging to a saint or sacred person

See color plate 3, vol. 1

as JEWELRY, ARMS AND ARMOR, tapestry, embroidery, woodwork, and ceramics were popular. Both wealthy and middle-class people collected decorative objects. But, for the most part, only the nobility and high-ranking church officials could afford expensive, high-quality items.

**Gold Work.** Elaborate objects made of gold served as a symbol of status in the Renaissance. Often decorated with precious stones, they reflected the wealth and prestige of their owners. Rulers displayed their impressive collections of gold items and presented some as gifts to important visitors. Members of the middle class also collected gold objects, such as drinking bowls, utensils, jewelry, and statuettes. However, they tended to purchase ready-made pieces, rather than works created specially for the owner.

Renaissance gold work served both secular* and sacred purposes. Secular items ranged from elaborate centerpieces to crowns, chains, pendants, and rings. Religious items included vessels to hold relics*, ceremonial objects, crosses, and statuettes. They were used in churches or displayed in private homes as a symbol of the owner's religious devotion.

The major centers of gold work were Florence, London, Nürnberg, and Venice. A number of famous artists, including Filippo BRUNELLESCHI, Lorenzo GHIBERTI, and Albrecht DÜRER, trained as goldsmiths. In addition, painters such as Hans HOLBEIN the Younger and RAPHAEL produced designs for gold objects.

**Medals, Arms, and Armor.** Portrait medals made of gold, silver, bronze, or lead were popular in the Renaissance, particularly in Italy. Members of the nobility distributed the medals to their friends and supporters. Inspired by ancient coins, the medals portrayed distinguished individuals, usually in profile and identified by an inscription. The Italian artist Antonio PISANELLO (ca. 1395–1455) was one of the great masters of this form.

Metalworkers also produced arms and armor for individuals participating in tournaments or preparing for war. The best weapons and pieces of armor, finely crafted and decorated with gold and gems, became a symbol of status among the upper classes.

**Textiles.** Decorative textiles were highly prized in the Renaissance. Tapestry, one of the most splendid art forms of the period, required hundreds of hours of skilled labor to produce. Woven of expensive materials such as gold, silver, silk, and wool, tapestries often contained mythological, religious, or historical scenes. People hung them in palaces, churches, and even military tents to create elegant and impressive settings. Philip the Good, duke of BURGUNDY, stored his extensive collection of tapestries in a specially designed fireproof hall staffed with guards and menders (those who repaired tapestries).

Embroidery, ornamental needlework, was another popular art form. Members of the upper classes wore clothing decorated with silk, gold, pearls, and gems. The ceremonial garments of high church officials

* **guild**   association of craft and trade owners and workers that set standards for and represented the interests of its members

* **perspective**   artistic technique for creating the illusion of three-dimensional space on a flat surface

often included richly embroidered panels. In addition, guilds* sometimes commissioned pieces of embroidery.

**Woodwork and Enamel.** The art of creating images with pieces of inlaid wood reached Europe in the mid-1300s from the Islamic world. Italian woodworkers produced benches, cabinets, and wall paneling featuring intricate inlaid pictures. In the early 1400s they began incorporating three-dimensional scenes in their designs, drawing on new theories of perspective*.

Works decorated with enamel were popular in France in the mid-1500s. Applied to a metal surface and then heated at extremely high temperatures, enamel produces a glossy, jewellike finish. The French used enamel for paintings as well as beautiful vases, candlesticks, and other household objects. Themes for the designs ranged from biblical and mythological stories to portraits and scenes from everyday life.

**Ceramics.** During the Renaissance, ceramics (objects made from clay) developed into a high art form. Artists were inspired by glazed pottery from China and Muslim regions of the Middle East and Spain. In Italy potters developed a technique known as majolica, which involved glazing a clay object, painting a design on it, coating it with a clear glaze, and firing it. A similar type of ceramics, known as faience, emerged in France.

Distinctive ceramic styles emerged in different parts of Europe. Spanish potters produced wing-handled vases and colored tiles. Italian artisans used a technique known as sgraffito, which features designs scratched into the surface to reveal a darker clay beneath. Luca della Robbia of Florence developed a method for producing colored, glazed clay pieces that were widely used in architectural decoration. (*See also* **Art; Art in France; Art in Italy; Art in the Netherlands; Art in Spain and Portugal; Coins and Medals; Luxury.**)

| **Demography** | **See** *Population.* |

| **Despotism** | **See** *Government, Forms of.* |

* **theologian**   person who studies religion and the nature of God

* **treatise**   long, detailed essay

**Devotio Moderna**

The spiritual movement known as Devotio Moderna ("modern devotion") arose in the Netherlands in the late 1300s. Its followers aimed to imitate Christ by living a simple and humble life. The movement also stressed quiet reflection and spiritual self-knowledge. The German theologian* Thomas á Kempis expressed these ideals in the early 1400s in his famous treatise* *On the Imitation of Christ.* Followers of Devotio Moderna formed religious societies and opened schools to promote Christian education.

Devotio Moderna arose out of the ideas of Geert Grote (1340–1384), a preacher in the town of Deventer. Grote began his career as a scholar, studying subjects such as philosophy and church law. Many years after obtaining a master's degree from the University of Paris, Grote decided to devote his life to God. In 1374 he converted his parents' former house into a home for women who wanted to serve God. He received a church position that allowed him to preach in public and spent four years traveling around, converting many people. However, Grote's bishop took away his preaching license when he became too harsh in his criticisms of priests who lived with women.

Grote and his followers established several communities based on the ideas of Devotio Moderna. Around 1381 Grote's friend, the priest Florentius Radewyns, made his house in Deventer the home of a group called the Brethren of the Common Life. Members pooled their earnings, gained mostly through writing, to support their community. They obeyed a chosen leader but, unlike monks, they did not take holy vows. Communities of this type spread throughout Germany, the Netherlands, Belgium, and France. Women formed similar groups, calling themselves the Sisters of the Common Life.

In 1387, after Grote's death, Radewyns gave the Brethren a more traditional role in the church by founding a monastery in Windesheim. This body followed monastic* rules, but remained dedicated to Grote's principles. The congregation grew as many established monasteries joined. Similar convents for women arose in several areas.

* **monastic**   relating to monasteries, monks, or nuns

The Brethren founded schools in many northern cities. Several prominent thinkers of the time studied at them, including Desiderius ERASMUS and Martin LUTHER. The Brethren's school system influenced educational practices throughout Europe. (*See also* **Netherlands; Religious Orders.**)

## Diplomacy

During the Renaissance, diplomacy—the practice of conducting relations between nations—developed into a permanent activity of government. European rulers began to send ambassadors to live in foreign lands to gather information and to represent their countries. In the Middle Ages, by contrast, rulers usually sent representatives to other states for short periods of time to accomplish specific tasks.

**The Rise of Diplomacy.**   Resident ambassadors first appeared in Italy. The growth of Italian city-states created a need for governments to communicate with their allies and to gather information about their rivals. By the 1450s the dukes of Milan had established embassies in Naples, Genoa, Rome, and Venice. Various Italian city-states followed Milan's example and set up diplomatic posts in other states. Florence appointed an ambassador to France in 1474.

* **Holy Roman Empire**   political body in central Europe composed of several states; existed until 1806

This new focus on diplomacy slowly spread to northern Europe. Various conflicts involving Spain, France, England, and the Holy Roman Empire* led nations to see the usefulness of skillful diplomats. In the late 1480s Spain established embassies in several northern European

countries, and by 1547 the king of France had ten resident ambassadors distributed across the continent.

In the 1560s, religious conflicts led Catholic and Protestant states to withdraw their ambassadors from each other's courts. Many of these countries did not reestablish diplomatic relations until the early 1600s. However, numerous states in eastern Europe, Scandinavia, and the OTTOMAN EMPIRE did not use resident diplomats during the Renaissance.

**Diplomatic Qualifications and Rank.** Governments looked for certain skills in the individuals they appointed as resident ambassadors. The most important qualifications were a knowledge of Roman law and a humanist* education. Latin was the common language of diplomacy, but ambassadors also used vernacular* languages to communicate with their home governments. Many Renaissance humanists were skilled at languages and rhetoric* and served as diplomats.

Renaissance diplomats held various ranks. The two lowest-ranking officials were nuncios, who delivered prepared messages, and procurators, who could carry out certain negotiations. Ambassadors and legates had more power; they could speak and negotiate on behalf of major rulers. In the 1500s, only individuals with the title *majesty* had the authority to appoint ambassadors.

The relative status of different diplomats also depended on the power of the states they represented. In Catholic countries, nuncios representing the pope received greater respect than nuncios of other rulers. In the early 1500s Pope JULIUS II issued an order recognizing the superiority of the Holy Roman Emperor over the rulers of other states, and this distinction extended to representatives of the emperor.

In addition to resident ambassadors, Renaissance rulers sent special envoys* to represent them at important public occasions, such as the coronation of a monarch or the signing of a treaty. These envoys were usually men of great rank, often nobles. Their rich clothing, gold chains, and other signs of wealth reflected both their own status and the importance of their mission. Rulers received the special envoys with elaborate ceremonies and hospitality, and often gave them generous gifts as a sign of courtesy and respect.

Over time the diplomatic service grew to include other professionals. Resident ambassadors often employed assistants who organized the embassy's papers and maintained the codes used in writing secret communications. By the mid-1500s, European rulers began to appoint secretaries of state to manage the activities of their embassies. Often chosen from the ranks of experienced diplomats, the secretary of state would prepare instructions for ambassadors, oversee negotiations, and supervise the gathering of information.

**Working Conditions for Diplomats.** One of the most important elements of diplomacy was communication between ambassadors and their home governments. Messages sent to and from embassies often took weeks to reach their destinations. Moreover, rival governments sometimes tried to intercept messengers, to discover the contents of let-

* **humanist** referring to a Renaissance cultural movement promoting the study of the humanities (the languages, literature, and history of ancient Greece and Rome) as a guide to living

* **vernacular** native language or dialect of a region or country

* **rhetoric** art of speaking and writing effectively

* **envoy** representative of government sent on a special mission

The countries of Renaissance Europe sent ambassadors to other nations to gather information and represent their native lands. In this painting by Italian artist Vittore Carpaccio, English diplomats assemble outside the royal court after spending time abroad.

ters and documents or to prevent them from getting through. To make sure documents reached their destinations, officials sometimes sent multiple copies by various routes.

For the most part, ambassadors did not receive regular pay but were given money for particular activities. As a result, many faced financial difficulties. Some rulers took steps to pay their representatives more regularly. Nevertheless, many diplomats complained about late payments and the high cost of living and carrying out their duties far from home.

Another important issue was providing security for diplomats, to protect them from arrest or ill treatment in foreign countries. Most governments granted resident ambassadors some basic rights. However, rulers did not hesitate to imprison an ambassador who committed a crime or other serious offense. Political writers urged diplomats to avoid dishonest behavior and deceitful practices. Yet they also acknowledged that the main responsibility of these officials was to defend and advance the interests of their countries. (*See also* **Espionage; Transportation and Communication.**)

### Donatello

**ca. 1386–1466**
**Florentine sculptor**

Born Donato di Niccolò in Florence, the sculptor Donatello was one of founders of the Italian Renaissance style. He took a great interest in the art of ancient Greece and Rome, combining classical models with his own inspiration to create sculptures that influenced later genera-

* **terra-cotta** type of clay used for sculpture, pottery, and architectural features

tions of artists. Donatello worked with an impressive range of materials, including marble, wood, bronze, terra-cotta*, glass, and brick.

Scholars know a great deal about Donatello's life and work from the many written sources that recorded his activities. The first biography of him appeared in 1550 in *Lives of the Artists,* by artist and historian Giorgio Vasari. This and other biographies of Donatello stress his great talent and forceful personality.

**Career in Florence.** From about 1403 to 1407, the artist worked as an assistant in the Florence workshop of Lorenzo GHIBERTI, the famous goldsmith and sculptor. By 1408 he began receiving commissions of his own, mostly for statues of single figures in marble or terra-cotta. He first gained fame for the works he created for the cathedral of Florence, which included life-sized marble statues of the biblical figures King David and John the Baptist. Scholars often point to the highly realistic *St. John the Evangelist* as a forerunner of MICHELANGELO's well-known statue of Moses.

Between 1411 and 1420, Donatello created two marble statues of saints for the Orsanmichele, a multipurpose structure that served as a center for Florence's GUILDS*. His *St. George* won admiration for its realism. The artist also created a scene to accompany the statue, using a new technique called flattened relief*. Donatello treated the surface of the marble like wax, drawing on it with the corner of his chisel. This work pioneered the use of perspective* to give the illusion of depth. Donatello's other notable pieces from this period include the five marble sculptures he created for the bell tower of Florence's cathedral.

* **guild** association of craft and trade owners and workers that set standards for and represented the interests of its members

* **relief** type of sculpture in which figures are raised slightly from a flat surface

* **perspective** artistic technique for creating the illusion of three-dimensional space on a flat surface

* **gilded** coated with gold

**Later Career.** Between 1420 and 1440, Donatello created many pieces in bronze. He worked with Michelozzo, an experienced metalworker in Ghiberti's workshop, to produce his first gilded* bronze, *St. Louis of Toulouse.* This sculpture led the two artists into an official partnership that lasted from 1425 until the early 1430s. With his bronze bust of *St. Rossore,* Donatello revived the classical form of the portrait bust. In the 1420s the artist received one of his most important commissions, a marble and bronze tomb in the Baptistery* of Florence cathedral.

Donatello's technique developed rapidly throughout the 1420s. He took an increasing interest in narrative* art. In *Feast of Herod,* a bronze panel, he explored the use of perspective as a way to link the space within the work to time in the story, showing the head of John the Baptist moving closer and closer to the foreground. Donatello continued to experiment with new techniques, materials, and ways of expression in the 1430s. His interest in ancient art grew, and around 1432 he traveled to Rome to explore ancient ruins. Upon his return to Florence, he began his first large-scale work for the MEDICI family. This project involved decorating a room constructed by Filippo BRUNELLESCHI to house the tomb of Giovanni de' Medici.

Around 1443 Donatello left Florence for Padua. One of the most ambitious works he created during his 11 years there was a high altar complex with seven bronze figures and a series of narrative reliefs in

* **baptistery** building where baptisms are performed

* **narrative** storytelling

both marble and bronze. His monumental bronze mercenary (hired soldier) on horseback, known as Gattamelata, was the first life-size equestrian statue since ancient times. From 1457 to 1459, Donatello lived in SIENA, where he designed a set of bronze doors for the city's cathedral. He returned to Florence in 1459 and remained there until his death in 1466. His late works display a wide range of emotional tension and drama. (*See also* **Art; Art in Italy; Sculpture.**)

### 1572–1631
### English poet and preacher

* **Jesuit** refers to a Roman Catholic religious order founded by St. Ignatius Loyola and approved in 1540

* **satire** literary or artistic work ridiculing human wickedness and foolishness

* **elegy** type of poem often used to express sorrow for one who has died

Few, if any, English poets of the 1600s had a greater influence on later writers than John Donne. His intelligence, unique style, sophistication, and poetic skill inspired poets for generations after him. In his later years Donne became a minister, and his reputation reflects his achievements both as a poet and as a preacher.

**Education.** John Donne was born into a Catholic family in London during the reign of ELIZABETH I. At the time England was a Protestant country, and Catholics could not practice their faith openly. Donne received his early education at the hands of Catholic tutors, possibly including his uncle, a Jesuit*. At the age of 12, he entered Oxford University, along with his younger brother. Scholars know very little about the next six years of Donne's life. Some have suggested that he left the university before he turned 16 and spent some time traveling, possibly in France.

In 1591 Donne entered Lincoln's Inn, one of the four London law schools known as the INNS OF COURT. Many educated men in Renaissance England attended the Inns as a way to make social contacts with high society, rather than to study law seriously. Donne, like many of his fellow students, used his time at the Inns as a stepping-stone to the wealthy world of the royal court.

**Poetic Beginnings.** Donne wrote his first works of poetry and prose during his years at Lincoln's Inn. Like other writers who studied at the Inns, Donne created satires* ridiculing life in Elizabethan London. However, he also broke new ground, becoming the first writer to produce a collection of English love poems in the style of ancient Roman elegies*. Donne's early poems reveal his interest in philosophy, religion, science, and politics. Because it was considered tasteless at the time for educated writers to publish their works, Donne circulated his poems in manuscript form among a select group of readers.

Some time after 1593, Donne moved away from his Catholic faith and gradually came to embrace Protestant ideas. In the late 1590s he served as a volunteer in two of England's military efforts against Catholic Spain. On his return to England, he became a secretary to Thomas Egerton, Queen Elizabeth's chief officer of justice. In 1601 Egerton helped Donne secure a seat in Parliament.

At this time Donne, who was living in Egerton's house, also began to write love poems that reflected his social life in the court and high society. He addressed some of these love poems to Ann More, a young

DONNE, JOHN

John Donne was a major figure in the world of English poetry. His intelligence, skill, and unique style have inspired many famous English writers.

---

* **sonnet** poem of 14 lines with a fixed pattern of meter and rhyme

woman who was also living in Egerton's house. When Donne and Ann, who was only 17 years old, ran off to be married in 1601, Donne lost his position and ruined his career at court. For the next 14 years he was unable to find a secure job.

Many of Donne's love poems from these years discuss the events of his life—his marriage, his situation as a social outcast, and his lack of employment. During this period Donne also composed many of his Holy Sonnets*, a series of powerful, religious verses. These deeply thoughtful poems reveal some of the depression Donne felt during his difficult time of unemployment. The sonnets combine Catholic and Protestant ideas, including the teachings of the Protestant reformer John CALVIN. The most famous of them, "Death, be not Proud," expresses the author's steadfast belief in life after death.

**Religious Career.** Over the course of his unemployment, Donne grew more and more bitter about politics and society. The king, JAMES I, suggested that Donne abandon the field of politics and become a minister. In 1615 Donne was ordained as a priest in the Church of England, and King James made him a royal chaplain. The following year Donne accepted a position at Lincoln's Inn that required him to preach 50 sermons a year.

Donne became one of the most respected preachers of his day, giving sermons not only at Lincoln's Inn but also at court, in local churches, at St. Paul's Cathedral in London, and in many other public and private places. One hundred and sixty sermons survive from Donne's years as a preacher. Some of them were published during his lifetime, others after his death. Donne's religious writings reveal his highly intelligent mind and political awareness. Although he was committed to the Church of England, in many of his sermons he tried to find a bridge between Protestants and Catholics.

When Donne's wife, Ann, died in 1617, he wrote the sonnet "Since She Whom I Loved Hath Paid Her Last Debt." Some scholars believe that Donne's religious faith deepened after this loss. In 1619 he left England to serve as chaplain on a diplomatic mission to Germany. He wrote a special poem for this occasion: "A Hymn to Christ, at the Author's Last Going into Germany." Many scholars consider this one of Donne's best religious poems.

In 1620 Donne returned to his post at Lincoln's Inn. Through his connections at court, he gained a post as chief officer (dean) of St. Paul's Cathedral. In this position Donne frequently defended the policies of King James. For example, his first published sermon defended the king's "Directions for Preachers," a document calling on preachers to stop criticizing the king's handling of internal and international affairs.

When Donne became seriously ill in 1623, he wrote the poem "A Hymn to God My God, in My Sickness." This verse expresses the author's firm belief in salvation and the afterlife. Donne preached his last sermon at court in 1631, only a month before he died. Within two years, the first collection of his poems appeared in print, and his work became an inspiration to many of the most famous poets in England

over the next 200 years. (*See also* **Books and Manuscripts; English Language and Literature; Poetry; Protestant Reformation**)

### Drake, Francis

**ca. 1540–1596**
**English explorer**

* **apprentice**   person bound by legal agreement to work for another for a specified period of time in return for instruction in a trade or craft

An explorer, pirate, and military leader, Francis Drake earned fame as the first Englishman to sail around the globe. His raids on Spanish ships in the Americas brought gold and silver to England. He also played a key role in defending his country against the attack of Spain's great fleet of ships, the ARMADA.

Drake learned how to sail in his youth as an apprentice on a small coastal trade ship. In 1567 he accompanied John Hawkins, a prominent sea captain, on an ill-fated expedition to the Caribbean. Much of Hawkins's fleet was destroyed by the Spanish, but Drake returned home safely. In the following years he made three more trips to the Caribbean.

In 1577 an expedition aboard his ship the *Golden Hind* took him around the world—though that was not his original plan. On that voyage Drake explored the coast of California, which he claimed for England, and searched for the Northwest Passage. Failing to find that much-desired sea route across North America, he then headed west across the Pacific Ocean. By 1580 he had rounded the tip of Africa and returned to England. Drake became the first Englishman and second navigator of any nationality to sail around the world. On arrival in England, he was knighted by Queen Elizabeth.

During the 1580s Drake took part in actions against Spain. He led a fleet into the Spanish port of Cádiz, which the Spanish surrendered to him. During the fighting Drake burned many Spanish ships, a fact that delayed Spain's planned naval attack against England. When the Armada finally set sail for England in 1588, Drake played a leading role in defeating the fleet. The following year, Drake returned to Spain and destroyed much Spanish shipping. (*See also* **Americas; England; Exploration.**)

### Drama

* **classical**   in the tradition of ancient Greece and Rome

During the Renaissance, drama came into its own as an art form. Although early types of plays had appeared as early as the 1200s, they were usually performed as part of a festival, not as events by themselves. Scholars of the Middle Ages had studied the drama of the ancient world, but they treated it as literature, suitable for reading rather than performing. Playwrights of the Renaissance revived classical* comedy and tragedy and brought them from the bookshelf to the stage.

## RELIGIOUS DRAMA

Religious theater arose during the late Middle Ages. By around 1350, most of western and southern Europe had adopted three basic forms of religious drama: the passion play, the miracle play, and the morality play. These forms remained popular until the early 1600s.

Passion plays, also known as mystery plays, were elaborate outdoor presentations of scenes from the Bible, often featuring events from the life of Christ. Performances ran for days or even weeks, involving hundreds of people at various locations throughout a city or town. A play in progress dominated the social, economic, and cultural life of the city. This form of drama reached its height around 1400 in England and 1500 in France and the Holy Roman Empire*.

Miracle plays recounted the lives of saints and the miracles they performed. In Italy, especially in Florence and Rome, passion and miracle plays often formed part of great religious pageants in honor of Holy Week (the week before Easter) or of a city's patron saint. The actors set up carts and moved their performance throughout the city. The productions often featured music and elaborate costumes. Confraternities—groups of laypeople* who joined together for religious and social activities—often wrote and performed passion and miracle plays. Nuns in convents occasionally produced these types of plays as well.

Another form of religious drama, the morality play, became particularly popular in northern France and the Netherlands. These plays were allegories* in which each character represented some human quality. One of the most famous morality plays, *Everyman* (ca. 1495), retold the story of a human being's spiritual journey from birth to death. During the play Everyman encounters such characters as Strength and Good Deeds.

In the early 1500s church officials began to view passion and miracle plays as sacrilegious*. Authorities tried to ban them in France, England, Italy, and the Protestant lands of the Holy Roman Empire. However, many actors continued to perform them.

## TRAGEDY

Although scholars of the Middle Ages studied tragic drama, they tended to see it as poetry rather than theater. Humanists* began writing new tragedies, based on ancient Roman models, as early as the 1300s, but they did not produce these works on the stage. However, in the mid-1500s playwrights and critics began to see the spectator, rather than the reader, as the proper audience for tragedy. At the same time, the discovery of ancient Greek tragedies by Sophocles, Euripides, and other authors helped fuel interest in the genre*.

As dramatists set out to revive this ancient form, they turned to classical sources for guidance. Their main references were *Poetics*, by the Greek philosopher ARISTOTLE, and *Ars Poetica*, by the Roman poet Horace. Authors engaged in lively debates about whether it was better to imitate the Greeks or the Romans and about whether plots should be based on fictional or historical events.

Slowly, tragedy came out of the scholarly study and onto the stage. In 1541 the Italian playwright Giambattista Cinzio Giraldi became the first to present a tragedy on stage. The performance of his play *Orbecche* revived the tragic tradition, which became an immediate success.

* **Holy Roman Empire** political body in central Europe composed of several states; existed until 1806

* **laypeople** those who are not members of the clergy

* **allegory** literary or artistic device in which characters, events, and settings represent abstract qualities and in which the author intends a different meaning to be read beneath the surface

* **sacrilegious** disrespectful of sacred things

* **humanist** Renaissance expert in the humanities (the languages, literature, history, and speech and writing techniques of ancient Greece and Rome)

* **genre** literary form

Renaissance playwrights often took their work to the streets, where they staged performances that might involve music and elaborate costumes.

* **patron**   supporter or financial sponsor of an artist or writer

Patrons* commissioned new plays and financed stage productions. Because Italy had no public theaters at the time, these plays appeared in private homes or at court.

**Tragic Themes.** Renaissance playwrights believed that their art should educate audiences as well as entertain them. They often began their tragedies with a prologue* that explained how the forces of good and evil would appear in the dramatic action. The prologue advised the audience to learn from the tragic events they were about to see on stage.

* **prologue**   introduction to a literary work

However, the playwrights' ideas of right and wrong reflected the changing views of their societies. The many tragedies written about kings show how these ideals changed over time. Early humanists considered honor and glory the chief virtues of a ruler. However, a later generation of dramatists followed the model of author Niccolò MACHIAVELLI, who argued that a monarch should be ruthless. Therefore, the theater encouraged the audience to think about, and perhaps to question, their society's changing values and beliefs.

Tragedies also presented society's conflicting views about the role of women. Female victims in tragedy often appeared as weak, overemotional characters of limited intelligence. However, in other cases women were strong, intelligent individuals seeking the respect they deserved.

## A Typical Comedy

The play *Calandria* (The Follies of Calandro), by Cardinal Bernardo Dovizi da Bibbiena, provides a typical example of the plot of an erudite comedy. It involves a pair of abandoned twins, one male and one female, searching for each other throughout Rome. The male twin falls in love with the unsatisfied wife of an old man named Calandro. Through a series of tricks, disguises, and mistakes, managed by a clever servant, the female twin eventually becomes engaged to Calandro's son, while the male twin becomes the lover of Calandro's wife.

Their courage in the face of death inspired admiration from audiences, both at court and in the general public.

**Tragic Effects.** The power of theater as a cultural force depended largely on its ability to draw the audience into the story. Playwrights struggled to make the world on stage seem more real through their use of language and stage effects.

Dramatists drew their audiences in by writing in the local language, rather than in Latin. They also updated the settings, costumes, and actions of their plays to reflect the society of their time. However, writers continued to rely on the classical tradition in their use of language. They tended to include many verbal flourishes and to show off their knowledge of ancient literature.

This emphasis on language has earned Renaissance tragedies the reputation of being too "talky," better for reading than for performing. However, this complaint overlooks the other devices playwrights used to add interest to their tragedies, such as costumes, movement, sound, and blocking (the placement of characters on stage). Dramatists developed a clever trick for presenting events such as murders and crowd scenes, which they could not easily show on the stage. They had characters onstage watch events occurring offstage and describing what they saw. This technique expanded the world of the play beyond the borders of the stage, enabling the audience to witness the action without seeing it directly. Playwrights also used sound and lighting to signal events taking place offstage. A blare of trumpets could hint at a procession, while thunderbolts and flashes of lightning suggested a violent storm.

## ERUDITE COMEDY

Popular as tragedy became, it never achieved the same appeal as comedy. During the Renaissance, playwrights developed a new style of comedy based on the works of ancient Roman dramatists, such as Plautus and Terence. They referred to this form as erudite (learned) comedy. The name suggests that they viewed it as a serious art form, suitable for noble or scholarly audiences.

Erudite comedy began in Italy in the 1400s. Its basic features were copied from classical comedy. Playwrights divided their works into five acts, all occurring on the same day and in the same place—usually an Italian city street or courtyard. They populated the stage with characters who fit the setting, such as servants, soldiers, innkeepers, and peddlers. Most dramatists reinforced the familiar feeling of the setting by writing in prose rather than verse. They also used the language the audience knew, although some characters might speak in foreign languages or regional dialects.

Erudite comedies often had complicated plots with two or more story lines entwined together. They tended to rely on devices such as tricks, disguises, mistaken identities, and practical jokes. The heroes of the piece were often young lovers who, with the help of their clever servants, outwitted the old men who tried to keep them apart. Broad phys-

ical humor, known as slapstick, played a major role in the action. However, within these silly and twisted plots, playwrights found room to slip in comments about politics, local events, and issues ranging from education and marriage to the use of cosmetics.

Certain plot devices became standard features in erudite comedy. Eavesdropping, cross-dressing, misunderstood letters, and switching bedmates in the dark all appeared repeatedly in different plays. Comedies also relied heavily on specific types of action, such as commenting on the action in asides*, exchanging insults, and talking from windows. As late as the 1600s, playwrights such as William SHAKESPEARE and the French dramatist Molière continued to use these elements in their works. (*See also* **Commedia dell'Arte; Drama, English; Drama, French; Drama, Spanish; Middle Ages; Theaters.**)

* **aside** remark made by a character onstage to the audience or to another character, not heard by other characters in the same scene

The dramatic arts grew and flowered in England during the Renaissance. This period produced some of the most distinguished names in the history of drama, including William SHAKESPEARE, Christopher MARLOWE, and Ben JONSON. Even today, their work continues to provide matter for scholars and entertainment for viewers, in England and elsewhere.

## ELIZABETHAN DRAMA

Scholars often refer to the English plays of the late 1500s and early 1600s as either Elizabethan drama or English Renaissance drama. However, neither of these terms is completely accurate. The term *Elizabethan* refers to ELIZABETH I, whose reign began in 1558. However, there was no system of scheduled play performances in England until the 1580s. Also, although Elizabeth died in 1603, English drama continued to flourish until 1642.

The term *Renaissance* also poses problems. It is true that the English drama of this period reflected the new artistic ideas of the Renaissance, which had spread to England from other parts of Europe. However, "Renaissance" art generally grew out of a desire to revive the culture of ancient Greece and Rome. English drama, by contrast, was mostly a business, aimed at attracting the money and applause of the semieducated masses.

In general, the term *Elizabethan* is more appropriate than *Renaissance* for referring to the plays written and performed during Elizabeth's reign. However, the two terms put together reflect a tension in the English drama of this period—and, in fact, in English society as a whole. Authors wanted to show respect for English traditions while making a place for new ideas. Elizabethan drama reflected common social views about the love of God, of country, and of community. Yet at the same time, it relied on strange and unusual images that alarmed many religious and public officials. Some authorities saw theaters as a threat to society and tried repeatedly to shut them down.

The most famous English playwright of the Renaissance was William Shakespeare. This picture illustrates the scene from Shakespeare's tragedy *Macbeth* in which the title character meets the three witches who predict that he will one day be king.

**London's Theaters.** Elizabethan London had two distinct types of theaters. Large, open-air playhouses, such as the Globe, the Red Bull, and the Rose, first appeared in the late 1500s. These theaters attracted a mixed audience. Wealthy patrons sat in the upper levels, while the lower classes stood in front of the stage. These large playhouses made it necessary for plays to include broad, bold effects that appealed to the lower-class spectators.

Refined, upper-class viewers came to associate the large theaters with loud overacting, sensational drama, and rowdy audiences. In the early 1600s, the large playhouses fell out of style with the well-to-do. They turned instead to smaller, more expensive private theaters that offered seating for everyone, such as the Phoenix and the Blackfriars. Historians of the late 1600s, looking back on the Elizabethan theater scene, argued that the indoor theaters stood for the respected dramatic tradition, while the large public playhouses served only to suit the tastes of "the meaner sort of people."

The private theaters resembled the playhouses that had existed at the court early in Queen Elizabeth's reign. At that time companies of choirboys, aged 12 to 16, had performed plays written especially for the queen. However, the child actors also presented "rehearsals" of their plays to the paying public. The queen closed these theaters down in 1590, probably because of some political blunder on the part of the acting companies. When the playhouses reopened ten years later, they had to survive in a more commercial world. They began putting on more

sophisticated plays designed to appeal to young gentlemen, such as the law students at London's INNS OF COURT. However, young boys continued to play all roles.

Companies of adult men (women never appeared on the Elizabethan stage) had to compete with these child actors. Over time, the adult companies won favor with the court. In 1608 the King's Men, the most respected and financially successful of the adult companies, took over the Blackfriars playhouse from the boys.

**The Playwright's Profession.** In Elizabethan England, the theater was a business, much like the modern movie industry. Wealthy investors financed the commercial playhouses where actors performed, while dramatists supplied the public's demand for new plays. However, audiences seldom knew the names of the authors who created the plays they watched. Most people at this time did not see drama as a form of literature. In fact, society looked down on those who wrote plays for money, tailoring their artistic vision to the tastes of the masses.

Although few people respected the playwright's profession, it still attracted many well-educated writers. The theater gave them a chance to display their broad range of knowledge and their skill with language. It also provided a better income than they could earn in most other professions available to educated men, such as preaching and teaching.

To keep thousands of spectators coming, acting companies had to produce a different play every afternoon of the week—and a new play once every two weeks. As a result, playwrights had to write quickly, often working in groups to complete a piece. They tailored their work to the acting companies they wrote for, creating plays that took advantage of the actors' strengths. They also paid careful attention to their audiences' tastes. Like the modern public, Elizabethan audiences enjoyed stories of great misfortune and disaster. Playwrights borrowed many of their plots from local scandals and crimes. In many ways, an Elizabethan dramatist's job was similar to that of a modern newspaper reporter.

In general, the most popular plays of this time are not the ones most admired by scholars. However, scholars tend to consider the plays as texts, while Elizabethan viewers saw them as events. Plays competed with other popular forms of entertainment, such as fencing, acrobatics, and bearbaiting—a spectator sport in which dogs attacked a chained bear. Like these spectacles, drama had to provide a show of energy and activity. The connection between the actors and the audience played a major role in the Elizabethan theater.

**The History Play.** English playwrights worked with many dramatic forms that were familiar throughout Europe, such as comedy and tragedy. However, they also created a type of drama rather specific to England: the history play. In these plays, dramatists drew on the events of the past to shed light on their own times.

Early history plays appealed to many viewers because they portrayed glorious English victories over foreign enemies. The play *The Famous Victories of Henry V,* written by an unknown author in the 1580s, offers

an example of this type of unquestioning patriotism. It relates the adventures of Henry V, king of England from 1413 to 1422, who attacked France and brought it under English rule. The playwright presented the young king as both a war hero and a champion of the individual.

Later playwrights used similar themes in their plays, but they explored the issues in more depth. For example, Shakespeare's three plays about Henry V examine the moral questions surrounding the king's attack on the French. Shakespeare's history plays about England's rulers posed difficult questions about the clash between politics and morality: Does a good king have to be a good man? Do national goals reflect national good, or only the ego and ambition of leaders? These complex views of history transformed drama from simple entertainment to food for thought.

Over time, history plays came to focus less on the military deeds of their kings and more on the rulers' personal lives. Marlowe's *Edward II,* written around 1591, focuses on the king's love for two male courtiers who are not of noble birth. His willingness to share power with them violates the accepted social structures of his country and ultimately leads to his downfall.

The last Elizabethan play to deal with a real political situation was probably John Ford's *The Chronicle History of Perkin Warbeck: A Strange Truth.* This play centers on the figure of Warbeck, an imposter who tried to seize the English throne from Henry VII. The sham king, a lively figure who dominates the stage, makes a vivid contrast to the dull yet competent ruler who controls the country. Ford's play cast suspicion on the very idea of celebrating the glory of kingship on the stage. Many scholars see this production as the end of the history-play genre*.

**Problem Plays.** Scholars label many popular plays of the English Renaissance as "problem plays." One of the "problems" with them is that they do not fit easily into the mold of comedy or tragedy. They often combine humor with disturbing elements. They also tend to be unclear in their moral position. Sometimes characters are rewarded for acts that seem morally questionable. Even when these plays end happily, some doubts linger about whether everything has truly worked out for the best.

Many problem plays draw on familiar stories, such as the "prodigal son," a young man who leaves his family, wastes all his money, returns home in disgrace, and finds forgiveness. Playwrights created several variations on this basic theme. They presented sons refusing to marry, husbands being unfaithful to their wives, and foolish country gentlemen falling victim to slick city merchants. However, the playwrights also put a twist on the basic plot. The young men who rebel against their families often embody the kind of manly vigor that Elizabethan society admired. These plays forced viewers to question their own standards.

Some of Shakespeare's plays, including *Measure for Measure* and *All's Well That Ends Well,* fall into the category of problem plays. A less famil-

* **genre**   literary form

* **dowry**   money or property that a woman brings to her marriage

* **Moor**   Muslim from North Africa; Moorish invaders conquered much of Spain during the Middle Ages

iar example is *Captain Thomas Stukeley* (1596), a play by an unknown author about a man who needs money for a military career. Stukeley's ambition enables him to convince his best friend to break his engagement and let Stukeley marry his fiancée. The "hero" then runs off with her dowry*. Stukeley's desperate search for glory eventually leads him into North Africa, where he dies in a contest between two groups of Moors*. The play leaves the audience uncertain about whether to honor the character's ambition or condemn his morals.

The idea of moral uncertainty also appears in "city comedies," plays that focus on the changing economy and social structure of London. In this harsh environment, the success of the hero often is not a victory of good over evil, but a matter of the survival of the fittest. The central character is typically a noble lover or soldier cheated out of his rightful estate by villains who reject traditional values. The only way he can defeat his enemies is by beating them at their own game. In the end he wins his love and recovers his losses, but the unworthy methods he has used leave a stain on his character. The city comedies raise questions about society's values and the conflict between economic success and honorable behavior.

## JACOBEAN DRAMA

The reign of JAMES I, which lasted from 1603 to 1625, is known as the Jacobean period. Many of the king's subjects disapproved of him because he gave political favors to his courtiers (much like Marlowe's *Edward II*) and sold noble titles for money. These concerns affected the tone of English drama during this period.

Jacobean drama focused mainly on the court and on London. Female characters took on larger roles than they had in Elizabethan drama, often appearing as shrewd schemers. Wicked or incompetent rulers also became common figures in drama. City comedies, with their biting wit and harsh view of the world, remained popular during this time. The other common type of drama was the satiric* tragedy, usually set in an immoral foreign court—a thinly disguised version of the English one. Plays of this time featured dark plots filled with horror and violence. Some critics have called them "tragedies of state" because they deal with diseased societies that lack a moral foundation.

* **satiric**   involving the use of satire, the ridicule of human wickedness and foolishness in a literary or artistic work

**Leading Dramatists.**   One of the most productive playwrights of the period was Thomas Middleton. Many scholars see Middleton's play *The Revenger's Tragedy* (1607) as the first drama in a distinctively Jacobean style. In this grim play about revenge, vicious humor overpowers any sense of moral certainty. This use of dark comedy is a common feature of Jacobean tragedy.

Most of Middleton's plays deal largely with money and sex. His comedies are energetic, featuring huge numbers of characters and complex intersecting plots. In 1624 Middleton scored a huge success with *A Game at Chess*. This biting satire broke all records for attendance when

it played for nine straight days. Scholars also note that Middleton's work shows particular sympathy for women. The character of Beatrice-Joanna in *The Changeling,* Middleton's most famous tragedy, is one of the greatest female roles in Jacobean drama.

The practice of collaborating, or working together on a play, remained common during this period. For example, Ben Jonson worked with fellow playwrights George Chapman and John Marston on his play *Eastward Ho!* One particularly well-known team was Francis Beaumont and John Fletcher. They achieved great success in the new genre known as tragicomedy, which blended elements of tragedy and comedy. Their three most famous plays—*Philaster, The Maid's Tragedy,* and *A King and No King*—all focus on one of the favorite topics of Jacobean theater: a king neglecting his duties.

One of the last great Jacobean dramatists was John Ford. Although he created most of his plays during the reign of James's son, CHARLES I, they reflect the style and ideas of Jacobean drama. Many of Ford's plays reworked plots and themes from Shakespeare. His most famous play, *'Tis Pity She's a Whore* (1633), retells the story of Romeo and Juliet with a shocking twist: the lovers are also brother and sister. Incest* was a common theme in Jacobean drama, but Ford was the first to deal with it so openly.

**The Court Masque.** One form of drama did not share in the general darkness and heaviness of the period. This was the court masque, a popular form of entertainment that combined words, music, dance, and elaborate scenery. Masques formed a part of the Christmas festivities at court and celebrated important state events, such as the marriage of Princess Elizabeth in 1613. They also served to display the splendor of the court to an audience that often included diplomats from foreign nations.

A masque began with the entry of members of the court in disguise. These courtiers performed a series of staged dances, then led members of the audience out into the social dances (known as "revels"). The plot of the masque served to explain the courtiers' entry, often by introducing them as foreign visitors coming to honor the monarch. The plot also had to praise the monarch, its most important spectator.

Playwright Ben Jonson and set designer Inigo JONES produced most of the masques at the court of King James. Jonson laid out his theory of masque writing in 1606. He saw the masque as a serious genre, suited to an educated audience and able to serve moral and educational purposes. Jonson transformed the genre by introducing the "antimasque," which opens the masque by introducing a series of evil or deceitful characters. Their actions provide a contrast with the heroic virtues of the figures in the real masque. Jonson created his first antimasque at the request of Queen Anne, who wanted her own entrance to follow a "false masque" of witches. (*See also* **Art in Britain; Censorship; Dance; Drama; England; Theaters.**)

* **incest** sexual relationship between blood relatives

## Women Who Wrote

Although the professional playwrights of the Elizabethan era were all men, women produced "closet dramas," which were meant to be read rather than performed. The most famous play by a woman was *The Tragedy of Mariam* (1613), by Elizabeth Cary. The author, a wealthy and well-educated heiress, angered her husband when she converted to Catholicism. Her play about Mariam, the wife of the biblical king Herod, deals with women's role in marriage and their right to speak.

## Drama, French

During the Renaissance, theatrical events formed a part of everyday life in France. Churches and cities often organized dramatic ceremonies and spectacles. The court took delight in elaborate weddings, military contests, and carefully staged processions to mark a royal entrance into an important city. As a result, scholars find it difficult to label specific types of performance as "Renaissance drama."

Another problem with the term stems from the fact that there was no clear distinction between the Middle Ages and the Renaissance in France. Medieval* ways of thinking gave way slowly to a renewed interest in classical* ideas. In the same way, the types of drama popular in the late Middle Ages gradually developed into the typical forms of the Renaissance between 1450 and 1620.

**Popular Theater.** During the Middle Ages, several types of plays had appealed to large and varied audiences. One example was the mystery play, a form of religious drama based on biblical stories. Some of these productions went on for days and involved much of the population in the towns where they appeared. Such performances continued until 1548, when the king banned them, fearing they would spread Protestant ideas. However, they left a continuing legacy in French drama. Some of these religious plays had included short, comic scenes called farces*. The farce became a dramatic form in its own right and remained popular throughout the Renaissance.

Actors of the 1500s staged several types of popular plays on makeshift platforms in the marketplace. One type, the morality play, served—as its name suggests—to teach a moral lesson. It featured either biblical characters or symbolic figures who stood for abstract qualities. For example, in one play a character named Charity must fight and win a battle with Cheating, Greed, and Death. Plays called *sotties,* or fools' plays, also tended to feature moral themes. However, they also sometimes included political satire*. Some of their characters served as symbols, like those in the morality plays, but the most common figures were the "fools" from which the plays took their name. Modern scholars find these fools' plays extremely difficult to translate because they relied heavily on complicated wordplay.

Hundreds of French farces have survived from the Renaissance. These comic plays tend to use a handful of standard plots, such as a violent quarrel between a husband and wife, an unfaithful wife tricking her husband, or a fond mother who believes that her idiot son will become a priest. Unlike morality plays and *sotties,* farces feature characters drawn from everyday life, such as servants, soldiers, shoemakers, and priests. Farces appealed to both intellectuals and common people. They had an influence on later dramas, including the works of the famous French playwright Molière (1622–1673) and possibly the Italian form known as COMMEDIA DELL'ARTE.

Two of the most famous French farces are still popular with actors today. *The Tub,* a piece from the late 1400s, tells the story of a weak husband bullied by his wife. When she falls into her washtub and gets stuck, he refuses to help her out until she agrees to obey him. *Master*

* **medieval**    referring to the Middle Ages, a period that began around A.D. 400 and ended around 1400 in Italy and 1500 in the rest of Europe

* **classical**    in the tradition of ancient Greece and Rome

* **farce**    light dramatic piece that features broad comedy, improbable situations, stereotyped characters, and exaggerated physical action

* **satire**    literary or artistic work ridiculing human wickedness and foolishness

### A Solo Soldier

Perhaps the simplest form of popular theater during the French Renaissance was the monologue. The most famous surviving French monologue is *The Bowman from Bagnolet* (ca. 1470). In this speech a soldier boasts about his cowardly behavior and his robbery during a war. He then mistakes a scarecrow for an enemy soldier and talks to it at length before realizing his error. Many scholars view this humorous little play as another form of the French farce.

Robert Garnier was the leading French writer of tragedies during the Renaissance. He also introduced into France the Italian form known as tragicomedy, which blended elements of comedy and tragedy.

* **humanist**   Renaissance expert in the humanities (the languages, literature, history, and speech and writing techniques of ancient Greece and Rome)

* **genre**   literary form

* **monologue**   long speech by one character

*Peter Pathelin* (ca. 1460)—the most famous of all French farces—relates the adventures of a trickster who outwits a greedy merchant, but then is himself outwitted by a shepherd. This play's language was more sophisticated than that of most farces, leading some critics to label it the first true French comedy.

**Humanist Comedy.** In the mid-1500s, French humanists* began attempting to revive the literary forms of ancient Greece and Rome. In 1552 playwright Étienne Jodelle restored the five-act play structure of ancient drama in *Eugène*. Jodelle intended this piece to be the first classical comedy of the French Renaissance. However, many modern critics note that the play actually combined elements of ancient Roman comedy and French farce. The plot centers on a tangled web of romances involving a wife, her uncultured husband, her former lover Florimond, her current lover Eugène, and his sister—who is in love with Florimond.

Tangled romantic plots became standard for French humanist comedy. Many playwrights borrowed ideas from the comedies of two ancient Roman playwrights, Plautus and Terence. Examples include an unfaithful wife juggling two lovers and an unfaithful husband who tries to take advantage of an orphaned girl, only to learn that she is a wealthy heiress. Certain standard characters appear in many French humanist comedies: family members, irresponsible young men who would rather make love than study, and servants (either helpful or disloyal). Doctors, law officials, and military men also turn up in several of these plays.

**Humanist Tragedy.** Tragedies, both in Latin and in French, were even more popular in the French Renaissance than comedies. Writers of this genre* often copied the style and subject matter of ancient authors, such as the Greek playwright Euripides and the Roman philosopher Seneca. Étienne Jodelle worked to revive classical tragedy, as he had done with comedy.

Scholars have labeled Jodelle's *Cleopatra in Prison* (1552–1553) the first French tragedy in a distinct Renaissance style. However, they do not consider it the very first French tragedy. That honor goes to *Abraham's Sacrifice* (1550), by Théodore de Bèze, even though it has a happy ending. Several other authors chose religious subjects for their plays, but most drew their ideas from the ancient world.

Scholars agree that the most important writer of French Renaissance tragedies was Robert Garnier. Between 1568 and 1583, he published eight plays, including seven tragedies. Garnier followed the five-act structure and many other features of ancient drama. These included the chorus (a character who introduces and comments on the action), large numbers of monologues*, and a style of rapid-fire dialogue. Garnier also took most of his plots from the history and mythology of ancient Greece and Rome.

**Tragicomedy and Pastoral.** In the 1580s, Garnier imported an Italian form known as tragicomedy into France. This style of drama

* **pastoral**   relating to the countryside; often used to draw a contrast between the innocence and serenity of rural life and the corruption and extravagance of court life

blended elements of tragedy and comedy. The genre remained popular well into the 1600s, reaching its greatest heights between 1620 and 1640. Another popular form of the early 1600s was the pastoral\*, a style imported from both Italy and Spain. Pastoral plays were set in the countryside, which often represented a quiet and simple way of life. This form of drama flourished for only a short time, but pastoral themes lingered in French literature throughout the 1600s. Playwright Jean Mairet combined the pastoral and the tragicomedy in several plays, but most of them were written too late to be considered Renaissance drama. (*See also* **Classical Scholarship; Drama; French Literature and Language; Pastoral; Theaters.**)

## Drama, Spanish

B y the 1400s, a flourishing religious drama existed in the Spanish kingdom of Castile. Two playwrights of the late 1400s helped develop this early theater into the forms of the Renaissance. Juan del Encina, who wrote 14 plays in verse over the course of his career, gradually expanded his works from short plays with only a few hundred lines to much longer pieces. Bartolomé de Torres Naharro transformed the theater by creating an illusion of the real world on the stage, rather than relying on artificial customs and rules.

Spanish drama in the 1500s took several forms, each appealing to a different audience. The general public enjoyed the popular religious plays performed on major feast days. Schools and universities put on plays in Latin, in Castilian Spanish, or in a mixture of the two, for a more learned audience. Traveling companies of actors performed nonreligious plays, often based on classical\* or Italian models. And at court, royalty and nobles watched types of entertainment based on the masques\* of the Middle Ages.

* **classical**   in the tradition of ancient Greece and Rome

* **masque**   dramatic entertainment performed by masked actors, or a ball or party at which all guests wear masks or costumes

* **theology**   study of the nature of God and of religion

* **Counter-Reformation**   actions taken by the Roman Catholic Church after 1540 to oppose Protestantism

During the 1600s, the popular religious theater of the 1500s developed into a more formal type of drama. These sacred plays celebrated the Catholic ritual of communion. They drew their plots from biblical stories, ancient mythology, or current events. By giving dramatic form to abstract religious ideas, these plays functioned as both theater and theology\*. They became an important means of transmitting the religious ideas of the Catholic Counter-Reformation\*.

The other popular form of drama during the 1600s was the *comedia*. This word, which literally means "comedy," became a general term for "play," reflecting the fact that most Spanish drama at this time took a comic form. The works sometimes had serious or tragic themes, but the characters inevitably overcame their problems to arrive at a happy ending. A typical *comedia* featured a pair of lovers and the people who threatened their union, such as a rival suitor or a stern father or brother. Another character, often a servant, provided comic relief through clever wordplay or comic imitation of the main plot. Audiences generally preferred swiftly moving plots filled with disguises, deceptions, and duels.

Lope Félix de VEGA CARPIO played a large role in developing the Spanish *comedia* from the dramatic practices of the 1500s. Most plays had three acts, plus a short introduction and comic skits, dancing, or

singing between the acts. Almost anything could provide the basis for a *comedia,* from proverbs and short stories to history, mythology, and the lives of the saints. Written entirely in verse, the *comedia* featured witty wordplay and complicated imagery*. The style of the poetry form varied from scene to scene. Peasants often spoke in traditional Spanish verse patterns, while nobles tended to use more formal Italian styles.

The Spanish *comedia* arose at the same time that Spain built its first public theaters. Plays took place during the day in courtyards surrounded by houses. Upper-class spectators sat in the houses and watched through the windows, while others sat or stood in the courtyard. The stage, at one end of the courtyard, was relatively bare, and the poetry of the play served to "paint" the scene and setting. Special stage machinery created spectacular scenic effects, which were extremely popular. One notable feature of the Spanish theater was the presence of women on the stage, which was forbidden in other European countries. (*See also* **Calderón de la Barca, Pedro; Drama; Humor; Spanish Language and Literature; Theaters.**)

* **imagery**   pictorial quality of a literary work, achieved through words

## Dubrovnik

The Republic of Dubrovnik, a city-state in what is now Croatia, reached its "golden age" of prosperity and culture in the 1400s. It boasted a large merchant fleet that rivaled those of VENICE and Genoa, and its wide-ranging trade extended from England to the eastern Mediterranean.

Dubrovnik (also known as Ragusa) enjoyed remarkable political stability. Archbishop Elias de Saraca played a major part in freeing the city from Venetian control and putting it under the protection of Hungary in the 1350s. Dubrovnik gained autonomy* after 1358 and over the next 50 years steadily extended control over neighboring lands. At its peak, the city population reached about 7,000, and the countryside had another 25,000. Although located between two powerful neighbors, Venice and the OTTOMAN EMPIRE, Dubrovnik maintained peaceful relations with both. It also established a diplomatic service that greatly aided its trade. Though generally avoiding foreign alliances, the republic came under Spain's protection during the 1500s.

Dubrovnik's system of government spread power among the noble families and prevented any single individual from gaining political control. The executive officer only held power for a six-month term. Real power lay with the Grand Council, made up of all noblemen over age 20. Authors and travelers spread word of Dubrovnik in western Europe as a "perfect republic." William SHAKESPEARE even used it as the setting of his play *Twelfth Night.*

The local language of Dubrovnik was Slavic, although the nobility spoke a dialect called *Old Ragusan* in the Grand Council. Culturally, Dubrovnik's greatest achievement was probably the vernacular* Slavic literature that developed there. Its plays by Marin Drzic and Ivan Gundulic are among the greatest works in the Slavic languages. Writers and artists in Dubrovnik combined local influences with Italian human-

* **autonomy**   independent self-government

* **vernacular**   native language or dialect of a region or country

* **humanism**   Renaissance cultural movement promoting the study of the humanities (the languages, literature, and history of ancient Greece and Rome) as a guide to living

ism* brought back from travel and study abroad. (*See also* **City-States; Government, Forms of; Hungary.**)

**Duel**

* **medieval**    referring to the Middle Ages, a period that began around A.D. 400 and ended around 1400 in Italy and 1500 in the rest of Europe

* **treatise**    long, detailed essay

* **Jesuit**    refers to a Roman Catholic religious order founded by St. Ignatius Loyola and approved in 1540

* **humanist**    Renaissance expert in the humanities (the languages, literature, history, and speech and writing techniques of ancient Greece and Rome)

* **aristocracy**    privileged upper classes of society; nobles or the nobility

Duels, combats between two armed individuals, are usually associated with affairs of honor. The duel had its roots in the medieval* practice of trial by battle, a method often authorized by officials to settle disputes between gentlemen in a public arena. This type of dueling ended by the mid-1500s. Thereafter, dueling came under fire and efforts were even made to prosecute duelers. At the Council of TRENT (1545–1563), the Roman Catholic Church condemned dueling. In 1566 France declared unauthorized dueling punishable by death. JAMES I of England waged a personal crusade against dueling and even wrote a treatise* against it.

None of these measures ended dueling, which continued to be popular in the late 1500s and early 1600s. According to estimates of the day, hundreds of European noblemen died every year in duels. The greatest number of duels took place in Italy, France, and England. The practice was rare in Spain, and only became popular in Germany and Holland in the late 1600s. Stage plays of the time, particularly in England, frequently featured scenes involving duels.

Many people criticized dueling, but others defended and glorified it. Despite the church's position, the Jesuits* tended to support the practice on the grounds that a man's honor was as valuable as his property and should be defended. French philosopher Jean BODIN believed that dueling offered an outlet for aristocrats and kept them from rebelling against the government.

Why did dueling become so popular during the Renaissance? Part of the answer is the elaborate code of honor developed by Italian humanists* of the 1400s and 1500s. The code specified how gentlemen should relate to each other, described various levels of insults, and explained how to respond to them. It became a mark of noble birth to settle matters of personal honor by dueling. Another factor in the increase in dueling was the development of the rapier—a light, thin, needle-sharp sword. Easier to handle than older, heavier swords, the rapier enabled gentlemen to walk around armed, to draw at a moment's notice, and to inflict grave injury.

Changes in the status and role of the aristocracy* also contributed to the growth of dueling. On the battlefield, military training and teamwork became more important than individual heroism and noble birth. Common foot solders, rather than nobles on horseback, now decided battles. At the same time, the ranks of the nobility grew as kings handed out many new titles. James I of England, for example, raised money in the early 1600s by selling titles to many commoners. Aristocrats worried about losing their special status. Dueling allowed them to show their nobility through a concern for personal honor, which would set them above the rest of society. (*See also* **Aristocracy; Chivalry; Honor; Violence; Warfare.**)

DÜRER, ALBRECHT

**1471–1528**
**German artist**

* **apprentice**   person bound by legal agreement to work for another for a specified period of time in return for instruction in a trade or craft

* **woodcut**   print made from a block of wood with an image carved into it

* **journeyman**   person who has completed an apprenticeship and is certified to work at a particular trade or craft

* **perspective**   artistic technique for creating the illusion of three-dimensional space on a flat surface

* **classical**   in the tradition of ancient Greece and Rome

A remarkably talented painter, printmaker, and designer, Albrecht Dürer was perhaps the best-known artist in Renaissance Europe. His prints spread his work far and wide throughout Europe, extending his influence as an artist well beyond his homeland of Germany. Dürer's work came to embody German art for audiences of later generations.

**Early Years.** Dürer was born in Nürnberg. His father, a noted goldsmith, trained him in the art of metalworking. The young Dürer's talent for drawing was already evident in 1484, when he produced a delicate self-portrait. Created at a time when artists rarely focused on their own images, this work became the first of many self-portraits by Dürer.

In 1486 Dürer became an apprentice* to Michael Wolgemut, Nürnberg's leading painter. Under Wolgemut, the young artist learned the arts of drawing, painting, and printmaking. Dürer may have assisted his master in designing and producing woodcuts* to illustrate two books.

Upon finishing his training in 1489, Dürer began a period of travel as a journeyman*. His travels took him to Basel and Strasbourg, two leading publishing centers, where he produced illustrations for books. Returning to Nürnberg in 1494, Dürer married Agnes Frey, the daughter of a well-known coppersmith. Agnes supported her husband throughout his art career, helping to manage his large workshop and often traveling to fairs to sell his prints.

Later that year Dürer visited Venice and other towns in northern Italy, where he discovered the work of Andrea MANTEGNA and Giovanni BELLINI. Mantegna inspired Dürer with his powerful images of the ancient world, his attention to the human body, and his use of perspective*. Bellini taught Dürer new approaches to the use of color.

**Woodcuts, Engravings, and Paintings.** Back in his native Nürnberg in 1495, Dürer established a workshop and entered one of the most productive periods of his career. During this time Dürer focused primarily on woodcuts and engravings. In his woodcuts, he experimented with ways to organize space and with varied material surfaces, using the white background of paper to suggest both solid matter and open areas. Dürer also explored the use of lines to express form, texture, and light. Through prints of these works, Dürer's artistic ideas and fame reached a growing audience well beyond Nürnberg.

Dürer's early skill with metalworking tools attracted him to the art of engraving as early as 1494. Several of his engravings reveal his growing fascination with the ancient world and with the human body. In a work entitled *Nemesis,* featuring a figure of a winged nude woman, Dürer followed a precise formula for human proportions laid out in the writings of the ancient Roman architect Vitruvius. By drawing on these ancient sources, Dürer attempted to ground his art in theory.

Dürer's 1504 engraving *Adam and Eve* also shows his interest in the classical* tradition of portraying the human form. He based his figures on two ancient works of sculpture, the *Apollo Belvedere* and the *Medici Venus.* However, the way he presented them strongly reflects the artistic

German artist Albrecht Dürer produced carefully observed studies of the human form. His drawing *Praying Hands* from 1508, done in chalk on paper, is a detailed look at the human hand.

* **patron** supporter or financial sponsor of an artist or writer

* **Holy Roman Emperor** ruler of the Holy Roman Empire, a political body in central Europe composed of several states that existed until 1806

styles of northern Europe, with a stress on surfaces, lighting, and vivid contrasts between the figures and the backgrounds. His *Adam* and *Eve* are among the most complex and fascinating nudes in German art, and they inspired dozens of copies by other artists.

Throughout this period, Dürer also painted and produced designs for stained glass and various other decorative objects. In 1496 he did a portrait of Frederick III, the ruler of the German state of SAXONY. Frederick became a regular patron*, commissioning Dürer to create many works on religious themes.

**Italy and Nürnberg.** In 1505 Dürer returned to Venice, this time as a renowned artist. He observed in a letter that many jealous Italian artists criticized his works as "not antique and therefore not good," yet copied them at every opportunity. While in Venice, and during travels to Bologna, Rome, and Florence, Dürer continued his studies of perspective and the human form. In Rome, he copied several sketches of the human body by LEONARDO DA VINCI.

Back in Nürnberg by early 1507, Dürer entered another highly productive period. His life-sized paintings of *Adam* and *Eve* illustrate the lessons he had learned in Italy. In Dürer's earlier engraving, the two biblical figures had appeared rigid and formal, but the new works made Adam and Eve softer and more graceful. Dürer also produced many series of woodcuts and engravings during this period. Some of these, such as the *Life of the Virgin* and the *Engraved Passion,* are among the most technically brilliant and emotionally expressive works of his career.

Sometime between 1510 and 1512, Dürer began working for the Holy Roman Emperor* MAXIMILIAN I. He created several sketches for bronze statues of kings that the emperor wished to have decorating his tomb. With the help of other artists in his workshop, Dürer also produced nearly 200 woodcuts for a massive collection called the *Triumphal Arch.* In 1515 Maximilian rewarded Dürer with an annual salary paid out of Nürnberg's taxes.

**Final Years.** Dürer made another journey in 1520 to 1521, this time to the Netherlands. According to the notes in his diary, wherever the artist went the locals treated him as a celebrity. Dürer paid for the trip by selling prints, drawing portraits, and producing a few paintings. During the journey, however, he developed a fever that permanently damaged his health.

In the last years of his life, Dürer concentrated on portraits and writing about art. He became a pioneer in the field of art theory, which until then had been undeveloped in Germany. In fact, he often had to invent his own artistic terms. Although his texts became popular with scholars, they had little practical impact on artists of his time.

After Dürer's death, his reputation continued to grow, and collectors eagerly searched out his drawings, prints, and paintings. The period between about 1570 and 1620 was called the "Dürer Renaissance" because of the great popularity of his work and of new works in his style. (*See also* **Anatomy; Architecture; Art in Germany; Art in Italy; Books and Manuscripts; Printing and Publishing.**)

## Dynastic Rivalry

**\* prince**   Renaissance term for the ruler of an independent state

**\* succession**   determination of person who will inherit the throne

**\* Holy Roman Empire**   political body in central Europe composed of several states; existed until 1806

During the Renaissance the ruling families of Europe competed for power and territory. Princes\* viewed each other as rivals in building alliances, trading networks, and overseas empires. Although rulers did not try to eliminate other dynasties, they watched the activities of rivals closely and took steps to protect their own interests. Sometimes competition over power or land triggered conflicts that continued from one generation to the next.

**Territorial Claims and Disputes.**   The race for wealth and influence was one factor in dynastic rivalry during the Renaissance. Even more important, though, were disputes over land and succession\*. These often affected numerous states and contributed to continuing instability in Europe. Many of the conflicts involved the HABSBURG DYNASTY, a family that controlled the Holy Roman Empire\* and various other kingdoms for centuries.

Questions about succession arose when rulers lacked a suitable heir to assume power after their death. In such situations, the prince often drew up an agreement naming a successor from another ruling family. However, these agreements were difficult to enforce. In some cases the local nobility challenged the agreement and refused to recognize the new leader. In others, distant relatives of the deceased suddenly appeared to claim the title and land. To make matters worse, princes frequently signed succession agreements with more than one family, increasing the likelihood of conflicting claims. Although marriages between ruling families were designed to strengthen dynastic relationships, they frequently created problems, such as disagreement over the transfer of land called for in a marriage contract.

Dynastic disputes resulted in bitter struggles between powerful families. Many princes viewed the loss of land or title as personal insults and defended their rights as a point of honor. Some spared no expense in pursuing their claims. In the early 1500s, for example, the Habsburgs and the VALOIS DYNASTY of France were engaged in a fierce rivalry. Eventually the military costs of defending their claims caused serious financial problems on both sides, and the competition came to a temporary halt.

**Extinction of Houses.**   The possibility that a ruling family would become extinct always increased the likelihood of conflict. In fact, between the 1300s and early 1600s, a large number of the ruling families of Europe did die out. Other families rushed in to try to gain control of the unoccupied seats of power.

A rivalry based on the end of a dynasty led to the Hundred Years' War (1337–1453) between France and England. Economic and political differences had long been a source of disagreement between the two countries. However, when the last male heir to the French royal house of Capet died in 1328, competing French and English claims to the throne led to a full-scale war.

Another succession rivalry involving the duchy\* of BURGUNDY pitted the Valois dynasty of France against the Habsburgs. After the death of

**\* duchy**   territory ruled by a duke or duchess

Charles the Bold of Burgundy in 1477, the Valois king tried to incorporate parts of Burgundy into France. His campaign angered the Habsburgs, who also laid claim to the duchy.

Central Europe lost all its royal families in the 1300s and 1400s. The end of the Piast dynasty of Poland in 1370 set the stage for a contest between the king of Hungary and the prince of Lithuania for control of Poland. The Jagellonians, a Lithuanian family, took over. Then the Jagellonian dynasty died out in 1572, leading to competition between the Habsburgs, the Valois, and other royal families.

**Armed Conflicts.** In western Europe, dynastic conflicts sometimes led to war. One of the major power struggles of the Renaissance occurred in the early 1500s between the Spanish branch of the Habsburg family and the French Valois. The dispute revolved mainly around the Italian cities of NAPLES and MILAN, which had succession problems. In 1499 the French seized Milan. When the Habsburg ruler CHARLES V became king of Spain in 1516, he challenged the French for the right to Milan, and the Spanish eventually won control of it.

Seeking to hold back Habsburg advances, the Valois kings of France allied themselves with German Protestant princes and the OTTOMAN EMPIRE. By the late 1500s, however, both Spain and France became preoccupied with internal affairs. The rivalry cooled, only to resurface in later conflicts, including the THIRTY YEARS' WAR (1618–1648). (*See also* **Aristocracy; Borgia, House of; Bourbon Family and Dynasty; City-States; Este, House of; Farnese, House of; Gonzaga, House of; Guise-Lorraine Family; Medici, House of; Monarchy; Montefeltro Family; Montmorency Family; Princes and Princedoms; Stuart Dynasty.**)

## Economy and Trade

* **feudalism**   economic and political system in which individuals gave services to a lord in return for protection and use of the land

* **capitalism**   economic system in which individuals own property and businesses

* **medieval**   referring to the Middle Ages, a period that began around A.D. 400 and ended around 1400 in Italy and 1500 in the rest of Europe

During the Renaissance, the European economy grew dramatically, particularly in the area of trade. Developments such as population growth, improvements in banking, expanding trade routes, and new manufacturing systems led to an overall increase in commercial activity. Feudalism*, which had been widespread in the Middle Ages, gradually disappeared, and early forms of capitalism* emerged. The changes affected many aspects of European society, forcing people to adapt to different kinds of work and new ways of doing business with others.

**Agriculture.** Medieval* Europe was overwhelmingly rural, and its economy depended almost entirely on agriculture. Towns and cities did not become significant centers of production until the late Middle Ages, but after that time their economic importance increased rapidly.

During the Middle Ages most peasants were serfs, individuals tied by law to the land they worked. By the late 1400s, however, serfdom was declining throughout Europe and peasants were freer to move about and to rent farms for themselves. At about this time peasants in many parts of Europe faced a shortage of open land. Most of the best fields were already being farmed. Moreover, high prices for wool encouraged

During the Renaissance, Europe's economy began to focus more on manufacturing. As depicted in "De Sphaera" from the illuminated manuscript of the *Book of Astrology*, merchants set up shops to sell goods such as cloth, spices, food, and metalwork.

nobles to enclose pastures for herding sheep, denying the peasants access to the land. As a result, thousands of peasants moved to urban areas looking for jobs, and cities and towns swelled in size.

As populations grew, the demand for food rose. Meanwhile, the new freedom of peasants meant that landowners had to pay more for their labor. These developments made goods more expensive and produced inflation—a general increase in prices—across Europe. The combination of rising prices and a growth in the number of people needing goods and services encouraged merchants to expand their businesses.

**The European Economy.** Renaissance Europe had a very diverse economy, in which many different goods were produced by various regions. Over time, some parts of the continent grew economically, while others declined.

In the 1300s and 1400s Italy dominated European trade and manufacturing. Merchants in Florence, Milan, and Venice developed large business organizations to carry on their activities across Europe. They manufactured, sold, or traded a wide variety of products. They also provided banking services for governments and other merchants in many areas of Europe.

Some cities specialized in particular areas of trade and manufacturing. Florence was known for the production of woolen cloth and silk. Milan produced metal goods, such as armor. Venice dominated Mediterranean trade. Venetian merchants bought spices and other goods from Arab and Ottoman* traders in eastern Mediterranean ports and shipped the goods to buyers in Italy and northern Europe.

In the early 1500s mining became an important economic activity in southern Germany. The silver, copper, tin, and iron produced by the mines were used to make various metal items, including silver coins. Funding from merchants and bankers in the cities of Nürnberg and Augsburg helped mine operators introduce new techniques and increase productivity. However, after 1550 the flow of silver from Spanish mines in the New World made silver mining in Germany unprofitable.

Overseas exploration contributed to the rapid development of Spanish and Portuguese trade in the 1500s. Spain brought silver from the Americas, and Portugal imported slaves, sugar, and other goods from Africa. The Portuguese also began to trade with Asia, breaking the Venetian monopoly* on goods such as spices, which were highly prized in Europe. However, Spain and Portugal did not profit as much as they should have from their overseas trade. They both borrowed heavily from banks in Italy and Germany to finance their voyages. Moreover, the two countries shipped much of the silver, spices, and other overseas goods to northern Europe. Merchants in northern ports such as Antwerp profited as much as—or more than—the Spanish and Portuguese from the overseas trade.

After the 1550s the center of Europe's manufacturing, trade, and banking moved from Italy and the Mediterranean to northern Europe, especially the Netherlands and England. Amsterdam and London became major centers of commerce, in part because of the increased importance of transatlantic trade routes. Italy remained a leader in the production of luxury goods such as works of art and fine silk cloth, but the balance had shifted.

**Manufacturing.** A number of changes in the organization of manufacturing and trade occurred during the Renaissance, especially in the 1500s. Major guilds*, such as those for the production of woolen cloth, changed character. Owners and investors dominated the guilds, making all the decisions. Investors had considerable political power, which they used to advance their interests, sometimes at the expense of the workers. Moreover, some laborers, such as many wool workers, were not even members of the guild, but they depended on the owners for their jobs.

During the Renaissance the European economy experienced a mix of crises and opportunities. Nevertheless, people showed remarkable skill

* **Ottoman Turks** Turkish followers of Islam who founded the Ottoman Empire in the 1300s; the empire eventually included large areas of eastern Europe, the Middle East, and northern Africa

* **monopoly** exclusive right to engage in a particular type of business

* **guild** association of craft and trade owners and workers that set standards for and represented the interests of its members

## Transfer of Power

Between 1550 and 1650 northern Europe replaced Italy as the center of the continent's economic activity. The growth of the cities of Amsterdam and London during this period reflects that change. In 1500 Amsterdam, under Spanish rule, had some 11,000 residents. After expelling the Spanish 78 years later, the city's economy and population both grew rapidly. Amsterdam had 50,000 residents in 1600 and a population of 150,000 by 1650. It became one of the most important commercial centers in northern Europe. London experienced similarly explosive growth. A city of 100,000 in 1500, London doubled in size by 1600 and doubled again by 1650. By that date it had 400,000 inhabitants and was the largest city in western Europe.

in adapting to change. If one promising trade route failed, merchants developed others. If one industry declined, another took its place. When Venice lost its leading role in the Asian spice trade, it became a center for printing. In 1500 Venice printed more books than any other city. Yet, in the 1570s, printing declined in Venice, and Paris became the printing capital of Europe, continuing the process of growth and change in the Renaissance economy.

**Banking.** Much of the increase in commercial activity during the Renaissance occurred in the area of international trade. This led the banking industry to expand to provide financial services that made it easier for merchants to conduct business far from home.

In the Middle Ages merchants had developed long-distance trade routes to bring their customers exotic goods from faraway lands. During the Renaissance merchants made use of their knowledge of international markets and trade goods to expand their operations. Some of these merchants became important bankers. They began making loans, transferring funds to different locations, and exchanging various forms of money. As the need for financial services increased, banks emerged as important institutions. Two of Europe's most prominent banks were run by the MEDICI of Florence and the FUGGER FAMILY of Augsburg in Germany.

Banks lent entrepreneurs the money to buy materials and equipment, to hire workers, and to pay for transporting goods. Without these funds, few people would have been able to develop large-scale trading enterprises. Banks also simplified the handling of money by introducing bills of exchange, notes that allowed merchants to borrow or deposit money in one city, then repay or withdraw money in another city. Merchants could then transfer money over long distances without the risk and inconvenience of carrying coins.

**Trade Routes and Trading Centers.** Political developments and overseas exploration had a profound effect on European trade. At the beginning of the Renaissance, the Mediterranean Sea was the main arena of international trade. Venice dominated commerce in the region because of its powerful merchant fleet and strategic location. The Venetians controlled the flow of luxury goods and spices between Asia and Europe.

In the early 1400s the OTTOMAN EMPIRE expanded westward, and Venice lost vital bases in the eastern Mediterranean. Then in the late 1400s the Portuguese discovered a sea route to Asia by sailing around Africa. This broke the Italians' monopoly over the profitable spice trade. Spain, France, England, and the Netherlands soon followed Portugal in opening up overseas markets in Asia. In the 1500s, merchants began to develop trade routes across the Atlantic Ocean to supply colonies being settled in the Americas. This contributed to the decline of Venice, Genoa, and other Mediterranean ports.

During the Middle Ages, much trading in Europe had taken place at regional fairs, such as those held in the Netherlands and the

Champagne region of France. By the Renaissance many of the fairs had disappeared and some of those that survived had begun to specialize in particular goods or services. For example, the fair in Lyon, France, concentrated on international money exchange. Meanwhile, many Renaissance cities became centers of trade and banking, reducing the need for fairs as a place to buy and sell goods. In the Netherlands, local fairs declined when Antwerp emerged as a commercial hub.

**Trade Goods.** A wide variety of goods were traded in Europe, with each country known for certain products. Although Italy suffered a general decline in trade after 1500, it was still the main source for fine arts and crafts such as painting, woodcarving, sculpture, silver and gold objects, glasswork, and silk. The Spanish prospered during the 1400s from trade in crafts such as leather processing and metalworking. Spain also produced olive oil, wine, fruit, and grain. However, Spanish agriculture, which depended on the labor of the Moors*, suffered heavily when the Moors were expelled from the country in 1492.

England exported raw wool and competed with the Netherlands in the market for woolen cloth. France sold grain and linen cloth to England and Spain, and wine and fruit to England, the Netherlands, and Switzerland. The Netherlands, famous for its cloth products, developed an important banking industry during the late 1500s and 1600s. (*See also* **Accounting; Agriculture; Artisans; Exploration; Fairs and Festivals; Guilds; Industry; Luxury; Mercantilism; Mining and Metallurgy; Money and Banking; Peasantry; Ships and Shipbuilding; Taxation and Public Finance; Transportation and Communication.**)

* **Moor** Muslim from North Africa; Moorish invaders conquered much of Spain during the Middle Ages

* **humanism** Renaissance cultural movement promoting the study of the humanities (the languages, literature, and history of ancient Greece and Rome) as a guide to living

* **classical** in the tradition of ancient Greece and Rome

* **rhetoric** art of speaking or writing effectively

The rise of humanism* had a great impact on education during the Renaissance. Schools began to focus more on the language and literature of the ancient world. They also adopted teaching methods based on classical* texts, with the study of rhetoric* occupying a particularly important place in the classroom. The spread of humanist education helped promote a common culture among people of different nations, languages, and religions. However, this change was limited mostly to the upper classes.

## FOUNDATIONS OF RENAISSANCE EDUCATION

Most Renaissance schools based their educational practices on the theories of ancient Greece and Rome. Italian educators were the first to adopt the models offered by ancient writers. Their approach to education later spread to all corners of Europe.

**Beginnings in Italy.** In 1350 the early humanist PETRARCH unearthed parts of a work called *Instruction in Oratory,* by the ancient Roman teacher Quintilian. The full text, discovered in 1416, inspired a new humanist approach to education. It outlined a training program that

As schools adopted a classical curriculum during the Renaissance, the demand for new grammar texts increased. This wood-cut of a Renaissance classroom appeared in a 1573 Latin grammar book.

lasted from birth to adulthood and aimed to provide both excellent public speaking skills and sound morals. Quintilian suggested that teachers begin with simple exercises and progress over time to more complex ones, with constant support tailored to the student's specific needs. He also believed that children should balance their studies with recreation. Rigid rules and harsh punishment had no place in Quintilian's program because he believed that young people are naturally inclined to learn.

Quintilian focused on reading, composition, and especially rhetoric. This focus carried over into Renaissance education. A complete copy of the *Instruction* was one of the first printed books in Italy. One hundred editions of the work appeared over the next 80 years.

Another work that had a great influence on education was *On Noble Customs and Liberal Studies of Adolescents*, by Pier Paolo VERGERIO. Written in 1404, it argued for the importance of history, moral philosophy, and poetry. Vergerio's ideas echoed Quintilian's in several ways. He advised instructors to consider the different characters and mental abilities of students and to avoid harsh punishments. He also stressed the importance of physical training as well as study. In Vergerio's system, students had to master each lesson before moving on to the next. Students could also act as teachers to other students.

Many Italian writers claimed that humanist education could benefit

the community by improving the character and culture of its future leaders. They believed that an ideal citizen should be familiar with classical culture and able to speak with grace and style. Knowledge of the humanities became the mark of an educated person and a basic requirement for political posts in Italy.

**Educational Practice.** Humanist education began among private tutors in wealthy households in Italy but soon spread into Latin grammar schools. In 1423 VITTORINO DA FELTRE founded one of the first humanist schools at the court of the Duke of Mantua. He taught the children of the duke and other noble families as well as promising students from poor families. They began their instruction with reading and spelling as young as age four or five.

Vittorino's goal was to teach students to write and speak Latin and Greek. He taught all lessons in Latin and expected his students to memorize large amounts of text. Pupils read works by Latin poets and historians to learn vocabulary, syntax (word usage), and pronunciation. The curriculum also included philosophy, mathematics, astronomy, and geometry. Vittorino stressed the development of the mind, body, and character of his pupils. Physical exercise and religious services were part of their daily routine.

Guarino GUARINI, another noted Italian educator, opened a humanist school at the court in Ferrara. Like Vittorino, he required his students to memorize passages, but he focused more on understanding the meaning of the works. He worked through texts carefully, defining terms and explaining background. The ideas of Vittorino and Guarini spread to towns throughout northern and central Italy in the mid-1400s. By the end of the 1400s nearly all Latin schools in Italy followed the humanist program.

**Textbooks.** In the early 1400s, teachers were still using grammar texts that had been popular during the Middle Ages. The shift to classical Latin texts during the Renaissance created a demand for new grammars. One of Vittorino's students published a Latin grammar in Rome in 1473. In 1487 Antonio de Nebrija wrote a Latin grammar that featured columns of Spanish text alongside the Latin. This work was used widely throughout Europe and was the only Latin grammar allowed in Spain or Portugal. Nebrija later compiled the first Spanish-Latin dictionary.

Johannes Despauterius of the Netherlands produced the most popular Latin grammar text of the Renaissance. His 1520 book *Grammar* became the model for all Latin grammars in France, Scotland, and the Netherlands until the 1900s. In Germany, Philipp MELANCHTHON produced a basic Latin grammar in 1524 that remained in use until the 1700s. The leading grammar text in England was William Lily's *Rudiments of Grammar,* which became the basis for later Latin grammars approved by the crown. These descendants of Lily's work were used long after the end of the Renaissance.

Along with grammars, students used phrase books and grammar exercises created by their instructors. Many humanist schools also used commonplace books, notebooks of quotations from classical texts. Pupils

---

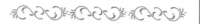

## Jesuits and Jesuitesses

In 1548 the Jesuits founded their first school for students outside of the religious order. Twelve years later, instructing others became part of Jesuit training. Students at Jesuit schools learned grammar, rhetoric, poetry, logic, philosophy, religion, mathematics, and astronomy from Latin texts. In 1609 a similar system of schools for girls, known as the Institute of the Blessed Virgin Mary, opened in England. By 1631 the Institute had 300 female instructors (popularly known as Jesuitesses). One of its schools, located in Vienna, had as many as 500 pupils.

---

often translated material from Latin to the vernacular* and back again. Many humanists believed that students should learn grammar by imitating classical authors, rather than by following "the naked rules of grammarians." The Dutch scholar Desiderius ERASMUS aimed to promote this method of learning in *Foundations of the Abundant Style,* a collection of texts by ancient writers. The work became a standard in schools throughout northern Europe.

The humanist curriculum also relied on colloquies, fictional dialogues in the classical style. These works provided models for speaking Latin outside of class, a practice that many schools encouraged. Erasmus published the first edition of his *Colloquies* in 1518, and it quickly became the most popular work of this type. Teachers also made extensive use of original Latin works by authors such as VIRGIL, Ovid, CICERO, and Livy. In addition, students read parts of the BIBLE and some works by early church fathers (figures who shaped Christianity in its early centuries).

## SPREAD OF HUMANIST EDUCATION

The humanist educational system soon spread beyond Italy, although it took slightly different forms from one country to another. Each nation adapted the course of study to fit its cultural and religious needs.

**Education in France.** The elite* in French towns and cities quickly embraced humanist education, as did the French king FRANCIS I. During the 1520s and 1530s city leaders funded many classical grammar schools, called *colleges.* The French adapted the Italian-Latin tradition, adding elements of Christian philosophy and French culture to the curriculum. Students worked their way through a series of classes, beginning with basic Latin works before proceeding to more challenging texts. They also had lessons in Greek grammar and read the works of Greek authors such as PLATO, ARISTOTLE, and Xenophon. By the mid-1500s nearly every town of reasonable size had a public school with four to six instructors teaching several hundred students.

Town elites encouraged the rapid growth of humanist schools in France. They felt that a humanist education honored the king, strengthened the country as a whole, and was "of greater profit to a community than are all the hospitals in the world." Despite the enthusiasm for humanist education in towns and cities, it had almost no impact in villages or rural areas. It also failed to appeal to French nobles, who continued to prefer military and practical training.

By the 1570s France's classical grammar schools had fallen into decline. Funds ran short, and qualified teachers were scarce. Religious politics also affected schools as the state tried to enforce Catholicism at a time when many teachers were attracted to Protestantism. In the early 1600s Catholic priests and religious orders began to combine classical studies with religious training. However, by this time both the church and the crown felt that there were too many educated laypeople* in

France. Renaissance education gradually gave way to an emphasis on French language and culture and on Christian thought.

**Education in Spain and Portugal.** Humanist education became popular at Spanish and Portuguese courts in the mid-1400s. Humanist ideas reached Spain largely through the court of Alfonso V in Naples, as well as through contacts with Rome and Florence. In addition, many Spanish students attended Italian universities, while the royal court of Portugal sent pupils to study in PARIS. By the late 1400s humanism had taken root in Spain, with the support of the queen, ISABELLA OF CASTILE. Spain's royal court hosted two schools of classical Latin, and noble families regularly hired humanist tutors. Humanist education in Spain and Portugal tended to place a heavy emphasis on Spanish Roman writers such as Quintilian.

By the year 1600, hundreds of Spanish towns boasted Latin grammar schools. However, church schools were also on the rise in the late 1500s. By 1600 the Jesuits* dominated Spanish education. There were more than 100 Jesuit colleges in Spain's major towns and cities, educating as many as 10,000 to 15,000 boys each year.

**Education in England and Scotland.** Erasmus was a major force in the spread of humanist education to England. He visited the country several times between 1499 and the early 1500s and wrote his text *On the Method of Study* there in 1511. He argued that children should begin life speaking Latin and read widely to improve their skills, not just memorize rules of grammar. In his last essay on education, Erasmus criticized the teaching practices of his day, particularly those used in monastery schools. He urged parents to send their children to public schools or educate them at home.

St. Paul's, founded by John Colet, was the best-known humanist school in England. William Lily, a scholar who had studied classical Latin and Greek in Italy, served as schoolmaster. St. Paul's used texts by Erasmus and the instruction had a strong Christian emphasis. Colet considered school a sacred space, a view that contributed to the popularity of English schools. Colet's successor at St. Paul's favored a more classical program of education.

Humanism was not as popular in northern England and Scotland as it was in the south. Documents dating from the mid-1500s indicate that most schools in northern England were large public schools. Although they may have promoted classical studies, their teaching methods continued to focus on firm discipline. There is little solid evidence of humanist education in Scotland prior to the 1560s, although the Latin grammar of Despauterius was apparently popular. In 1563 educator George Buchanan proposed a humanist program for the University of St. Andrews. Parts of this program may have found favor at grammar schools in several Scottish cities. Overall, however, Scottish schools did not follow a consistent curriculum. Many grammar teachers created their own Latin texts based on classical models.

**Education in Germany and the Netherlands.** Humanism began to affect education in Germany and the Netherlands by the late 1400s

* **Jesuit** refers to a Roman Catholic religious order founded by St. Ignatius Loyola and approved in 1540

and early 1500s. City schools throughout the Netherlands were modeled after Italian schools, although they sometimes showed French influences as well. Education in this part of Europe was very organized, with specialized subjects and classes divided into grades. Students began studying Latin in their first class. They added Greek in the second, and their lessons increased in difficulty with each level.

The Protestant Reformation* had little effect on the curriculum in German schools. However, both Protestant and Catholic schools added more religious instruction. Melanchthon introduced a model Latin curriculum that combined classical studies with Scripture, music, and some Hebrew. This program was particularly popular in Germany and Denmark. The school in the city of Strasbourg offered the most thorough humanist education in Germany. It had eight classes arranged according to a strict hierarchy*. Students had to pass a thorough exam to move from one level to the next.

**Education of Women.** Many humanist thinkers took a favorable view of the education of women. Quintilian's works had included examples of learned Roman women and had recommended that both fathers and mothers be as well educated as possible. The many female rulers throughout Europe, as well as the powerful women in the courts of northern Italy, may also have had an impact on humanist attitudes.

Most writers, however, saw education as a way to prepare women for their roles as wives and mothers, rather than an end in itself. One early letter addressing female education recommended all of the "new learning" as appropriate for girls, but noted that debate and public speaking "are of the least practical use, if indeed they are not positively unbecoming" to a woman. Despite this advice, some learned Italian women gave public speeches and corresponded on learned topics with men. Women in other nations also began to take on less traditional roles in society. In Spain, for example, Francisca de Nebrija, the daughter of Antonio de Nebrija, may have substituted for her father as a lecturer at the University of Alcala. Many learned women from Spain, Italy, and other parts of Europe entered convents.

Women in England had few opportunities for classical training. Education remained restricted to households and to elementary schools, where girls received instruction in English. Some women, such as the daughters of HENRY VIII, benefited from humanist tutors at the royal court. (*See also* **Academies; Classical Scholarship; Humanism; Latin Language and Literature; Literacy; Printing and Publishing; Science; Translation; Universities.**)

* **Protestant Reformation** religious movement that began in the 1500s as a protest against certain practices of the Roman Catholic Church and eventually led to the establishment of a variety of Protestant churches

* **hierarchy** organization of a group into higher and lower levels

**1537–1553**
**King of England**

Edward VI, the only son of England's king HENRY VIII, succeeded his father on the throne at the age of nine. Edward's reign was cut short by his death from tuberculosis six years later. During his reign the Protestant Reformation* took root in England, but Edward himself played little part in national politics.

* **Protestant Reformation** religious movement that began in the 1500s as a protest against certain practices of the Roman Catholic Church and eventually led to the establishment of a variety of Protestant churches

* **humanist** referring to a Renaissance cultural movement promoting the study of the humanities (the languages, literature, and history of ancient Greece and Rome) as a guide to living

* **mystery play** early form of drama based on biblical stories

* **patronage** support or financial sponsorship

The young king received a thorough humanist* education that reflected the influence of the Renaissance in England. His studies were based on the curriculum designed for undergraduates at Cambridge University. He learned ancient history, Latin and Greek, geography, mathematics, astronomy, music, and a variety of other subjects. He also received a thorough grounding in Protestant beliefs from his tutors and from preachers at the royal court. Edward's guardians were fervent Protestants who sought to instill in him the principles of "true religion."

Edward's uncle Edward Seymour, duke of Somerset, acted as the young king's protector and assumed political power in his place. Somerset abolished the Roman Catholic Mass and Catholic symbols such as candles and shrines. He also suppressed traditional religious practices such as maypoles and mystery plays*. However, a costly war with France and a peasant rebellion at home led a group of royal advisers to put an end to Somerset's protectorate in 1549. John Dudley, duke of Northumberland, took control of the government for the remainder of Edward's reign. Before his death, Edward tried to prevent his Catholic sister Mary (MARY I) from succeeding him.

Renaissance styles reached England during Edward's reign. Under the patronage* of the Duke of Somerset, artists from the Netherlands and Italy brought new French styles to England. Somerset's house in London, built in 1550, marked the arrival of Renaissance architecture in England. The English artist John Shute went to Italy in the same year to study the architecture of ancient Greece and Rome. His descriptions and engravings of the ancient structures were the first to be published in England. (*See also* **Art in Britain; England.**)

### El Greco

ca. 1541–1614
**Greek painter in Spain**

* **Byzantine** referring to the Eastern Christian Empire based in Constantinople (A.D. 476–1453)

* **humanist** Renaissance expert in the humanities (the languages, literature, history, and speech and writing techniques of ancient Greece and Rome)

* **patron** supporter or financial sponsor of an artist or writer

* **naturalistic** realistic, showing the world as it is without idealization

The artist known as El Greco (Spanish for "the Greek") developed a truly distinctive style of painting that combined methods of Byzantine* and Renaissance Italian art. His vibrant works were filled with turmoil and great religious feeling. The portraits he painted reveal remarkable psychological insight into the character of his subjects.

Born Doménikos Theotokópoulos on the island of Crete, El Greco was the son of a tax collector. He received artistic training in the Byzantine tradition of icon painting, the highly stylized religious art associated with the Greek Orthodox Church. At the time Crete belonged to Venice, and in 1567 El Greco established himself in Venice.

Under the influence of Renaissance Italy, the artist slowly transformed his style of painting. He particularly admired the work of the Venetian masters TITIAN and TINTORETTO. By November 1570 El Greco had moved to Rome, where he continued his study of Renaissance painting. He also became acquainted with a group of humanists* associated with Fulvio Orsini, a great scholar of CLASSICAL ANTIQUITY.

El Greco had trouble finding patrons* in Italy, so he moved to Spain in July 1577 and settled in the city of TOLEDO. One of the artist's first commissions was for a painting for Toledo's cathedral. In the work, the *Disrobing of Christ,* he combined a vivid naturalistic* style with idealized

forms. Cathedral officials criticized various elements of the picture, but El Greco refused to make the changes they requested.

While in Italy, El Greco had absorbed Renaissance ideas about artistic freedom and mastery of technique. The Spanish audience for which El Greco was working found these ideas unacceptable. In Italy he had become interested in Mannerism, an artistic style popular in the late 1500s. The style, characterized by elongated and twisted figures, strange spatial relationships, and harsh lighting, did not find favor in Spain.

Nonetheless, El Greco was among the artists selected to provide altarpieces for the royal complex of El Escorial, built by the Spanish king PHILIP II. El Greco's work, the *Martyrdom of St. Maurice and the Theban League,* was completed in 1582. However, Philip disliked the painting, perhaps because it introduced new methods of narrative* and composition. Although Philip kept the work, he paid less for it than the artist had requested and ordered a new picture of the same subject from another artist. Thus, El Greco had failed to please two of the most powerful patrons in Spain—the king and the cathedral officials of Toledo.

After the disappointment of El Escorial, El Greco returned to Toledo. By 1585 he had established a workshop that produced copies of his paintings, as well as frames and statues. In 1586 he received an important commission for the chapel of Santo Tomé in Toledo. The monumental painting he created, *The Burial of the Count Orgaz,* is one of the artist's masterpieces.

Although El Greco rarely painted landscapes, his brooding *View of Toledo* opened a new chapter in the history of landscape painting by using nature to express emotion. In portraits and religious scenes, El Greco created elongated, otherworldly figures, strong diagonal lines, and abrupt contrasts of tone and color in an effort to rise above earthly matters and express the divine. Many elements of his work seemed perfectly suited to express Spanish religious fervor. (*See also* **Art; Art in Spain and Portugal.**)

* **narrative** storytelling

**1533–1603**
**English queen**

* **adultery** sexual relationship outside of marriage

* **classical** in the tradition of ancient Greece and Rome

Daughter of one monarch and sister of two others, Elizabeth I became queen of England in 1558 and ruled for 45 years. Her long reign, often referred to as the Elizabethan Age, was notable for war with Spain, religious tension, and the flourishing of a brilliant Renaissance court.

**Life and Reign.** Elizabeth was born in 1533 to HENRY VIII of England and Anne Boleyn, his second wife. Three years after Elizabeth's birth, her father accused her mother of adultery* and had her beheaded. In the years that followed, Elizabeth was raised to be married to a European king or prince, the usual life for princesses during the Renaissance. Hence, she received an excellent education that included training in the Greek, Latin, Italian, and French languages and exposure to classical* literature. She also received training in the Protestant faith—not surprising, because her father, the king, had broken off from the Roman Catholic Church over the issue of divorcing his first wife.

This picture of Elizabeth I, known as the Armada Portrait, celebrates England's victory over the Spanish Armada in 1588. The victory was a proud moment for Elizabeth, and she became very popular among her troops.

When Henry VIII died in 1547, Elizabeth's nine-year-old brother became EDWARD VI of England. The young king died six years later, and the throne passed to Elizabeth's older sister, Mary (MARY I). The new queen brought Catholicism back to England, and Elizabeth was in some danger of execution as a Protestant threat to the monarchy. However, Mary's closest advisers argued against such an act. A few years later, on the verge of death, Mary reluctantly acknowledged Elizabeth as her heir.

When Elizabeth assumed the throne of England in 1558, she assembled a team of advisers and officials who would govern the country for much of her reign. William Cecil, Lord Burghley, led the government until 1598. Francis Walsingham, one of Elizabeth's chief advisers on foreign affairs, managed a network of spies. He provided proof that Elizabeth's cousin Mary (MARY STUART), the Catholic queen of Scotland, was involved in treasonous plots. Mary had fled to England in 1568, where she was imprisoned by Elizabeth and finally executed in 1587.

Robert Dudley, earl of Leicester, became the queen's favorite courtier in 1559. Her affection for Dudley, a married man whose wife died in suspicious circumstances, gave him great power in court. After Dudley's death in 1588, the earl of Essex emerged as Elizabeth's favorite. But then in 1599, returning from defeat in a war in Ireland, Essex rushed into the aging queen's chamber and saw her without her makeup and wig. Furious, the queen cast him off. Two years later Essex tried to seize control of the court and the queen. He was executed.

For the first 20 years of Elizabeth's reign, England's relations with other countries revolved around the question of which royal suitor the

queen would marry. But Elizabeth did not marry, and she refused to name a successor. By about 1578, when her subjects assumed that the queen was past the years of childbearing, she began to be honored as an almost mythical figure. Admirers called her the Virgin Queen and referred to her poetically as Gloriana and Virginia (the American colony was named for her). By the time of her death in 1603, however, Elizabeth had grown unpopular with her subjects because of high taxes. Elizabeth refused to name a successor, but on her death the throne went to JAMES I, the son of the Scottish queen whom Elizabeth had ordered killed.

**Conflicts.** The first task of Elizabeth's government was to restore the Protestant religion in England after her sister Mary's rule. At first she did not punish Catholics simply for their faith. But after English Catholics tried to mount a rebellion against her in 1569, she became more aggressively Protestant. Elizabeth considered it her right and duty to lead the Anglican Church, the official Protestant church in England, and would not allow Parliament to discuss further religious reforms. Her reign saw increasing tension between her determination to keep the Anglican Church as it was and the Puritans* and other groups who wished to change it. As Elizabeth grew older, she became less tolerant of both Catholics and Protestants who expressed disagreement with the established church.

During the first 20 years of her reign, the queen kept England out of wars on the European continent. Eventually, however, Elizabeth and England were drawn into conflict with Spain. In 1588 Spain sent a vast fleet of ships against England, but this Spanish ARMADA suffered a crushing defeat because of weather and the superior guns of the English ships. The victory was a glorious moment for England. Elizabeth won great affection by appearing before her troops in armor and declaring that she had "the heart and stomach of a king" and would stand by them in the fight. Yet war with Spain dragged on for another decade. In addition, the Spanish stirred up new uprisings in Ireland, an English possession where many costly and bloody rebellions erupted during Elizabeth's reign.

**Court Culture.** Elizabeth presided over a glittering court. In the early years, its members were influenced by models from ancient times. Later a guide to courtly behavior by the Italian writer Baldassare CASTIGLIONE, *The Book of the Courtier* (1561), became quite popular. English courtiers began adopting the manners and ideals of European courts.

The queen spent most of her summers traveling about southern England, visiting the homes of her courtiers. Although Elizabeth built no palaces, members of the court erected a number of huge homes and palaces to welcome her. Courtiers both sought and dreaded these visits. Entertaining the queen and her court could be devastatingly expensive—among other costs were the spectacles and pageants that hosts arranged to honor, amuse, and impress her. In 1591, for example, Elizabeth and the court visited the earl of Hertford and were entertained by an elaborate pageant enacted on an island crowned with a mock castle.

* **Puritan** English Protestant group that wanted to simplify the ceremonies of the Church of England and eliminate all traces of Catholicism

Elizabeth spent the early years of her reign concentrating on laying the foundations of her state, establishing the beliefs and practices of her church, and restocking her treasury. After the mid-1570s, however, cultural life gained importance as Elizabeth's court stimulated new literary, artistic, and musical achievements. Plays were popular at court, and when Elizabeth visited the university towns of Oxford and Cambridge, students presented plays on classical themes. Chivalry* was also an important theme of the Elizabethan court, and many Elizabethan masterpieces contained elements drawn from romances of the Middle Ages. Among these works are Edmund SPENSER's long poem *The Faerie Queene* (1590–1596) and Sir Philip SIDNEY's *Arcadia* (1581–1584), in which knights fight for the love of a fair and chaste queen. Other artistic achievements of the age include the music of English composers William BYRD and Thomas Tallis and the paintings of Nicholas Hillyard. (*See also* **Court; Drama, English; England; English Language and Literature; Espionage; Patronage; Protestant Reformation; Puritanism.**)

* **chivalry**   rules and customs of medieval knighthood

## England

The course of the Renaissance in England corresponds closely with the history of the Tudor dynasty. Ideas associated with the Renaissance began to take hold in the country around the time that HENRY VII, the first Tudor monarch, assumed power. The Renaissance reached its peak in England during the reign of ELIZABETH I, the last Tudor monarch. Although Renaissance thought continued to flourish during the rule of her successor, JAMES I, it lost momentum after his death.

**The Birth of the Tudor Dynasty.**   When Henry VII took the throne in 1485, he put an end to the Wars of the Roses, a long struggle for power between the noble houses of York and Lancaster. Henry, a relative of the Lancasters, united the two families by marrying Elizabeth, the daughter of a Yorkist king. To strengthen his new dynasty, he arranged matches for his four children with foreign royals. His daughter Mary wed Louis XII of France, while his daughter Margaret married James IV of Scotland. The heir to the throne, Arthur, wed the Spanish princess CATHERINE OF ARAGON. When Arthur died in 1502, his younger brother Henry became heir and eventually married his brother's widow.

An able but rather colorless ruler, Henry VII firmly established the Tudor dynasty on the English throne. He made the government more efficient and raised money for the royal treasury. During his reign, the humanist* ideas that had begun to enter England took firm root. Latin and Greek, which only a few university scholars had studied before 1485, became a regular part of the curriculum around 1500. At the same time, the printing industry was established in England. The king took little personal interest in intellectual matters. However, his mother, Lady Margaret Beaufort, became a patron* of scholars and founded two colleges at Cambridge University.

* **humanist**   referring to a Renaissance cultural movement promoting the study of the humanities (the languages, literature, and history of ancient Greece and Rome) as a guide to living

* **patron**   supporter or financial sponsor of an artist or writer

This painting, called *Allegory of the Tudor Succession,* portrays Henry VIII surrounded by his three children, each of whom ruled England in turn after his death. Edward VI, who appears at the king's right, died in his teens. The throne went next to Henry's elder daughter, Mary I, shown here with her husband, Philip II of Spain. After her death the crown passed to her half-sister, Elizabeth I, who stands next to the young Edward.

---

* **theology**   study of the nature of God and of religion

* **Protestant Reformation**   religious movement that began in the 1500s as a protest against certain practices of the Roman Catholic Church and eventually led to the establishment of a variety of Protestant churches

* **papal**   referring to the office and authority of the pope

In the past, most historians labeled Henry VII England's first Renaissance ruler. However, modern scholars believe that Renaissance ideas truly came to dominate the country in the 1530s, during the reign of his son Henry VIII. Well educated in Latin and theology*, and a strong supporter of learning and the arts, Henry VIII embodied many of the qualities of the Renaissance. Art and humanism flourished under his rule. The great Renaissance scholar Sir Thomas MORE served as Henry's lord chancellor in the 1530s, and German-born artist Hans HOLBEIN became the official court painter. The founding of St. Paul's School, the first grammar school in England to provide thorough instruction in ancient Greek and Latin, also encouraged humanist studies during Henry's reign.

**The Reformation in England.**   The growth of Renaissance thought in England went hand in hand with the Protestant Reformation*. The changes in the English church began in 1527, when Henry VIII sought the pope's permission to divorce Catherine of Aragon. The couple had no sons, and Henry wanted a new wife who could give him a male heir to the throne. When the pope denied the king's request, Henry decided to reject papal* authority. In 1533 and 1534 Parliament passed laws that cut England's ties to the Roman Catholic Church and named the king as head of the new Church of England.

Henry's divorce from Catherine became official in May 1533. The king had already taken a new wife, Anne Boleyn, in secret several months earlier. Anne bore Henry a daughter that September, but the couple had no more children. In 1536 Henry accused Anne of being unfaithful and had her beheaded. He then married Jane Seymour, who bore his long-awaited son in 1537. The queen died shortly after childbirth. Henry married three more times, but none of these marriages produced additional children.

After breaking away from the Catholic Church, Henry began taking over the monasteries in England. This change had a major impact because at the beginning of the Tudor period, monasteries had owned as much as a quarter of the country's land. Parliament passed acts in 1536 and 1540 that closed the monasteries and turned their property over to the crown. By the time Henry VIII died, most of the former monastic lands had been sold to nobles and members of the gentry*. Their valuable libraries went to universities, cathedrals, and private collectors.

Much of the wealth seized from the religious houses was spent on warfare. Henry had already taken part in wars earlier in his reign. As a Catholic king, he had made England part of the Holy League, an alliance designed to prevent the French from gaining territory in Italy. The king had personally commanded troops at the famous Battle of the Spurs (1513), in which the hasty French retreat had left several towns in northern France under English control. After establishing a Protestant church in England, Henry and his advisers feared that Catholics would attempt to invade the country and restore the old religion. They spent vast amounts of money on fortifications and on renewed wars against France and Scotland, its longtime ally.

The relationship between the Renaissance and the Reformation in England is complex. Renaissance ideas about questioning traditional views may have paved the way for rethinking church government. Also, classical* learning had an impact on several early leaders of the Church of England. At the same time, however, the Reformation drew interest away from the Renaissance. Humanist learning generally became less important after 1540, as religious concerns absorbed the nation.

**Shifts in Power.** In his will, Henry VIII named his son, Edward, as his heir. However, he also decreed that his daughter Mary, the child of Catherine of Aragon, would inherit the throne if Edward died without children. Elizabeth, the daughter of Anne Boleyn, was third in the line of succession*.

EDWARD VI became king in 1547, when he was only nine years old. Henry had named a large group of advisers to act as his son's regents*, but Edward's uncle, the duke of Somerset, soon took control of the government. Somerset ruled effectively for several years, but rebellions in 1549 caused him problems. He lost power to John Dudley, the duke of Northumberland, who remained the most important figure in the government for the rest of Edward's reign.

Edward and his regents brought new reforms to the English church. In 1549 Archbishop Thomas CRANMER introduced the first Book of

* **gentry**   people of high birth or social status

* **classical**   in the tradition of ancient Greece and Rome

* **succession**   determination of person who will inherit the throne

* **regent**   person who acts on behalf of a monarch who is too young or unable to rule

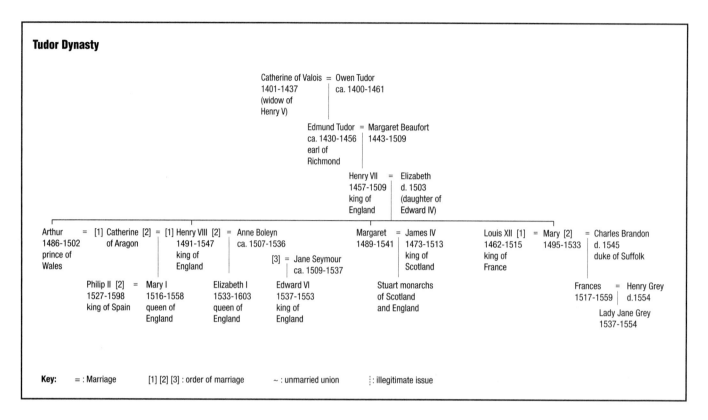

**Tudor Dynasty**

Catherine of Valois = Owen Tudor
1401-1437　　　　　ca. 1400-1461
(widow of
Henry V)

Edmund Tudor = Margaret Beaufort
ca. 1430-1456　　1443-1509
earl of
Richmond

Henry VII = Elizabeth
1457-1509　　d. 1503
king of　　　(daughter of
England　　　Edward IV)

Arthur = [1] Catherine [2] = [1] Henry VIII [2] = Anne Boleyn　　　Margaret = James IV　　　Louis XII [1] = Mary [2] = Charles Brandon
1486-1502　　of Aragon　　1491-1547　　ca. 1507-1536　　1489-1541　　1473-1513　　1462-1515　　1495-1533　　d. 1545
prince of　　　　　　　king of　　　　　　　　　　　　　　king of　　　king of　　　　　　　　duke of Suffolk
Wales　　　　　　　　England　　　　　[3] = Jane Seymour　　Scotland　　France
　　　　　　　　　　　　　　　ca. 1509-1537

Philip II [2] = Mary I　　　Elizabeth I　　Edward VI　　　Stuart monarchs　　　　　　Frances = Henry Grey
1527-1598　　1516-1558　　1533-1603　　1537-1553　　of Scotland　　　　　　1517-1559　　d.1554
king of Spain　queen of　　queen of　　king of　　　and England
　　　　　　England　　England　　England　　　　　　　　　　　　　Lady Jane Grey
　　　　　　　　　　　　　　　　　　　　　　　　　　　　　　　1537-1554

**Key:**　　= : Marriage　　　[1] [2] [3] : order of marriage　　　~ : unmarried union　　　⋮ : illegitimate issue

Common Prayer in the English language. This volume did not stray too far from Catholic practices, but a revised version that appeared in 1552 contained more sweeping changes. The following year, Cranmer issued the Forty-Two Articles of Religion, which laid out the doctrines of the English church. Many of these beliefs represented a sharp break from Catholic views.

King Edward died of lung disease in 1553. During the last days of his reign, his advisers tried to steer the succession to Lady Jane GREY, a distant relative of the king's and a supporter of Protestant causes. They feared that if the crown passed to Edward's Catholic sister Mary, she would try to restore the old religion. However, Mary had enough popular support to take the throne as MARY I.

Queen Mary undid the English Reformation in two stages. In 1553 she restored the Latin Mass (the Roman Catholic religious service), and in 1554 she brought England back under the authority of the pope. The Protestant Archbishop Cranmer was dismissed, arrested, and finally executed. A Catholic noble, Reginald Pole, took his place. Many people supported Mary's restoration of the Catholic faith, believing that earlier reforms had gone too far in doing away with beloved church ceremonies and religious beliefs. Those who held on to their Protestant beliefs continued to worship in secret or fled the country.

**The Golden Age.** When Mary died in 1558, her younger sister Elizabeth took the throne. Many historians have called her reign the golden age of England. The young queen began by trying to resolve the

### Perkin Warbeck

In 1491 Henry VII faced a threat to his rule from an imposter named Perkin Warbeck. Warbeck was posing as Richard Plantagenet, the younger son of the Yorkist king Edward IV. Richard and his brother had disappeared from public view after their father's death. Members of King Henry's own household promoted Warbeck's rebellion, and several foreign monarchs briefly supported him. The king finally captured Warbeck in 1497, and he was hanged two years later.

* **Puritan** English Protestant group that wanted to simplify the ceremonies of the Church of England and eliminate all traces of Catholicism

conflict in the English church. She restored the Church of England in 1559 but attempted to steer a middle course between Protestant and Catholic ideas. For example, the Elizabethan prayerbook allowed worshipers to hold different views on some points of theology.

The Renaissance reached its fullest flower under Elizabeth. Educated by humanist scholars, the queen spoke many languages and was an accomplished musician. During her long reign, classical ideas dominated literature. Noted writers such as William SHAKESPEARE, Philip SIDNEY, and Christopher MARLOWE drew ideas from ancient history and mythology. Grammar schools and universities began to emphasize Greek, Latin, and ancient history in their courses of study. Even areas such as state pageants and medical practice reflected the influence of classical thought.

During Elizabeth's reign, England devoted much of its energy to opposing Catholic powers in Europe. PHILIP II, the Catholic ruler of Spain who had been married to Mary I, sought Elizabeth's hand. When Elizabeth rejected his offer, she gained an enemy and brought England into the conflict between Spain and the pope and other Protestant states. In the Netherlands, Protestants were struggling against Spanish rule and persecution by Catholics. At first Elizabeth avoided taking sides. However, in time she decided that England, the main Protestant power in Europe, had a duty to aid Protestants elsewhere. Angry at Elizabeth's support for the rebels, Philip sent a fleet called the Spanish ARMADA against England in 1588. England defeated the Armada, scoring a decisive victory in its battle with Spain.

Elizabeth also faced Catholic threats closer to home. Various Catholic plots centered on MARY STUART, the former queen of Scotland, whose Protestant subjects had driven her from her homeland. For years Elizabeth allowed Mary to live under guard in England, even though this granddaughter of James IV of Scotland was the leading Catholic rival for the English throne. In 1586 Elizabeth learned of Mary's involvement in a plot against her life. The queen arrested her cousin and in 1587 ordered her execution. Catholic rebellion in Ireland also caused difficulties in Elizabeth's final years.

**A Troubled Reign.** When Elizabeth died in 1603, she left no children, and the Tudor dynasty came to an end. The crown passed to James VI of Scotland, the son of Mary Stuart and Lord Darnley. James took the throne as James I of England, the country's first monarch of the STUART DYNASTY. His court was more troubled than Elizabeth's had been. Under his rule the country suffered severe economic problems, and political leaders disapproved of the king's favorite courtiers.

Soon after taking the throne, James called a special conference to respond to Puritan* requests for church reform. The attempt at cooperation failed, however, when the Puritans demanded that James eliminate bishops. James refused, believing that a structured church was an essential partner to the monarchy. The only lasting result of the conference was the King James BIBLE, a new translation that remained popular for centuries.

ENGLAND

**masque** dramatic entertainment
performed by masked actors, or a ball
or party at which all guests wear masks
or costumes

King James made peace with Spain and proposed a marriage between
his son Charles and the daughter of Philip II. However, the Spanish
princess refused to wed a Protestant. A marriage between the king's
daughter Elizabeth and the German ruler Frederick V had unfortunate
results as well. Frederick's attempts to take the throne of BOHEMIA led to
the outbreak of the bloody THIRTY YEARS' WAR (1618–1648). James tried
to remain outside this conflict, but many of his subjects believed that
England should support fellow Protestants. As a result, England was
dragged into unsuccessful naval campaigns against Spain and France.

Throughout the early years of the Stuart dynasty, classical learning
continued to dominate education and literature in England. Playwrights
such as Ben JONSON based court masques* on stories from ancient
mythology. At the same time, architect Inigo JONES introduced classical
styles into English architecture. With the death of King James in 1625,
the English Renaissance faded.

**Economic and Social Changes.** The population of England grew
rapidly in the 1500s, straining the country's resources. At the same time,
changes in agriculture caused economic problems. Many large landowners had begun replacing their grain fields with fenced pastures for sheep.
This process, called enclosure, increased their profits because wool was
England's most valuable export. However, it also forced many peasants
off the lands they had farmed all their lives. They moved into the cities
seeking work, but many lacked the skills to find jobs and ended up as
beggars or robbers. Although the government tried to deal with this
social problem by banning enclosure, most landlords ignored the law.
England eventually passed a series of poor laws to provide relief for
those in need.

Inflation, an increase in prices, contributed to economic distress as
well. To meet their expenses, kings Henry VIII and Edward VI had
reduced the amount of precious metal in the coins they issued. When
merchants realized that the coins had less value, they began to raise
their prices. Elizabeth I recalled all the "debased" coins in 1560 and
replaced them with coins of higher value. However, prices continued to
rise, causing hardship for many.

At the height of the Renaissance, England began expanding its naval
power. Voyages of exploration and discovery began in 1497, when John
Cabot sailed to North America. In the 1500s, Captain John Hawkins
opened up trade with the Caribbean and Sir Francis DRAKE gained fame
for his voyage around the world. In the early 1600s England began to
establish colonies in the New World, laying the foundations of what
would eventually become the mighty British Empire. (*See also*
**Americas; Art in Britain; Classical Scholarship; Drama,
English; English Language and Literature; Humanism;
Libraries; London; Money and Banking; Netherlands; Poetry,
English; Poverty and Charity; Protestant Reformation;
Puritanism; Spain; Universities.**)

**English Language and Literature**

At the end of the 1400s, most scholars in England still relied on Latin rather than English in their writings. A standard version of written English existed, which was used by merchants and printers in London. In everyday speech, however, the people of England used a great variety of dialects.

During the 1500s, English began to outstrip Latin in importance. After the nation broke away from the Roman Catholic Church in the 1530s, English, rather than the Latin of Rome, became the preferred language for Bibles and prayer books. During the reign of ELIZABETH I (1558–1603), English literature blossomed, and the English language became a symbol of the nation as well as the national church.

## THE GROWTH OF THE ENGLISH LANGUAGE

As English grew in importance during the Renaissance, scholars disagreed about its suitability for literary and scholarly works. Many feared that the vocabulary of the English language was too limited. Writers and translators developed two different views on how to add words to the language.

One group of authors favored expanding English by borrowing words from other languages, especially Latin, French, and Italian. Rather than waiting for English to absorb words from French and Latin, as it had done in the past, translators and other scholars began inserting foreign words into their texts. They hoped these words would make their way into the English language. Scholars who supported borrowing words from other languages also argued that English words did not sound as good as some foreign words.

The members of the opposing camp were the purists. In the words of one prominent purist, their aim was to keep English "clean and pure, unmixed … with borrowing." They formed new words from existing English words by compounding, adding prefixes and suffixes, and changing the way they used words. English writers such as Edmund SPENSER also favored bringing outdated English words back into circulation as a way to extend the language.

Both sides had some success. Between 1580 and 1600, the purists fueled the largest expansion of English vocabulary in the Renaissance. By the end of the 1500s, however, many people considered native English to be "low." The highest circles of society—including the royal court—spoke a refined form of English that relied heavily on Latin.

## WRITING STYLE

* **classical** in the tradition of ancient Greece and Rome

* **humanist** referring to a Renaissance cultural movement promoting the study of the humanities (the languages, literature, and history of ancient Greece and Rome) as a guide to living

While the English language was growing in size and importance, English writers were still looking to classical* models for style. One of the greatest challenges for English authors was learning to balance these classical styles with the unique patterns of the English language.

**Prose Styles.** Most English schools of the 1500s followed a humanist* program. As a result, English prose writing strongly reflected classical

**\* rhetoric**   art of speaking or writing effectively

styles. Rhetoric\* formed a major part of the curriculum. Even when students wrote in English, they drew on ancient Greek and Roman models for structure and style. The idea of "originality" in prose writing came to mean going back to the origins of literature—by imitating and modifying antique texts—rather than creating something entirely new. Writers showed their individuality in the way that they blended these ancient sources with their own everyday experience.

Writing style took on great importance for authors of the 1500s. In fact, many writers believed that the form of expression was as important as the ideas they expressed. These authors filled their work with elaborate figures of speech and sound patterns. Other writers followed an approach based on the ideas of the ancient Greek philosopher ARISTOTLE, which involved blending style with substance.

Modern scholars identify two extremes in Elizabethan writing styles, using terms drawn from the ancient Roman writer CICERO. The so-called Asiatic style is elaborate and ornate, while the Attic style is tight and focused. The most complex form of Asiatic writing appears in the work of English writer John Lyly. His style, known as euphuism, carefully balanced the length, structure, and sound patterns of phrases within a sentence. Lyly hoped that this highly polished form of English would give his nation's court the kind of elegance that other European courts seemed to have. Other writers, such as the essayist Francis BACON, cared more about force and precision than about elegance. Bacon represents the most extreme example of the Attic style. His sparse, direct writing conveyed his ideas clearly and with an air of authority.

**Poetic Styles.** During Elizabeth's reign, English poets developed a clear understanding of prosody, the study of meter in poetry. Although poets of the mid-1500s used fixed patterns of meter in their verse, they had trouble making these patterns fit the rhythm of human speech. The rhythms of their poems were either awkward and uneven or technically perfect but stiff and unnatural. In the decades that followed, poets learned how to use meter in a more flexible way, and by the year 1600, they had mastered the technique.

One of the most important lessons the poets learned was that meter was not rigid. They realized that they did not need to place exactly the same amount of stress on each accented syllable. A writer might choose to use strict meter, as Edmund Spenser did in the following line of iambic pentameter\* from "Mother Hubberd's Tale":

**\* iambic pentameter**   line of poetry consisting of ten syllables, or five metric feet, with emphasis placed on every other syllable

To *fawn,* to *crouch,* to *wait,* to *ride,* to *run*

However, a line of iambic pentameter did not have to bounce violently and predictably between hard and weak syllables. Instead, it might keep the ups and downs of the meter without interfering with the normal pattern of speech. Christopher MARLOWE used this approach in the following line from *Tamburlaine the Great*:

My *nature and* the *terror of* my *name*

Elizabethan poets also learned to make effective use of monosyllabic, or single-syllable, words. The English language's wealth of monosyllabic words kept English poets from using some of the meters of ancient

*The Shepheardes Calender,* by Edmund Spenser, was a collection of poems, one for each month of the year, accompanied by woodcut illustrations. The print shown here illustrated the month of May, complete with dancers in a meadow.

* **sonnet**   poem of 14 lines with a fixed pattern of meter and rhyme

* **epic**   long poem about the adventures of a hero

* **elegy**   type of poem often used to express sorrow for one who has died

* **literacy**   ability to read

* **genre**   literary form

* **romance**   adventure story of the Middle Ages, the forerunner of the modern novel

verse, which depended on words of many syllables. However, English poets came to realize that a monosyllabic word could serve as either an accented or an unaccented syllable, depending on where it is used. SHAKESPEARE illustrated this idea in Sonnet 129, making the same words, "well" and "knows," both stressed and unstressed in the same line:

All *this* the *world* well *knows,* yet *none* knows *well*

Finally, Elizabethan poets argued over the question of rhyme. Some believed that rhyme made their poems more beautiful. Others considered it an unnecessary frill that English poets should avoid, as classical poets had done. Neither side won the argument, and today volumes of both rhymed and unrhymed Elizabethan poetry survive. Poets such as Shakespeare, Marlowe, Philip SIDNEY, John DONNE, and Ben JONSON wrote rhymed verse in many forms, including the sonnet*, the romantic epic*, the narrative, and the elegy*. Meanwhile, blank (unrhymed) verse became the favored form for dramatic verse, as in the plays of Thomas Kyd, Robert Greene, Marlowe, and Shakespeare.

## ELIZABETHAN GENRES

The Elizabethan age was a rich period for English literature. As literacy* rates increased, a variety of genres* became popular. Although Elizabethans enjoyed drama, they tended to think of it as a type of performance rather than a form of literature. However, they read many forms of poetry and prose. Popular works included romances*, reports of

---

**You and Thou**

As the English language evolved, the old plural pronoun "you" gradually replaced the pronoun "thou" for speaking to an individual. During the Renaissance, people used both terms, depending on whom they were addressing. "You" was the more polite form, used between social equals and by servants speaking to their superiors. People used "thou," the more casual form, to address a social inferior. This term could also show affection between very close friends and family members. In any other situation, however, "thou" became an insult that showed anger or a lack of respect.

\* **chivalric**   referring to the rules and customs of medieval knighthood

---

voyages to the New World, stories of England's glorious past, and pamphlets describing witchcraft and society's underworld. The new genres enabled the public's political, social, and even sexual values to find their way into print.

**Elizabethan Fiction.** At the beginning of the Renaissance, England had a well-developed tradition of oral (spoken) storytelling. Reading aloud in a group, as a social activity, was much more common than solitary reading. Therefore, writers of fiction often designed their works to be engaging when read aloud. John Lyly's elaborate style, with its patterns of rhythm, sound, and repetition, is an example of this technique.

After the development of commercial printing, books became more widely available—more than 100 works of fiction were published during the Elizabethan period. These printed texts were much cheaper than handwritten manuscripts. For the first time, anyone with a little extra money could own books. As printed works became more common, many of the strategies that had worked well in oral reading came to seem clumsy. By the end of the 1500s, writers had adapted their styles to fit the format of the printed book. They also changed their subject matter to suit the tastes of their larger audiences. Romances and crime stories were some of the most popular genres.

Publishing also changed the nature of writing in other ways. Before publishing, most authors were upper-class men who circulated their manuscripts only among friends. As printing rapidly became a business, these authors feared that other people might consider their writing to be paid labor—something they saw as disgraceful. Therefore, early published writers often made excuses for going into print, denying that they were writing for money. One author claimed that a friend had taken his book to a printer without his approval; another said that his friends had demanded that he publish his work.

By the end of the 1500s, print had become the accepted format for written works, and these kinds of excuses were the subject of mockery. The first English author to make a living by writing was Robert Greene (ca. 1558–1592). Greene wrote more than 30 works of fiction, many of them openly commercial. His work marks the shift in English literature from a mainly oral form to a printed one.

**Romances.** Chivalric\* romances, which told of the adventures of knights, were widely popular in Elizabethan England. The chivalric tradition drew on the British legends of King Arthur and his Knights of the Round Table. However, during the Renaissance the romance also served a political function. The English interest in chivalry was largely imported from the Netherlands, a trading partner of England and home to many Protestants. The Dutch had revived the tradition of chivalry to add vigor to a revolt against the Catholic Spanish, who controlled the Netherlands at the time.

English writers who sympathized with the Dutch cause showed their support through chivalric literature. *The Faerie Queene* (1596), a chival-

* **allegory**  literary or artistic device in which characters, events, and settings represent abstract qualities, and in which the author intends a different meaning to be read beneath the surface

* **satire**  literary or artistic work ridiculing human wickedness and foolishness

ric romance by Edmund Spenser, contained an allegory* of the Dutch struggle against the Spanish. Sir Philip Sidney, who wrote the romance *Arcadia* (1590), believed that chivalric romances had a natural link to military service. Sidney died in 1586 as a soldier fighting for the Protestant cause in the Netherlands. The chivalric romance remained popular throughout Elizabeth's reign but fell from favor after her death.

**Satire.** Satire* played a major role in Elizabethan literature. Renaissance satirists saw themselves as doctors to society, diagnosing its disorders in an attempt to restore its health. Like other literature of the Elizabethan era, satire reflected classical models, particularly those of ancient Rome.

Many well-known Renaissance poets produced satirical verses. Edmund Spenser accused the royal court of envy, malice, and laziness. John Donne imagined London as hell on earth. Ben Jonson urged Elizabethans to return to the basic values of friendship and honesty, rather than the commercial values then on the rise in England.

Elizabethan prose satirists adopted a hard-boiled style. Writers such as Thomas Nashe exposed the immoral elements of society in much the same way that today's tabloids do. They also targeted people or groups that they found corrupt. One of the satirists' subjects, the church establishment, defended itself from their attacks by issuing restraining orders, burning books, and banning satires.

Satirists also wrote for the stage. Ben Jonson described his play *Every Man Out of His Humor* (1599) as a "comical satire." This dramatic form, also known as "city comedy," used exaggerated characters to portray specific cultural or moral types. Shakespeare's *Troilus and Cressida* (ca. 1601–1602) is a biting example of dramatic satire. It warns audiences that pursuing individual passions will lead to a breakdown of morals.

**Elizabethan Bawdy.**  Bawdy—a form of indecent humor, often dealing with sex—appeared in many forms of Elizabethan literature. Bawdy humor often took the form of a simple joke or a pun. In other cases, an actor might make a vulgar gesture onstage for comic effect or to give the playwright's words a humorously suggestive alternate meaning. Same-sex love was a common topic of bawdy humor. Bathroom humor was also popular.

Foreign works written entirely in a bawdy style were also popular in England. They included classical poetry addressed to a god of fertility, Italian poems with hidden sexual meanings, and Spanish chivalric romances that included sexual situations. Thomas Nashe used elements of these works in his own bawdy writing. Shakespeare, Marlowe, and Donne also penned bawdy poems. Such works reflect the standards of the Elizabethan age about what was indecent and what was funny. Their jokes about women, the mentally ill, and the uneducated might seem tasteless to modern audiences. (*See also* **Bible; Chivalry; Drama, English; Poetry, English; Humor; Literature.**)

## Erasmus, Desiderius

**ca. 1466–1536
Dutch scholar**

* **humanist** referring to a Renaissance cultural movement promoting the study of the humanities (the languages, literature, and history of ancient Greece and Rome) as a guide to living

* **classical** in the tradition of ancient Greece and Rome

* **illegitimate** refers to a child born outside of marriage

* **theology** study of the nature of God and of religion

* **medieval** referring to the Middle Ages, a period that began around A.D. 400 and ended around 1400 in Italy and 1500 in the rest of Europe

* **Holy Roman Emperor** ruler of the Holy Roman Empire, a political body in central Europe composed of several states that existed until 1806

* **Protestant Reformation** religious movement that began in the 1500s as a protest against certain practices of the Roman Catholic Church and eventually led to the establishment of a variety of Protestant churches

* **satire** literary or artistic work ridiculing human wickedness and foolishness

* **pagan** referring to ancient religions that worshiped many gods, or more generally, to any non-Christian religion

* **Spanish Inquisition** court established by the Spanish monarchs that investigated Christians accused of straying from the official doctrine of the Roman Catholic Church, particularly during the period 1480–1530

The Dutch humanist* Desiderius Erasmus was one of the most celebrated scholars of his time. He corresponded with kings, popes, princes, and fellow scholars, and his works were translated into many languages. Toward the end of his career, Erasmus drew criticism from both Roman Catholics and Protestants for his religious ideas. Still, his works remained popular, continuing to influence Christian thought, classical* learning, and education for centuries after his death.

**Life and Career.** The illegitimate* son of a priest, Erasmus was born in Rotterdam in the Netherlands. He attended a school run by monks and eventually entered the Augustinian order. Later, after complaining that he had been pressured into joining the order, he received permission from the pope to live outside the monastery.

In 1492 Erasmus became a priest. Several years later he went to Paris to study theology*. However, he disliked his studies because of his professors' use of Scholasticism, a medieval* method of studying religion. He began to focus more of his attention on the study of classical literature. Eventually he left Paris and began working as a tutor while pursuing his own studies. In 1499 he traveled with one of his pupils to England, where he made lifelong friends, including the humanist writer Thomas MORE. Seven years later Erasmus accompanied some other pupils to Italy, where he received a degree in theology from the University of Turin. However, the theologians who had completed the strict course of studies in Paris looked with scorn on his achievement, believing his degree from Turin had little academic value.

After a second stay in England, Erasmus settled near Brussels (in present-day Belgium), home to one of the courts of BURGUNDY. Already well known through his publications, Erasmus served as an adviser to the prince who later became Holy Roman Emperor* CHARLES V. In the 1520s his writings on religion drew him into debates surrounding the Protestant Reformation*. Although he agreed with some of the ideas proposed by Martin LUTHER and his followers, he strongly disapproved of their efforts to break away from the Catholic Church. However, some people at the court accused him of supporting the Lutherans. To escape this uneasy situation, Erasmus moved to Basel, Switzerland, where he remained until 1529. At that time, the city formally turned Protestant, and Erasmus moved to Freiburg, Germany.

**Works and Thought.** A scholar of unusually broad learning, Erasmus produced many written works during his career. Writing only in Latin, he created essays, satires*, letters, collections of proverbs, textbooks containing amusing stories, advice to princes, and biblical studies. He also penned books on preaching, morals, religion, and the value of marriage. When his complete works were published in the early 1700s, they filled ten very large volumes.

Some of Erasmus's most influential works were his books on religion. He edited and translated volumes by the church fathers (figures who shaped Christianity in its early centuries) and wrote a biography of one of them, St. Jerome. He also produced works criticizing the church and

Dutch humanist Desiderius Erasmus was one of the leading scholars of the Renaissance. This 1523 painting by German artist Hans Holbein the Younger shows Erasmus at work.

### Champion of the Young

Erasmus spoke up for young people at a time when they received little respect. He claimed that both boys and girls should develop their minds through good educations. He believed that learning should be fun, and he criticized teachers who punished students for their mistakes. Also, in an age in which arranged marriages were common, Erasmus argued that young men and women should be free to marry as they wished. In one story about an arranged marriage, he made fun of a doddering old husband and expressed sympathy for his lively young wife.

spelling out his recommendations for reform. Erasmus's most important contribution to religious scholarship was his work on the BIBLE. He applied to Scripture the same critical method that many Renaissance scholars were using to edit classical manuscripts. His edition of the New Testament (1516) contained both a Greek text (the first available in print) and a Latin one, with notes on the revisions he had made to correct errors found in earlier Latin versions.

In the area of politics, Erasmus promoted the goal of peace and universal fellowship among human beings. In works such as *War Is Sweet to the Inexperienced* (1515), he urged leaders to look for ways to resolve their differences without the use of military force. Erasmus also applied this principle to conflicts within the church, recommending that rival religious groups hold a council to settle their disagreements.

Erasmus's works on education reflect the views of many Renaissance humanists. In *On the Education of Children* (1529) he declared that parents had a duty to choose teachers who could provide moral and intellectual leadership for their children. He disapproved of physical punishment and believed in encouraging learners by challenging them, engaging their interest, and rewarding them for good behavior.

Erasmus recognized the value of classical literature, including various pre-Christian texts. He defended such works against those who wanted to keep pagan* ideas out of Christian education, promoting the study of classical works as examples of grammar and style. He also recommended that students learn Greek. During his own youth, books in Greek—and people qualified to teach the language—had been rare, forcing him to teach himself. To make the process easier for future students, he translated a Greek grammar into Latin. He also translated Greek plays and prose writings and produced new editions of ancient Latin works.

**Influence.** Both Catholics and Protestants attacked Erasmus during the final decade of his life. Catholics criticized his translation of the New Testament, which seemed to challenge the authority of the Bible by introducing changes in the words. In 1531 the professors of theology in Paris condemned Erasmus's religious writings. The Spanish Inquisition* also investigated his works. Eventually some of his works were banned in France, Italy, and Spain.

Meanwhile, Protestants were attacking Erasmus for withdrawing his support for the Lutherans when he realized that their movement would lead to a split within the church. His refusal to take sides in the Reformation debate made him unpopular with extreme groups on both sides. Still, the tradition of Christian humanism that Erasmus established remained alive, especially in England and the Netherlands. Readers of the 1700s admired him for creating a theory of religion based on reason. In the 1900s interest in his works revived again, and new editions of his writings began to appear. (*See also* **Catholic Reformation and Counter-Reformation; Christianity; Classical Scholarship; Humanism; Philosophy; Protestant Reformation; Religious Thought.**)

**Espionage**

* **diplomacy**   formal relations between nations or states

* **Protestant Reformation**   religious movement that began in the 1500s as a protest against certain practices of the Roman Catholic Church and eventually led to the establishment of a variety of Protestant churches

Espionage, the use of spies to obtain military and political secrets, is as old as human history. During the Middle Ages, states resorted to espionage from time to time, typically in periods of crisis. However, the development of a permanent system of diplomacy* in the Renaissance changed the nature of espionage. Although ambassadors, the official representatives of foreign governments, had access to a certain amount of information, top-level secrets were rarely shared. Besides, ambassadors were supposed to help countries avoid conflict, not spy on their hosts.

When European states began to establish embassies in rival countries, ambassadors came under considerable suspicion. After all, the main job of ambassadors was to provide information about the host country to their own governments. Some states assigned agents to watch ambassadors to make sure they were not collecting secrets. In Venice members of the government were not even allowed to speak privately with foreign diplomats. But the need for information about the plans and resources of political rivals ensured that spying would occur. Ambassadors and professional spies used whatever methods they could to gather intelligence, including bribing officials and paying informers.

The Protestant Reformation* and religious wars increased international tensions, making spying even more important. Both Catholic and Protestant countries expanded their spy networks as espionage became more elaborate. Bernardino de Mendoza, the Spanish ambassador to England during the reign of ELIZABETH I, recruited a large number of spies locally. He had agents in key ports as well as inside the English government. He used English Catholics to communicate with Mary, queen of Scots (MARY STUART), while she was in prison.

Queen Elizabeth preferred spies to resident ambassadors. Spies were less expensive and usually provided more accurate information. In the late 1500s, the English had the most effective and extensive spy network in Europe. Sir Francis Walsingham, who ran it, gathered agents from all walks of life: noblemen, criminals, and even famous individuals such as the philosopher Giordano BRUNO and the author Christopher MARLOWE. At one time Walsingham had dozens of spies in Spain, France, Germany, Italy, and as far away as Constantinople. At least one of Spain's top spies was actually a double agent working secretly for Walsingham.

Spies were always in danger of being caught, especially through intercepted communications. Agents often sent their messages in diplomatic pouches in the regular mail, but they might disguise the messages by using codes, ciphers (a system of mixing up letters or substituting numbers or symbols), and even invisible ink. Private couriers also carried many communications. Especially sensitive secrets might be sewn into clothing, put into a hidden compartment in a trunk, or memorized and delivered orally so they could not be discovered. (*See also* **Diplomacy.**)

## Este, House of

* **patron** supporter or financial sponsor of an artist or writer

* **humanist** referring to a Renaissance cultural movement promoting the study of the humanities (the languages, literature, and history of ancient Greece and Rome) as a guide to living

* **papal** referring to the office and authority of the pope

The House of Este was a noble family that ruled a region in northern Italy during the Renaissance. Among the cities under Este control at one time or another were FERRARA, Modena, Reggio, and Rovigo. The family also served as patrons* of the arts and learning. Este residences contained huge collections of art, and their libraries were filled ancient and humanist* manuscripts. In the 1400s, Este princes transformed Ferrara into a model Renaissance city and supported its university.

**Niccolò III.** Founded in the Middle Ages, the House of Este reached the peak of its power during the Renaissance. Niccolò III, one of the notable members of the dynasty, ruled from 1393 to 1441. He increased the family's power by playing his neighbors against each other. Niccolò's long rule brought stability to Este territory and consolidated the family's control over the lands. Under his successors, the court of the Este became one of the most brilliant in Europe.

Aware of strong local traditions and privileges, the Este did not try to unify their state. They made Ferrara their seat of power and governed other territories through appointed officials. Among the Este holdings were papal* lands ruled by the family. Beginning in the late 1300s, the Este headed off several attempts by the papacy to regain direct control of these lands. The pope finally succeeded in reclaiming Ferrara in 1598. The Este then moved their seat of power to Modena and ruled their remaining territories from that city.

During the Renaissance, the highest rank for the Este family was achieved by the son of Niccolò III, Borso (ruled 1450–1471). In 1452 the named Borso the duke of Modena and Reggio and count of Rovigo. In 1471 the pope added the Duke of Ferrara to Borso's titles. These titles were passed on to Borso's successors. The Este coat-of-arms reflected the family's status and appeared prominently on Este residences and public buildings.

**Alliances.** During the 1400s, the major powers on the Italian peninsula sought to expand their territory. Yet, remarkably, the Este family survived without major territorial loss until 1598. This success stemmed in part from the ability of family members to find powerful allies in times of crisis. The Este also avoided involvement in wars whenever possible. However, when forced to fight, their princes proved to be skillful military commanders.

The Este relied on marriage as a way to forge political alliances. The daughters of Este princes were raised to be suitable wives for other rulers. Through marriage, the House of Este created alliances with MANTUA, MILAN, and the kingdom of NAPLES. In 1502 Alfonso I d'Este reluctantly married Lucrezia BORGIA, the daughter of Pope ALEXANDER VI, in an effort to end papal military pressure against Este lands. Unfortunately, any advantage gained by the marriage was lost when the Borgia pope died a year later.

Este males often had children outside of marriage. Niccolò III is said to have fathered some 300 illegitimate children, including numerous sons. This led to many rivalries for power and even to assassination plots

by unhappy brothers. Este princes sought to steer surplus children to the church to become priests or church officials. From the late 1400s, the aim was to ensure that a member of the dynasty would become a cardinal, who could further Este interests through his papal connections. For a brief period, the family boasted two cardinals at the same time.

During the late 1500s, Este rule became increasingly despotic. Some princes were cruel, vengeful, and morally corrupt. Moreover, the heavy taxation necessary to support the Este patronage of the arts led to an unhappy and restless population. Any unrest that erupted in Este lands, however, was put down quickly and harshly. (*See also* **City-States; Italy; Princes and Princedoms.**)

**ca. 295 b.c.**
**Greek mathematician**
**and philosopher**

During the Renaissance, scholars rediscovered the writings of many ancient Greek and Roman thinkers. One of the most influential minds of the ancient world was the Greek mathematician and philosopher Euclid. His work became a major resource for scholars, who came to view mathematics as the foundation for science, technology, and many other fields.

Euclid's most influential work was *Elements,* a mathematical text. Its theory of proportion—that is, how to compare two objects that are the same shape but different in size—not only had many practical uses but also led to new advances in mathematics. The work also laid out strict rules for proving mathematical theories. Many Renaissance thinkers believed that Euclid's system of proof offered a sounder basis for knowledge than any other method.

Over the course of the Renaissance, versions of Euclid's writings appeared in Latin, Italian, German, French, and English. Many of these translations reached an audience of artisans* and other practical workers, as well as scholars. The prefaces of these texts often stressed the uses of mathematics in both practical and philosophical fields. One edition observed that Euclid's ideas could help sailors, architects, engineers, doctors, lawyers, scientists, and even theologians*.

* **artisan** skilled worker or craftsperson

* **theologian** person who studies religion and the nature of God

Many of the Renaissance's greatest minds drew on Euclid's ideas. For example, the astronomer Nicolaus COPERNICUS referred to Euclid's work on optics as evidence for his theory that the earth moves around the sun. Euclid's work also influenced Renaissance philosophers, who used his teachings to help them understand other ancient Greek thinkers, such as PLATO and ARISTOTLE. (*See also* **Astronomy; Classical Scholarship; Mathematics; Philosophy; Science.**)

**Europe, Idea of**

The idea of Europe as a specific geographic, cultural, and political region took shape during the Renaissance. Several factors led to this development, including the threat of Muslim invasion, the rise of powerful states in Europe, and the founding of overseas empires by

Europeans. The emergence of a new identity for the continent changed the ways in which Europeans viewed their own states and related to the rest of the world.

During the Middle Ages, rulers and scholars tended to use the word *Christendom*—meaning the region where Christianity was practiced—to refer to the continent of Europe. The Muslim lands surrounding Christendom determined its borders. However, in the late Middle Ages, the idea of Christendom began to disintegrate as Muslim invaders gained control of parts of the continent. Muslim armies invaded Spain in the 700s, briefly held Sicily in the 800s, and conquered the kingdoms of the Balkan Peninsula (Bosnia, Bulgaria, Croatia, and Serbia) in the 1300s and 1400s.

The word *Europe* came into use around 1400. A secular\* term, it originated in ancient myth and tradition as a name for the small continent west of Asia and north of Africa. In Greek mythology, the god Zeus rapes a beautiful woman named Europa and takes her to a land in the west. According to Jewish tradition, the descendants of one of Noah's sons settled in Europe. The word caught on during the Renaissance as influential leaders and humanists\* adopted it. In 1461 Pope PIUS II referred to the continent as *Europe* in a letter to Muhammed II, ruler of the OTTOMAN EMPIRE. The pope also described the area's inhabitants as *Europeans,* rather than *Christians*. This use of the term reinforced the emerging status of Europe as a cultural and political region.

Another factor that reinforced the idea of Europe was the global exploration that took place in the 1500s. Increasing contact with other parts of the world made Europeans more aware of their own geographic and cultural identity. Renaissance writers tended to describe Europe as more fertile, populous, and culturally advanced than other parts of the world. Illustrations of the time depicted Europe as a magnificently crowned figure, carrying complex weapons and scientific equipment. In comparison, other continents were shown as less powerful and sophisticated.

Various Renaissance intellectual movements contributed to the rise of a European identity. The use of Latin encouraged the exchange of ideas among scholars and the development of a shared point of view. A renewed emphasis on classical\* texts led scholars to study the works of the ancient Greek geographer Strabo. In Strabo's view Europe was distinguished from other continents by certain characteristics, including climate and cultural diversity, which made it superior. Meanwhile, writers such as the Italian statesman and political philosopher Niccolò MACHIAVELLI studied political developments in Europe. According to Machiavelli, Europe's cultures and political systems were much more diverse than those of other continents. By the 1600s, most scholars had adopted the concept of a European identity. However, it took most of that century for the idea to become more widely accepted. (*See also* **Africa; Americas; Asia, East; Exploration; Geography and Cartography; Ideas, Spread of; Political Thought.**)

**\* secular** nonreligious; connected with everyday life

**\* humanist** Renaissance expert in the humanities (the languages, literature, history, and speech and writing techniques of ancient Greece and Rome)

**\* classical** in the tradition of ancient Greece and Rome

See color
plate 4,
vol. 4

During the Middle Ages, Europeans knew little about the world beyond their lands and the seas around them. The Renaissance brought a great leap forward in geographic knowledge and interest in the rest of the globe. Beginning in the 1400s, Europeans made a series of remarkable voyages to Africa, Asia, the Americas, and the Pacific Ocean. This exploration led to the opening of new trade, the conquest of foreign territories, and the founding of colonies. From these colonies grew the overseas empires of Portugal, Spain, the Netherlands, Britain, and France.

Driven by economic, religious, and political forces, the great age of European exploration was unlike anything before or since. As Spanish chronicler Francisco de Jérez asked in 1547: "When, among the ancients or the moderns, have been seen such great undertakings of so few individuals to go conquering the unseen and the unknown ... in such diverse climates and reaches of the sea or across such distances?"

## ORIGINS OF EXPLORATION

Why did the great age of world exploration begin in Europe in the early 1400s? Some historians argue that new techniques and tools of shipbuilding and navigation launched a wave of ambitious voyages. However, before this time, three practical problems would have discouraged Europeans from sailing beyond the familiar Mediterranean Sea or the Atlantic coast. The problems involved maps, navigation, and ships.

First, mariners lacked maps and charts of foreign waters and possessed little useful knowledge of winds and currents. The only way to gather information and create maps was through voyages of discovery. Charting unfamiliar shores would be one of the great accomplishments of Renaissance explorers.

Second, mariners did not have much experience sailing out of sight of land, and their navigational tools and methods were primitive. They had crude compasses but did not really understand the differences between magnetic north and true north until the 1500s. They could measure latitude with instruments called astrolabes and quadrants, but using these instruments aboard moving ships was difficult. As the age of exploration progressed, sailors devised more efficient methods of measuring latitude. However, the accurate measurement of longitude at sea did not occur until the 1700s.

Third, few ships were well equipped for long ocean voyages or unfavorable winds. Explorers in the early 1400s used caravels—small, triangular-sailed ships built for coastal cruising. Over time, Atlantic sailors adapted caravels to handle square sails as well, making them better suited to wind conditions on the high seas. As voyages became longer, the need for bigger storage areas led to the development of a larger ship called the *nao* or carrack. By 1500 carracks might be as much as four times as large as caravels.

Solutions to the problems of maps, navigation, and ships arose during, not before, the age of exploration. The Europeans of the early

Renaissance pushed out into the unknown with inadequate equipment from the past. The spark that drove them did not come from advances in technology but from forces within society.

European exploration during the Renaissance grew out of various motives and factors. One was simple curiosity, the growing interest in the world that was a key feature of the dawning Renaissance. Economic motives played a key role as well. Contact with the Muslim world had given Europeans a taste for the spices, silks, and other luxury goods of Asia. When the city of Constantinople fell to the Ottoman Turks* in 1453, the overland trade route to the East was disrupted. The European demand for luxury goods fueled the search for a sea route to Asia.

Religion also played a part in the growth of exploration. Some European rulers who sponsored voyages felt a sincere duty to carry Christianity to other parts of the world. Others wanted to gather allies to fight the growth of the Muslim empire. Finally, political ambition was an important force that propelled exploration. European nations that discovered new territories could acquire great riches, power, and prestige through trade and colonial outposts.

* **Ottoman Turks** Turkish followers of Islam who founded the Ottoman Empire in the 1300s; the empire eventually included large areas of eastern Europe, the Middle East, and northern Africa

## THE PORTUGUESE AND THE EASTERN ROUTE

Historians date the great age of exploration from 1415, when a Portuguese prince named Dom Henry helped capture Ceuta, a Muslim city in North Africa. This adventure inspired the prince, later called Henry the Navigator (1394–1460), to sponsor a series of voyages of exploration. Over the next century, such expeditions would eventually bring Portugal colonies in Africa, Asia, and South America.

**Prince Henry the Navigator.** In 1419 Henry began outfitting ships for missions into the Atlantic. Some of these voyages led to the establishment of colonies on the islands of Madeira and the Canaries. Other expeditions probed southward along the west coast of Africa. By 1434 one of the prince's navigators had passed Cape Bojador, the southern-most point reached by Europeans. From then on the Portuguese were venturing into unknown waters.

In a series of voyages from 1444 to 1460, the Portuguese found the mouth of the Senegal River, explored the Cape Verde Islands, and reached Sierra Leone. During that period, they began trading with Africans along the coast for ivory, gold dust, and slaves. By the time of Henry's death, Portuguese mariners had made at least 35 voyages to western Africa. Historians debate how many of these journeys Henry directly sponsored, but clearly he played the leading role in the nation's drive to explore other lands.

**Later Portuguese Exploration.** A succession of Portuguese kings sponsored voyages along the African coast to the mouth of the Congo River and beyond. These expeditions resulted in increased trade in gold, pepper, and slaves—one expert estimates that Portugal brought back 150,000 slaves from western Africa before 1500.

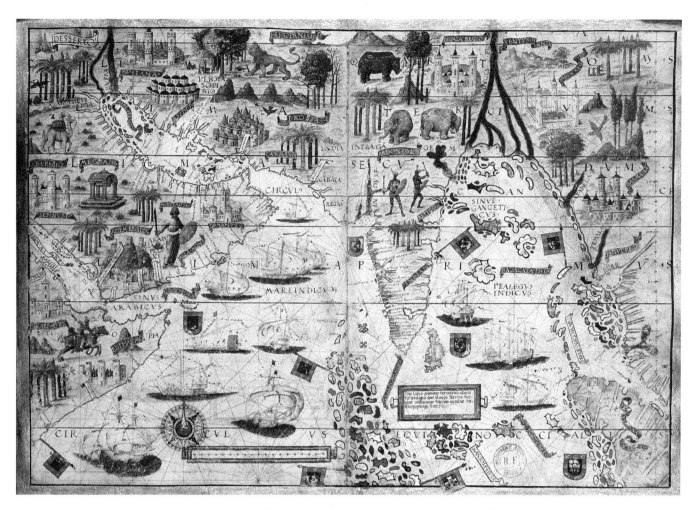

In the late 1400s Portuguese sailors explored the Indian Ocean. This map of the ocean, dated 1519, was dedicated to the king of Portugal.

See color plate 2, vol. 4

The voyages raised questions about the geography of Africa that led Portuguese king John II (ruled 1481–1495) to launch several expeditions in 1487. One group of explorers traveled by land in search of a route across Africa. Others went to India to learn about the commerce and navigation of the Indian Ocean. Most importantly, Bartolomeu Dias sailed off to find the southern tip of Africa and a route around it. In 1488 Dias returned to Portugal and reported that he had rounded the tip of Africa, which the king named the Cape of Good Hope. These trips produced two valuable pieces of information: that ships could sail around Africa and that regular commerce existed between eastern Africa and India across the northern Indian Ocean.

Nearly nine years passed before another Portuguese expedition set out to take advantage of these discoveries. In 1497 Vasco da GAMA left Portugal with four ships. The fleet rounded the Cape of Good Hope and stopped at several ports in eastern Africa before landing on the coast of India. Gama returned to Portugal in 1499, having found the basic sea route that would open to Europeans the trade of India and the Asian lands beyond.

About six months later, a much larger fleet under the command of Pedro Álvares Cabral sailed from Portugal for India. However, on the way the ships were blown westward by storms and ended up on the coast of Brazil. Cabral claimed the land for Portugal. After a few weeks he resumed his journey, reaching India in September 1500, and he set up several trading posts. Within a few years, other expeditions had built fortified trading posts along the eastern coast of Africa, at the entrances to the Red Sea and the Persian Gulf, and along the shores of the Indian peninsula. The Portuguese also created settlements farther east, eventually gaining control of the trade of the Spice Islands (now called the Moluccas).

## OTHER EXPEDITIONS

* **exploit**  to take advantage of; to make productive use of

While the Portuguese were opening and exploiting* the sea route that led eastward around Africa to the Indian Ocean and Asia, others turned westward. Christopher COLUMBUS hoped to reach Asia by sailing west across the Atlantic Ocean but landed instead in the Americas. His historic voyage across the ocean and back in 1492–1493 was just the beginning of transatlantic exploration.

**The Americas and Beyond.** Columbus made three more voyages, determined to find a passage to the markets of Asia. Even before his death in 1506, however, other navigators had visited the Americas. Although many of them focused their efforts on finding a way through or around the continents to Asia, others were interested in the geography, people, and resources of the uncharted lands. Mapmakers had begun to realize that these lands were part of the world previously unknown to Europeans. As early as 1493 Pietro Martire d'Anghiera, an Italian scholar in Spain, called Columbus's discovery "the New World."

One of the first to venture into that world was John Cabot, an Italian navigator working for England. In 1497 he sailed from Bristol to the island of Newfoundland, now part of Canada. On a second expedition a year later Cabot was lost without a trace. Soon afterward Portuguese mariners explored the region around Newfoundland; by 1506 they had begun fishing for cod in nearby waters.

Meanwhile, several Portuguese expeditions along the northern and eastern coasts of South America began to reveal the vast size of the continent. Spanish navigators looked along the coasts of Central America and the Yucatan Peninsula for an easy water passage through the Americas.

Geographers realized that these continents lay between Europe and Asia. It might be possible, however, to sail around the southern tip of South America as the Portuguese had sailed around Africa. In 1519 Portuguese navigator Ferdinand MAGELLAN led an expedition for Spain that would test that idea. Magellan, who believed that a narrow sea separated South America from the Spice Islands (Moluccas) and Asia, managed to find a route through the turbulent waters at the tip of South America and into the Pacific Ocean. Although Magellan had greatly underestimated the distance to Asia, he landed in the Philippines with his fleet after 106 days at sea. Magellan died in the Philippines in 1521,

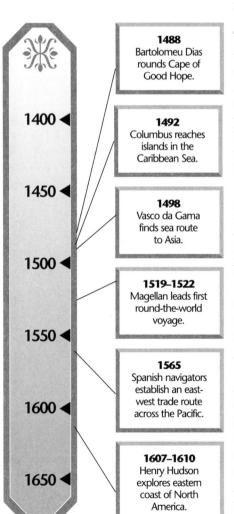

**1488**
Bartolomeu Dias rounds Cape of Good Hope.

1400 ◄

**1492**
Columbus reaches islands in the Caribbean Sea.

1450 ◄

**1498**
Vasco da Gama finds sea route to Asia.

1500 ◄

**1519–1522**
Magellan leads first round-the-world voyage.

1550 ◄

**1565**
Spanish navigators establish an east-west trade route across the Pacific.

1600 ◄

**1607–1610**
Henry Hudson explores eastern coast of North America.

1650 ◄

**Naming the New World**

Christopher Columbus "discovered" the Americas for Europe but thought they were part of Asia. Fifteen years later the Americas were named for a traveler who insisted that they were a "new world." Between 1501 and 1504, Amerigo Vespucci of Italy accompanied two Portuguese voyages of exploration along South America's coastline. His popular, colorful accounts of these missions greatly exaggerated his own importance in the expedition but made him famous. On his world map of 1507, Martin Waldseemüller labeled the new southern continent America (for Amerigo) and the name stuck.

---

\* **conquistador** military explorer and conqueror

See color plate 3, vol. 4

---

but Juan Sebastián del Cano took command of the remaining ship and returned to Spain in 1522. He was the first navigator to sail around the world. As a result of Magellan's voyage, Spain claimed the Philippines as a colony.

**Phantom Passages and Golden Cities.** During this first phase of Renaissance exploration, Europeans learned the shape and size of Africa, mapped many Asian islands and coasts, discovered new continents, and established European colonies in the tropics. Many later voyages and expeditions failed to reach their goals but still added to the accumulation of geographic knowledge.

One of the most frustrating goals was to find a Northwest Passage, a waterway that would enable ships to sail through North America to the Pacific Ocean. Between 1524 and 1610, Giovanni da Verrazano and Jacques Cartier for the French, Martin Frobisher and John Davis for the English, and Henry Hudson for the Dutch all tried to find the route and failed. However, Cartier's voyages up the St. Lawrence River launched French exploration and colonization in Canada, and Hudson's voyage into the bay that carries his name led to later expeditions and the establishment of the English fur trade in the region.

Far to the south, stories of legendary golden cities and kingdoms lured explorers. Such rumors drew adventurers such as Walter Raleigh and Francisco Vásquez de Coronado into the interior of South America and the North American southwest. No such cities were found, but each expedition resulted in more information about the American continents. Spanish military leader and conqueror Hernán Cortés and other conquistadors\* went deep into the interior and captured the fabulously wealthy empires in Mexico and Peru. By the mid-1500s Europeans had some knowledge of all the major river systems of South America and had traced most of the continent's coast.

The mammoth Pacific Ocean was the great unknown. A Spanish expedition meant to follow Magellan's route around the globe ended in disaster in the 1520s. Fifty years later, England's Sir Francis Drake made the second complete trip around the world, pioneering an alternate route around the tip of South America and possibly exploring part of the California coast. Perhaps more significant, though, was the achievement of Spanish navigators Felipe de Salcedo and Andrés de Urdaneta. In 1565 they established a practical east-west sailing route across the Pacific that took advantage of winds and currents. It became one of the world's great trade routes. Europeans could now travel and trade regularly across all the oceans of the world.

## EFFECTS OF EUROPEAN EXPLORATION

The age of European exploration yielded enormous improvements in geographic knowledge, travel, and trade. It had darker results as well. Many of the peoples that Europeans "discovered" in other continents had their lives violently disrupted. Whole civilizations in the Americas

were conquered and wiped out, and millions of Africans became merchandise in a growing international slave trade.

Earlier historians tended to celebrate the heroic achievements of Renaissance explorers. They also presented a positive view of the colonizers and missionaries whose work followed on the heels of exploration. In recent years, scholars have instead portrayed the legacy of Renaissance exploration as cruelty, environmental destruction, and the inability of cultures to communicate. Both views contain elements of truth, and each is one-sided and incomplete without the other. For better or worse, the explorers of the European Renaissance brought the various branches of the human family together and laid the foundations of the modern world. (*See also* **Africa; Americas; Asia, East; Geography and Cartography.**)

**Flemish painters**

* **Flemish**    relating to Flanders, a region along the coasts of present-day Belgium, France, and the Netherlands

See color plate 11, vol. 1

* **illumination**    hand-painted color decorations and illustrations on the pages of a manuscript

* **patron**    supporter or financial sponsor of an artist or writer

The brothers Jan and Hubert van Eyck came from a family of prominent Flemish* artists. Jan, the more successful painter, is often considered the founder of the northern Renaissance artistic tradition. His work influenced artists throughout Europe.

**Hubert van Eyck (ca. 1370–1426).** Little is known about Hubert van Eyck. Some experts identify him with an artist known as Master Hubert, who completed a number of works in the early 1400s. Sources confirm that Hubert van Eyck lived and worked in the Flemish city of Ghent between 1422 and 1426. He designed a painting for the city and began work on a monumental altarpiece for the church of St. Bavo. Hubert died before completing this work, the *Adoration of the Lamb,* also known as the Ghent Altarpiece.

The Ghent Altarpiece has been praised for its beauty, realism, and technical mastery. The most famous Flemish painting from the Renaissance, it consists of 24 panels that show Christ, the Virgin Mary, Adam and Eve, saints, angels, prophets, and other biblical figures. Experts disagree about Hubert's contribution to the work. Some believe that Hubert designed the altarpiece and began the painting and that Jan completed it. Others, however, credit the masterpiece entirely to Jan.

**Jan van Eyck (before 1395–1441).** Jan van Eyck probably studied art with his brother Hubert and began his career doing manuscript illumination*. By 1423 he had become an independent artist serving as court painter to John III, the count of Holland. Although Jan established an excellent reputation as an artist during this time, none of his works from the period survive.

After the death of John III, Jan went to the city of Bruges. In 1425 Philip the Good, the duke of BURGUNDY, appointed Jan as court painter and as *varlet de chambre,* a position that made Jan an official member of the duke's household. The duke valued Jan and provided generously for him, and the duke's prestige brought Jan great respect.

The artistic services that Jan provided to his patron* included decorating Philip's residences and helping to stage lavish festivities for spe-

Flemish artist Jan van Eyck is known for his rich textures and attention to detail. He painted *Virgin and Child with Chancellor Rolin* in the 1430s for a government official in Burgundy, where he served as court painter. Placing a wealthy patron in a historical scene was a fairly common practice among Renaissance artists.

* **Iberian Peninsula**  part of western Europe occupied by present-day Spain and Portugal

cial occasions. In addition, Jan acted as Philip's agent in buying works of art and hiring other artists. The artist also carried out diplomatic missions for Philip both within Burgundy and abroad. Between 1428 and 1429, he went to the Iberian Peninsula* to negotiate a marriage between the duke and Isabella of Portugal. During this trip, Jan painted a portrait of Isabella for Philip's approval, a standard practice for royal marriages.

**Works of Jan van Eyck.** Jan's paintings range from portraits and religious pictures to scenes of women bathing or merchants reviewing their accounts. He painted a map of the world, probably after consulting a mapmaker in Philip's court. Although many of these works have been lost, most of the surviving ones contain Jan's signature. In fact, the artist usually signed his works in Latin and often included his personal motto, *Als Ich Can* (As I was able).

Jan van Eyck's work is notable for its images of the rich textures and details of the physical world. His paintings are so precise that the viewer can see single strands of hair, the shimmer of silk, and highlights on jewels. Although his scenes incorporate a wide variety of human activities, his emphasis on lavish display reflects the values of his many upper-class patrons.

Jan created some of his best-known works for patrons associated with the Burgundian court. The *Arnolfini Betrothal,* for example, was painted for an Italian merchant who supplied Philip with fine textiles. This portrait of a bride and groom includes a remarkable reflected image in a mirror on the wall, showing the young couple as well as two other figures entering the room.

Jan van Eyck's fame as an artist spread well beyond Burgundy to Italy and other regions. Influential Italian humanists* and nobles from the MEDICI, ESTE, and other ruling families eagerly collected the artist's paintings. In the 1500s, the Italian painter and art historian Giorgio Vasari identified Jan van Eyck as the inventor of oil painting. Although artists had been working with oils since the Middle Ages, Jan took the technique to new heights. By using multiple layers of oil glazes, he was able to create enamellike surfaces that gave his paintings a feeling of great depth. The fine glazes also enabled him to blend brush strokes until they almost disappeared. The artist probably used other types of paints as well, including tempera (an egg and water mixture) and watercolors. (*See also* **Art in the Netherlands.**)

* **humanist** Renaissance expert in the humanities (the languages, literature, history, and speech and writing techniques of ancient Greece and Rome)

Factions—interest groups devoted to achieving particular political goals—existed throughout Renaissance society. They were formed to influence public affairs and often divided the population into rival parties. Some factions engaged in activities that disrupted the peace, destroyed property, and even led to war. Many Renaissance political thinkers disapproved of factions, arguing that individuals should set aside their personal interests to work for the common good. Others, however, accepted the idea that factions might have a legitimate basis.

**Reasons for Factions.** During the Renaissance, factions emerged as a result of personal loyalties, political rivalries, opposition to government policies, and other causes. Personal loyalties played a major role because people gained access to business opportunities and positions of privilege through their contacts with relatives, friends, and neighbors. Connections with important patrons* sometimes led people to favor a particular faction. Prominent individuals, such as members of the MEDICI family in FLORENCE, often acquired supporters by performing favors for others. Bonds formed in this way, however, were limited because people might receive favors from more than one patron.

Some factions developed around political rivalries. Government officials often divided into factions over policy issues, with each side claiming its own position to be better for the community. Competition for public office could also cause friction between the candidates' supporters. In monarchies, factions formed when a lack of strong leadership led to a power struggle. The rise of one family to a position of prominence might cause other families to band together. Hostility or rivalry between families could also result in the formation of factions.

Factions sometimes grew out of opposition to the government, particularly if rulers adopted unpopular policies or failed to carry out their

* **patron** supporter or financial sponsor of an artist or writer

* **republic** form of Renaissance government dominated by leading merchants with limited participation by others

* **elite** privileged group; upper class

* **ideology** belief system

duties. This type of opposition arose more often in republics\*, where issues were openly debated and large numbers of people participated in the political process. It was less common in states run by an established ruling family, where an elite\* group decided all major issues. In such an environment there was little opportunity for factions to develop. As long as the rulers acted according to expectations and satisfied powerful interests, peace and harmony could be maintained. Ideology\* also gave rise to factions. Groups cited principles such as the need for good government to justify their actions. Religion, in particular, often served as a powerful force in uniting people behind a common cause.

**Structure and Organization of Factions.** Some Renaissance factions, particularly those involved in long-term conflicts, developed a formal structure, with officials and councils like those of government. To help unify the group, members might wear certain colors or greet each other with a special handshake. However, most factions were relatively informal. They tended to be short lived because their followers shifted loyalties freely according to their interests and beliefs.

External factors played a role in the growth of factions as well. Sometimes minor disputes within a state turned into major crises because foreign powers intervened or factions received support from abroad.

**Controlling Factions.** Renaissance leaders sought to eliminate factions because of their disruptive effects. Rulers often appealed for peace or asked people to place public concerns above personal interests. They might also ask citizens to take oaths against participating in factional conflicts.

Some political thinkers suggested more formal means of limiting factions, such as placing strict controls on elected leaders. Italian writer Niccolò MACHIAVELLI proposed establishing public institutions to deal with personal disputes. Others concluded that the only way to achieve peace and stability was to give complete power to one individual.

In general, attempts to control factions were unsuccessful. However, a few republics, including VENICE and NÜRNBERG, managed to limit political rivalry by providing relatively good government and general prosperity. In this way they avoided provoking opposition that could lead people to form factions. (*See also* **Dynastic Rivalry; Patronage; Political Thought; Revolts; Wars of Religion.**)

## Fairs and Festivals

Fairs and festivals were special events that broke up the cycle of the Renaissance year. A fair was essentially an economic event—a large multiday market. A festival, by contrast, celebrated a holiday or other special occasion. Fairs and festivals not only spiced up Renaissance life but also gave people of different regions and social classes a chance to interact.

The typical Renaissance fair, really a large outdoor market, lasted several days. It often took place during an annual feast celebration. This painting shows vendors at a fair in Antwerp selling fruit, animals, and other goods.

* **Flemish**   relating to Flanders, a region along the coasts of present-day Belgium, France, and the Netherlands

# FAIRS

Fairs became a significant form of economic activity between the 1000s and the 1200s. A typical fair was simply an outgrowth of a town's weekly open-air market. Once a year, often at the time of a local saint's feast celebration, the town expanded this market into a multiday event. Such small fairs had little importance to anyone outside the town.

A few fairs became more major events that attracted buyers and sellers from throughout the region or nation—sometimes even from foreign countries. For example, Flemish* merchants brought their goods to English fairs at St. Ives and Winchester. The only truly international fairs took place in a few towns in northeastern France. There merchants from England, France, and the Netherlands traded cloth for Italian merchants' goods from the Mediterranean and the Near East. Before the 1400s these were the only fairs where different coins and currencies were exchanged.

The number of fairs declined when the European economy fell into a slump in the 1300s. During the unsteady recovery of the 1400s and 1500s, new fairs arose and old ones declined in importance. For much of the 1400s, Geneva, Switzerland, held four fairs throughout the year that attracted merchants and financiers from all over Europe. By the 1500s, however, the quarterly fairs in Lyon, France, had become the biggest in Europe. They supported a booming trade in merchandise,

especially silks and spices. They also played a major role in the international money market. Financiers met at the fairs to arrange loans and set interest rates.

Over time many fairs simply died out. In England, some fairs survived by specializing in one or two products or types of livestock, becoming "mop fairs" or "goose fairs." A few fairs also added an annual labor market at which employers could hire workers. The fair at Scania, Sweden, survived until the mid-1500s. It specialized in herring but also provided a general distribution point for goods across much of the region. Several German fairs also remained active. Frankfurt served as a major exchange for textiles, with cloth traveling north from Italy and southern Germany and south from England and the Netherlands. Frankfurt and Leipzig, another German town, held annual book fairs that still survive today.

## FESTIVALS

Renaissance festivals ranged from sober church ceremonies to wild street parties. Some festivals occurred every year. Others were one-of-a-kind events in honor of an important occasion, such as the wedding of a noble. Modern historians have noted that some Renaissance festivals celebrated and reinforced the existing, established order of society, while others appeared to overturn it for a period of time.

**Celebrating the Social Order.** Both religious and civic* festivals aimed to show the social order in a positive light and to make people feel safe and comfortable within it. The calendar of religious holidays reassured people by repeating itself year after year without change. Religious festivals also offered comfort with their references to salvation and the afterlife, which suggested that human life and the world as a whole had meaning and purpose.

Many festivals served both church and state interests. Local officials sometimes took part in religious processions, hinting at the idea of a link between the spiritual and worldly realms. In the city-states of Italy, the feast day of each city's patron saint was also a patriotic holiday, like the modern Independence Day in the United States and Bastille Day in France.

Public events often aimed to promote the idea of social unity. Processions might feature heads of state and government officials appearing in the company of foreign visitors, merchants, and representatives of local guilds* and other groups. These public displays hinted at harmony among the different social classes and among Christian nations. Processions of this sort could form part of the wedding festivities for royalty and nobles. Such events might also include banquets, decorations, fireworks, performances, and tournaments. Humanist* professors and students in various places revived classical* festivals and created new holidays to celebrate key events in Roman history. In Rome in the late 1400s, a small group began celebrating the Palilia, an annual ancient festival honoring the city's founding. In 1513, city officials used

See color plate 6, vol. 2

* **civic** related to a city, a community, or citizens

* **guild** association of craft or trade workers that set standards for and represented the interests of its members

* **humanist** referring to a Renaissance cultural movement promoting the study of the humanities (the languages, literature, and history of ancient Greece and Rome) as a guide to living

* **classical** in the tradition of ancient Greece and Rome

### Carnival Mockery

In Germany, Carnival celebrations often ridiculed religious authorities. Around the time Protestants first began to break away from the Roman Catholic Church, floats in several cities mocked the pope and Catholic clergymen. However, Protestants were not safe from mockery either. The main float in the Carnival parade at Nürnberg in 1539 made fun of a local Protestant preacher who had criticized Carnival pleasures. Nervous city authorities everywhere tried to prevent such embarrassments but did not always succeed.

* **secular**   nonreligious; connected with everyday life

the Palilia as an occasion to honor the new pope, LEO X. The result was the most remarkable scholarly festival of the Renaissance. The Romans built a huge theater in the ancient style, decorated with paintings and inscriptions. The celebration included a 20-course banquet, performances in Latin, and a Latin speech praising Rome and the pope's family. The festival was the ultimate expression of Renaissance humanism, celebrating literature, learning, and culture.

**Challenging the Social Order.**   Not all festivals celebrated order and harmony. Some popular and widely enjoyed events played with images of "misrule," an overthrowing or reversing of the social order. Some historians believe that such festivals undermined the established order of society by leading people to focus on physical pleasures rather than on reason and morality. Others, by contrast, see them as safety valves that allowed common people to voice their resentments in ways that would not actually threaten society. In this way, misrule may have actually reinforced the social order. In fact, Roman civic and religious leaders organized, approved, and even funded local festivals of this kind.

Festivals of misrule dated back to ancient times. During the ancient Roman Saturnalia, a midwinter holiday, masters had dressed in their servants' clothing and served them at the table. A Renaissance version of this event was the Feast of Fools, celebrated in most of western Europe. During this festival, people made fun of the things they normally held sacred by electing a young clergyman as "bishop" and holding mock church services. In some areas churchgoers also observed a related festival, the Feast of Asses, by bringing donkeys into church and braying during the service. Church authorities had largely suppressed these customs by the 1500s. However, secular* festivals of misrule continued to thrive.

During the 1400s and 1500s, young men in France and some other countries organized "abbeys" or "kingdoms" of misrule. These associations staged activities during regular festivals, such as Christmas, and also provided an outlet for high spirits. At times the groups conducted rituals to embarrass newlyweds, mocking henpecked husbands or old men with young wives.

By far the most popular festival of the Renaissance was Carnival, which came just before Lent, the 40-day period of fasting and sober living that led up to Easter. In contrast to Lent, Carnival was a time of rule breaking that encouraged eating, drinking, and sexual freedom. The length of the Carnival season varied, according to locality, from a week or so to several weeks. This festival was most widespread in southern parts of Europe.

The unifying theme of Carnival was the "world turned upside down." Normal rules of social order and Christian behavior were suspended, criticized, or mocked. Pageants and other entertainments explored such themes as servants giving orders to their masters, laborers pretending to be kings, and men and women dressing in each other's clothes. Carnival represented a temporary, brief triumph of the weak over the powerful, the young over the old, and the earthly over the sacred.

During the 1400s and 1500s Carnival was an unruly, grassroots expression of popular spirit. The common people both observed and

took part in the performances. By the 1600s, however, criticism from moralists and Protestant reformers had changed the nature of Carnival festivities. In some places, the festival faded out altogether. In others, it became formal and commercial. Professional actors, acrobats, and singers took the place of spontaneous, festive crowds. (*See also* **Economy and Trade; Money and Banking; Parades and Pageants.**)

## Family and Kinship

See color plate 14, vol. 2

The concept of family, or kin, had great importance during the Renaissance, especially among the upper classes. However, the definition of kinship was not always straightforward. The Roman Catholic Church defined kin as people who shared at least one common ancestor in the past four generations. In practice, most people saw only the relatives they knew by name and saw occasionally as kin.

**Kinship and Power.** Renaissance families traced their ancestry through the male line, so mothers played no official part in defining kinship. However, most people also paid attention to maternal bloodlines. Even relatives with no blood connection could be important, as the Catholic definition of kin included in-laws. Many marriages were arranged to create an alliance between two families.

Kinship had much more importance for the wealthy and powerful than for common people. The average person did not know many distant relatives, while members of wealthy families could often name even distant ancestors. The use of surnames, which identify people as members of a certain family, was a fairly new practice in the early 1400s. Prominent or noble families based their last names on the names of famous ancestors or the territory from which the family drew its power. Many of the most important names of the Renaissance belonged not to individuals, but to influential families—the MEDICI, the FUGGERS, the HABSBURGS.

Property passed from one generation of a family to the next through inheritance. Those who inherited property had a duty to preserve and improve it for later generations. Primogeniture, a practice by which the eldest son inherited all of the family property when his father died, spread to many sectors of society during the Renaissance. It provided a way to keep family property intact over several generations.

See color plate 15, vol. 2

**Family Obligations.** Great families were very aware of their image and the duty to live up to it. The genealogies (family trees) of noble houses often listed legendary heroes as distant ancestors as a way to add polish to the family name. All members of a noble family shared in its reputation, good or bad, and all relatives suffered if the family lost its honor. For example, the family of a noble who was convicted of a crime might lose the legal privileges enjoyed by other aristocrats. Noblewomen had to protect themselves against charges of sexual misconduct, which would damage the reputation of their husbands' families as well as their own.

Kinship carried certain obligations. Individuals commonly chose careers and marriage partners based on what was best for their family, not on what they personally preferred. Wealthy and powerful kinsmen had a responsibility to help less fortunate relatives. Members of wealthy families assumed they could approach even distant relatives for help. Kin were the first source of help among the lower classes also, but only very close relatives had a legal obligation to help each other.

In Renaissance society, nepotism (favoritism based on family ties) was normal and even admirable. For example, popes often assisted relatives by giving them titles and property, arranging favorable marriages, and naming nephews as cardinals. Anyone who was able to do so would put a relative in a position that could benefit the family in the future. Ideally, the position would have hereditary benefits that would stay in the family for future generations. (*See also* **Childhood; Honor; Love and Marriage; Social Status.**)

## Farnese, House of

* **duchy**  territory ruled by a duke or duchess

* **papacy**  office and authority of the pope

* **patronage**  support or financial sponsorship

* **prefect**  chief administrative official

* **Holy Roman Emperor**  ruler of the Holy Roman Empire, a political body in central Europe composed of several states that existed until 1806

During the Renaissance the Farnese, a family of military men and landholders, acquired a duchy* in northern Italy and became a great princely house. In the 1400s Farnese military commanders gained fame in the service of Venice, Florence, and the papacy*. The family also was known for its patronage* of the arts, contributing splendid buildings in Parma and Rome.

The fortunes of the Farnese family improved sharply in 1534 with the election of Cardinal Alessandro Farnese as Pope Paul III. The new pope used his influence to secure important positions for members of his family. Three of his grandsons became cardinals of the church, and a fourth held the office of prefect* of Rome. His son Pier Luigi was named commander in chief of papal troops. Then in 1545 Pope Paul III took church lands to form the duchy of Parma and Piacenza for his family, an action that caused some controversy. Pier Luigi became the first duke.

The Farnese acquired political power, wealth, and prestige through territorial gain as well as marriage alliances arranged by Pope Paul. One of the most important of these alliances was the marriage of his grandson Ottavio to the daughter of CHARLES V, the Holy Roman Emperor*. Another important match linked the pope's grandson Orazio and a daughter of French king Henry II.

Among the grandsons of Paul III, Cardinal Alessandro Farnese stands out. Named vice-chancellor of the church while still a teenager, he later became one of the richest cardinals. A shrewd and successful diplomat, Alessandro is remembered primarily as a great art collector and generous patron of the arts. He oversaw the completion of the magnificent Farnese palace in Rome and the building of many churches.

Alessandro's brother Ottavio, duke of Parma and Piacenza from 1547 to 1586, worked hard to preserve the duchy. After the death of Paul III, Ottavio became dependent on the king of Spain, his wife's half-brother. Ottavio's son Alessandro grew up in Spain and gained fame as a military leader for Spain in the wars of Dutch independence. Ranuccio, Ottavio's

grandson, ruled Parma from 1592 to 1622. During his long reign Ranuccio constructed massive monuments to the Farnese, including a huge ducal palace in Parma, founded the University of Parma, and brought about an absolutist* state.

The Farnese always sought first to maintain power in the duchy of Parma and Piacenza. Their close alliance with Spain in the 1500s gave way in the 1600s to more complex relations with the Holy Roman Empire, France, and the Italian states. The family line in Parma and Piacenza came to an end in the early 1700s, and the duchy passed through inheritance to the BOURBON FAMILY AND DYNASTY of Spain. (*See also* **Italy; Palaces and Townhouses; Popes and Papacy.**)

* **absolutist**    refers to complete control by a single ruler

### Feminism

For centuries prior to the Renaissance, men dominated European society and women lacked the power to challenge them. After about 1400, however, women began demanding greater equality, access to education, and control over their own lives. By the 1600s, women had begun to see themselves in new ways, and the first feminists—supporters of women's rights—had emerged.

Feminism had its roots in Renaissance humanism*. Women educated in the humanist tradition debated issues with male scholars, celebrated the achievements of women, and tried to promote greater equality between the sexes. The French writer Christine de PIZAN (1365–ca. 1430) was a pioneer in this area. She claimed that women and men were morally equal and that the only true difference between them was physical strength. For this reason she believed that any virtuous woman could achieve extraordinary things.

During the 1500s other French writers spoke out in favor of women's rights. The poet Louise Labé urged women to become scholars. Madeleine des Roches and her daughter Catherine maintained a salon, a regular gathering of individuals dedicated to learning and discussion. Unlike most learned women of the Renaissance, the des Roches participated fully in intellectual debates with men. The humanists who attended their salon encouraged them to pursue their studies and publish their work.

In England, writers such as Jane Anger wrote vigorous defenses of women as men's moral and intellectual equals, echoing Pizan's notion that virtue is the same for both sexes. Between the 1570s and the 1620s, a number of women in London dressed as men to demonstrate their belief that gender does not define virtue or identity. In 1620 the king, JAMES I, ordered ministers to preach against this practice.

During the 1600s more salons appeared in France. Men and women involved in these groups wrote novels based on the experiences of real women. Their plots featured both political and romantic adventures. Between 1620 and 1640, many novels portrayed women as adventurous hunters and warriors. Later works focused on women as scholars and on the intellectual life of the salon.

In Italy various women writers expressed strong feminist views. In 1600 Lucrezia Marinella published *The Nobility and Excellence of Women,*

* **humanism**    Renaissance cultural movement promoting the study of the humanities (the languages, literature, and history of ancient Greece and Rome) as a guide to living

*with the Defects and Vices of Men*. This text reveals great learning and skill in debate. In it the author expresses a hope that women will "wake themselves from the long sleep which oppresses them." That same year Moderata Fonte published *The Worth of Women*, in which seven Venetian noblewomen give examples of unequal treatment of women. One speaker urges women to "wake up, and claim back our freedom, and the honor and dignity men have usurped* from us for so long." Arcangela Tarabotti's *Innocence Deceived* (1654) condemned the practice by which girls—including the author—were forced into convents by parents unwilling to give them dowries*.

In many of these works, women began to see themselves as individuals who must shape their own destinies. By the end of the 1600s European feminists had developed an awareness of themselves as a group. The female intellectuals and feminists of the Renaissance prepared the way for later works, such as Mary Wollstonecraft's *Vindication of the Rights of Women* (1792), the first clear call to change the conditions of women's lives. (*See also* **Ideas, Spread of; Individualism; Querelle des Femmes; Salons; Sexuality and Gender; Women.**)

* **usurp**   to seize power from a rightful ruler

* **dowry**   money or property that a woman brings to her marriage

---

### 1503–1564
### Holy Roman Emperor, king of Hungary and Bohemia

* **Bohemia**   kingdom in an area of central Europe now occupied by the Czech Republic

* **patron**   supporter or financial sponsor of an artist or writer

* **Holy Roman Emperor**   ruler of the Holy Roman Empire, a political body in central Europe composed of several states that existed until 1806

* **Ottoman Turks**   Turkish followers of Islam who founded the Ottoman Empire in the 1300s; the empire eventually included large areas of eastern Europe, the Middle East, and northern Africa

* **classical**   in the tradition of ancient Greece and Rome

As king of Hungary and Bohemia*, Ferdinand I played an important role in keeping Turkish invaders out of central Europe in the 1500s. He was also a generous patron* of the arts and learning. A member of the powerful HABSBURG DYNASTY, Ferdinand was the second son of Juana, heir to the Spanish throne, and the Archduke Philip, son of emperor MAXIMILIAN I. When his older brother became Holy Roman Emperor* as CHARLES V, Ferdinand received Habsburg lands in Austria. This began the historic split between the German and Spanish branches of the Habsburg family.

Ferdinand married the sister of King Louis of Hungary and Bohemia. When Louis died in 1526, Ferdinand succeeded to the two thrones. His new position placed him on the front line of defense against the Ottoman Turks*, who controlled much of southeastern Europe. Ferdinand failed to recapture all of Hungary from his lifelong Ottoman opponent, SÜLEYMAN I. However, he did succeed in preventing further Turkish expansion. Late in his life, he took over the throne of the Holy Roman Empire from his brother.

An energetic and capable ruler, Ferdinand also had a great impact on religion, the arts, and scholarship. A faithful yet flexible Catholic, he supported church reforms and was a major force behind the Council of Trent. He also played a role in the Peace of Augsburg, an agreement that allowed citizens to worship as Protestants or Catholics and brought a temporary religious calm to Germany. His court employed many talented artists and musicians, and his reforms at the University of Vienna promoted the study of classical* languages. (*See also* **Austria; Councils; Dynastic Rivalry; Ottoman Empire; Spain; Trent, Council of.**)

## Ferdinand of Aragon

### 1452–1516
### Spanish king

* **Moor**   Muslim from North Africa; Moorish invaders conquered much of Spain during the Middle Ages

* **Spanish Inquisition**   court established by the Spanish monarchs that investigated Christians accused of straying from the official doctrine of the Roman Catholic Church, particularly during the period 1480–1530

* **Holy Roman Empire**   political body in central Europe composed of several states; existed until 1806

* **succession**   determination of person who will inherit the throne

* **humanism**   Renaissance cultural movement promoting the study of the humanities (the languages, literature, and history of ancient Greece and Rome) as a guide to living

During the 1400s Spain consisted of three separate Christian kingdoms—Aragon, Navarre, and Castile—and the Muslim kingdom of Granada. The marriage of Ferdinand of Aragon to ISABELLA OF CASTILE in 1469 brought two of these kingdoms together. Ferdinand and Isabella consolidated power in their lands and acquired foreign territory.

After Ferdinand became king of Aragon in 1479, he and Isabella cooperated in a "union of crowns." Their plan was to keep various rival groups under control through a series of wars. They joined in the struggle to drive the Moors* from Granada, the last Muslim possession in Europe. Granada fell in 1492, and the Moors who remained had to convert to Christianity. That same year, under pressure from the Spanish Inquisition*, Ferdinand and Isabella ordered the Jews in their realm to convert or leave.

The monarchs brought Italian lands under their control when they took NAPLES from France in 1503. Ferdinand became a major player in Italian politics. Isabella's death the following year ended the union of crowns. The throne of Castile went to their daughter Juana and her husband Philip (Philip I of Spain). After Philip's death in 1507, Ferdinand returned to claim the crown. Within a few years he had incorporated Navarre into Castile.

Before his death, Ferdinand prepared the way for his grandson to rule Spain (as Charles I) and the Holy Roman Empire* (as CHARLES V). That succession* created a united and powerful Spain, a kingdom that controlled part of Italy and the beginnings of an empire in the Americas. However, Ferdinand also left behind military conflicts that drained the country financially and a fierce Catholicism that divided society. On the positive side, Ferdinand's legacy includes his support for the arts, for humanism*, and for the historic voyages of Christopher COLUMBUS. The people of Spain admired Ferdinand because he was the last Spanish ruler before their land passed to foreign dynasties. (*See also* **Holy Roman Empire; Inquisition; Moriscos.**)

## Ferrara

* **patronage**   support or financial sponsorship

* **papacy**   office and authority of the pope

* **guild**   association of craft and trade owners and workers that set standards for and represented the interests of its members

Ferrara, an important Renaissance city in northern Italy, took its name from the wheat *(farro)* cultivated in the area by the ancient Romans. During the Renaissance, Ferrara increased dramatically in size, and its prosperity came largely from the rich agricultural lands that surrounded it. The city's ruling family, the House of ESTE, provided centuries of stability and patronage* of the arts.

**Este Rule.**   Legally, Ferrara and its territory fell under the authority of the papacy*. However, in the early 1200s the pope had granted control of the city to the House of Este. Ferrara's local government, run by male guild* members, had little real power. Whenever one Este ruler died, the council simply named another as the new *signore,* or lord—a position with almost absolute power in the city. The city government dealt with some matters, such as street cleaning and the maintenance of public

buildings, but all decisions required the approval of the *signore*. The Este dukes handled foreign relations and controlled appointments to all important government positions. The citizens of Ferrara were not unhappy with the rule of the Este, who promoted public well-being. Few revolts occurred, and most of those arose out of rivalry between Este family members.

Although the Este family controlled other large territories in northern Italy, the dukes usually lived in Ferrara and its surrounding lands. Throughout the 1400s, they provided generous support for the arts, particularly architecture. The Este castle, built in 1383, went through many renovations. The Este also constructed magnificent summer palaces, built and remodeled many churches, and erected statues at prominent locations in the city.

* **medieval**    referring to the Middle Ages, a period that began around A.D. 400 and ended around 1400 in Italy and 1500 in the rest of Europe

* **classical**    in the tradition of ancient Greece and Rome

**Architecture and Court Life.**  By the mid-1400s, the city of Ferrara had grown beyond its medieval* walls. Two successive rulers, Borso d'Este and Ercole I d'Este, extended the city walls, nearly doubling Ferrara's enclosed area. Duke Ercole also had the city within the walls remodeled along classical* styles. Architect Biagio Rossetti widened Ferrara's main thoroughfares and straightened crooked alleys. A wide new road ran in a straight line from the north gate of the city wall to the Este castle. New public squares also brought light and air into the city. Rossetti's changes placed three important buildings—the castle, city hall, and cathedral—at the heart of the city. His work represented the first example of large-scale urban planning during the Renaissance.

Culture in Ferrara centered on the Este court. The Este dukes promoted various public spectacles. Duke Borso sponsored tournaments, while Ercole I held theatrical performances in the courtyard of his palace. Lavish musical entertainments formed part of Este weddings and the city's annual carnival. The Este also promoted more serious activities. In 1442 duke Leonello d'Este established the University of Ferrara. It had some well-known professors and many foreign students over the next 100 years. In addition, the dukes supported charitable institutions within the city. The Hospital of Santa Anna, founded in 1444, received a generous contribution from the Este.

In the late 1400s, overspending by the Este rulers led to increased taxation and discontent. Over the next century, a general neglect of both public and private property caused the city's standard of living to decline, even as the life of the Este court grew increasingly luxurious. In 1598 the pope reclaimed control of Ferrara, ending Este rule in the city. (*See also* **Architecture; Cities and Urban Life; City-States; Italy; Princes and Princedoms; Universities.**)

---

| **Festivals** | **See** *Fairs and Festivals*. |

**Ficino, Marsilio**

### 1433–1499
### Italian translator
### and philosopher

* **theology**  study of the nature of God and of religion

* **medieval**  referring to the Middle Ages, a period that began around A.D. 400 and ended around 1400 in Italy and 1500 in the rest of Europe

* **villa**  luxurious country home and the land surrounding it

* **astrology**  study of the supposed influences of the stars and planets on earthly events

* **plague**  highly contagious and often fatal disease that wiped out much of Europe's population in the mid-1300s and reappeared periodically over the next three centuries; also known as the Black Death

* **metaphysical**  concerned with the nature of reality and existence

Italian scholar Marsilio Ficino became famous for his translations of the works of the ancient Greek philosopher PLATO. He was also a prominent philosopher in his own right, known for his attempts to merge Plato's ideas with Christian theology*.

**Translator and Author.** Ficino's father was the court physician to Cosimo de' MEDICI, the political leader of Florence. Marsilio received training to prepare him for a medical career, and he wrote about medicine in later life. However, his main interest from an early age was the ideas of Plato. After studying Plato through the writings of medieval* scholars who wrote in Latin, Ficino set out to learn Greek so that he could understand Plato more thoroughly. By the late 1450s he had acquired enough skill to translate several Greek texts. Cosimo, learning of Ficino's abilities, asked him in 1462 to translate some of Plato's works. Cosimo gave Ficino a house in Florence and a small villa* outside the city with some farmland attached to it, which provided him with income.

By 1468 Ficino had finished the first draft of his translation of Plato's complete works, but it took him another 16 years to revise and publish the work. A second edition, which appeared in 1491 and went through many printings, became the most widely accepted Latin version of Plato's works. Ficino also translated the works of other writers. In 1469 he created an Italian translation of *On Monarchy,* by the medieval writer Dante Alighieri.

At the same time, Ficino wrote several books of his own. His *Platonic Theology* (1482) was a major work on the religious ideas of Plato and other ancient writers. In other texts, Ficino attacked the use of astrology* to predict the future, proposed ideas on how to control the plague*, and commented on the works of Plato and other thinkers. Along with his writing and translating activity, Ficino served as a priest and held a position in Florence's cathedral.

**Thinker and Theologian.** Ficino generally based his philosophy on the ideas of Plato. However, he blended these beliefs with other ideas from fields as diverse as medicine and magic. His chief goal as a philosopher was to prove that the basic ideas of Christianity were compatible with Plato's philosophy. Ficino believed that God had given the ancient Greeks and Romans, such as Plato, prophets and belief systems similar to those of the ancient Hebrews, and that the two religious traditions had a common source. He claimed that ancient writings foretold the coming of Jesus and hinted at other Christian concepts, such as the Holy Trinity.

Ficino focused on the religious and metaphysical* ideas in Plato's work and linked them to Christian theology. He developed the concept that God is the source of both the human consciousness, or soul, and the greater Soul of the universe as a whole. This universal Soul, in turn, is the source of all physical reality. He believed that individual human souls could reunite with God through love, prayer, and thought. His idea of the soul's union with God led him to declare the soul is immor-

tal, a concept accepted as official doctrine of the Roman Catholic Church at the Fifth Lateran Council of 1512–1517. However, the church showed less support for Ficino's views on magic and on the nature of the universe, which he saw as a living, conscious spirit. His *On Life* (1489) emphasized the unity and harmony of all creation and described human beings as the link between the physical world and the ideal world of the mind. Ideas such as his emphasis on the power of intellectual love had a great influence on the development of Western thought. (*See also* **Councils; Humanism; Philosophy.**)

---

**Flanders**

**See** *Netherlands.*

---

**Florence**

* **patronage** support or financial sponsorship

* **Holy Roman Empire** political body in central Europe composed of several states; existed until 1806

* **faction** party or interest group within a larger group

* **Black Death** epidemic of the plague, a highly contagious and often fatal disease, which spread throughout Europe from 1348 to 1350

* **guild** association of craft and trade owners and workers that set standards for and represented the interests of its members

Located on the Arno River in Italy, the city of Florence flourished during the Renaissance as a center of banking, trade, and culture. The arts played a particularly important role in the life of the city, and the influence of Florentine artists, writers, and thinkers spread throughout Italy and Europe. For much of the Renaissance, the powerful and wealthy MEDICI family ruled the city, either officially or behind the scenes. Their patronage* helped make the city a leading force in the worlds of art and culture.

## HISTORY AND POLITICS

Florence was a small provincial center in Roman times. During the Middle Ages the city came under the authority of the Holy Roman Empire*, but by the early 1100s it had emerged as a self-governing community ruled by well-to-do merchants and landowners. However, a faction* called the Ghibellines continued to support the Holy Roman Emperor, while an opposing faction, the Guelfs, supported the pope. The struggle between these groups lasted into the 1300s.

Meanwhile, Florence prospered, developing into one of Europe's largest cities, with a population of about 120,000. Then in the 1340s the Black Death* struck, killing about half the city's inhabitants. Additional outbreaks every ten years or so kept the population from recovering completely.

**Structure of Government.** Florence had a complicated political history. During the Middle Ages, its merchant classes struggled with landowning nobles for political power. In the 1200s the trade guilds* took control of the city's political life. Only guild members—some 5 to 10 percent of the city's population—could hold political office. This law effectively barred nobles from government.

Even guild members had to meet certain standards to serve in government. Officials called *accoppiatori* screened guild members to determine who was eligible. They placed the names of approved candidates in a leather bag and pulled out names at random to fill vacant posts.

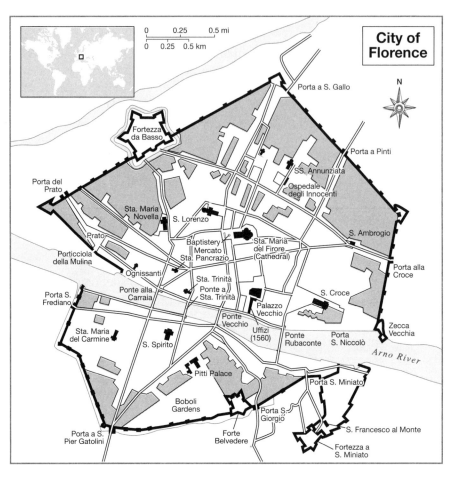

City of Florence

## The Giant Killer

One of the most famous sculptures of the entire Renaissance is Michelangelo's *David,* created in 1504 for public display in Florence. The sculptor Donatello created two pieces on the same subject in the 1400s. One of these, a bronze figure sculpted for Cosimo de' Medici, was the first freestanding nude sculpture since ancient times. David was a popular subject for sculpture because Florence strongly identified with this biblical figure. Many Florentines saw the boy-warrior who took on a giant as a symbol of their small republic struggling against tyranny.

Typically, the *accoppiatori* approved only 10 to 15 percent of guild members as candidates for office. As a result, any group that could influence the *accoppiatori* could effectively control politics in the city.

The chief governing body in Florence was the Signoria, or city council. Its nine members, known as *gonfalonieri* (standard-bearers), served two-month terms. Two other bodies existed to advise the Signoria; members of these groups also served short terms of three or four months. Separate departments dealt with such matters as war, public safety, and basic administrative duties. To balance the rapid turnover in government posts, the city also had a few officials who served for life.

The Signoria passed laws and controlled foreign policy. A temporary chairman presented bills for discussion within the group. In some cases, the Signoria invited interested outsiders to join in these discussions before voting. If more than two-thirds of the Signoria voted for a bill, it would pass to two larger councils, each with about 300 members. These councils could accept or reject proposed laws but otherwise had little power.

Florence also had a fairly complex court system. The chief officer of justice was the *podestà*. To make sure this official would be neutral, the city always selected a foreigner for the position. The *podestà* and two other courts tried most criminal cases. Another function of the justice

system was auditing—reviewing the accounts of those who controlled public funds. Beginning in the mid-1500s, auditors had the power to torture people they suspected of fraud or theft.

**Rise of the Medici.** The late 1300s and early 1400s saw Florence involved in a series of wars, first with the papacy* and then with other cities in Italy. During this time, the Medici—a family of wealthy bankers—emerged as the dominant power in Florence. The head of the family, Cosimo de' Medici, gained control of the *accoppiatori* and used his wealth to influence the city's leaders. However, he took care to remain behind the scenes to preserve the illusion of republican* rule in Florence.

Cosimo and his successors, Piero and Lorenzo the Magnificent, dominated the city until 1494. While maintaining the appearance of republican government, they established two new governing bodies that took power away from the older councils. The Medici kept nobles loyal by allowing them to hold important offices, and they made peace with their political rivals through marriage alliances. The Medici also formed ties with powerful families outside of Florence, such as the Orsini family of Rome. The Medici sought to maintain peace and a balance of power among the five major powers in Italy: Florence, Venice, Milan, Naples, and the papacy. They achieved this goal in 1454 to 1455, when the five powers signed a treaty called the Peace of Lodi.

In 1478 the Pazzi family, Medici rivals, tried to assassinate Lorenzo and his brother Giuliano. Lorenzo survived, and the Medici took bloody revenge on the Pazzi. The affair led Florence into war against Naples and the pope. Lorenzo eventually negotiated a truce between the parties, increasing his own political power in the process. However, Lorenzo's death in 1492 signaled the decline of Medici power. Two years later the French king Charles VIII gained control of Florence, and the Medici were exiled from the city. Florence eliminated the two councils the Medici had created and replaced them with a Grand Council of 1,000 members.

**Shifts in Power.** After the departure of the Medici, Florence fell under the leadership of a Dominican* friar named Girolamo SAVONAROLA. The monk had arrived in the city in 1489 and begun preaching to crowds of Florentines about doom and destruction, urging them to reform their lives and government. In particular, he encouraged them to destroy works of pagan* art and other "vanities." The painter BOTTICELLI fell under Savonarola's spell and burned some of his own works.

The arrival of Charles VIII in 1494 seemed to confirm Savonarola's warnings of disaster. With the Medici in exile, he and his followers seized power. However, Savonarola's policies angered the pope, who excommunicated* him. The monk lost power and was hanged in 1498. After Savonarola's fall, Florence's aristocrats assumed power. However, their leader, Piero Soderini, failed to strike a balance between a broad-based government and oligarchy*. In 1512 he fled the city and the Medici returned, backed by the papacy.

* **papacy**  office and authority of the pope

* **republican**  refers to a form of Renaissance government dominated by leading merchants with limited participation by others

* **Dominican**  religious order of brothers and priests founded by St. Dominic

* **pagan**  referring to ancient religions that worshiped many gods, or more generally, to any non-Christian religion

* **excommunicate**  to exclude from the church and its rituals

* **oligarchy**  form of government in which a small group of people holds all the power

Cosimo de' Medici, shown here in a painting by Italian artist Jacopo Pontormo, led the Medici family to power in Florence during the 1400s. He became the leading citizen, banker, statesman, and patron of the arts in the city.

* **sack** to loot a captured city

The Medici ruled Florence as lords for 15 years. In 1527, however their power suffered a severe blow. Holy Roman Emperor CHARLES V sacked* Rome, defeating the troops of Pope Clement VII, a member of the Medici family. The Medici left Florence, and the city returned to a republican form of government. However, before long Charles V and Clement VII made peace. Medici forces attacked Florence in 1529, and the republic collapsed the following year.

Many of Florence's public institutions changed when the Medici returned. In 1532 the city's nobles drew up a new constitution inviting Alessandro de' Medici to become head of the city, and a short time later they named him "duke of the republic of Florence." A ruling body called the Supreme Magistrate replaced the Signoria and shared power with

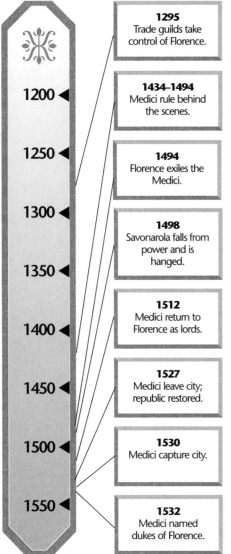

**1295**
Trade guilds take control of Florence.

**1434–1494**
Medici rule behind the scenes.

**1494**
Florence exiles the Medici.

**1498**
Savonarola falls from power and is hanged.

**1512**
Medici return to Florence as lords.

**1527**
Medici leave city; republic restored.

**1530**
Medici capture city.

**1532**
Medici named dukes of Florence.

1200

1250

1300

1350

1400

1450

1500

1550

See color plate 4, vol. 3

the duke. A new council with 200 members, along with a smaller senate, replaced the Grand Council. Members of the new bodies were appointed for life, not elected for short terms. These new arrangements gave the Medici dukes firm control over Florentine political affairs. Under the control of the Medici—especially the talented Cosimo I, who ruled from 1537 to 1564—Florence conquered its long-time rival SIENA and once again became a center of culture and art.

## ECONOMY, SOCIETY, AND CULTURE

Florence prospered during the Renaissance, and much of the city's wealth went into promoting the arts. Sponsoring art provided the city's great families with a way to promote both their own glory and that of their city. The works they commissioned made Florence the showplace of Italian Renaissance culture.

**Economy.** The economic power of Florence came mainly from banking and textiles. By the late 1200s, the city's banks were handling important business for the papacy and the kingdom of Naples. Great banking families such as the Bardi, Peruzzi, and Medici established branches throughout Europe.

The cloth industry had an even greater role in the city's economy, employing about 30,000 people in the early 1300s. Florence imported wool from England, Spain, and other areas and wove it into fine cloth that was sold throughout Europe. During the Renaissance, Florence had about 200 wool firms. The owners of these firms belonged to the wool guild, but most of the workers in the industry were not guild members and had no political power. The silk industry occupied a smaller, but still significant, place in the economy. Women filled many roles in the production of wool and silk, making up two-thirds of the city's wool weavers in the early 1600s.

Florence conducted its business in several types of currency. For international transactions, bankers and merchants used the gold florin, named for the city. This coin, first produced in 1252, contained about 3.5 grams of pure gold. In the 1500s, a less pure coin called the scudo replaced the florin. Local businesses generally used smaller coins of copper and silver. In addition to coins, Florentine banks employed "moneys of account" such as the lira. Money of account did not exist in a physical form, but bankers used it for bookkeeping purposes, such as transferring funds from one account to another.

**Society.** Various groups played a role in the social life of Florence. Many Florentines identified strongly with their local church parish or with their guild. However, the main unit of Florentine society was the family. Marriages that united two families were an important route for social advancement. The wealthy often hired marriage brokers to find favorable matches for themselves or for their children. Girls of the middle and upper classes generally married by their late teens. Men usually waited until they had established themselves financially, typically in

* **dowry** money or property that a woman brings to her marriage

* **humanist** Renaissance expert in the humanities (the languages, literature, history, and speech and writing techniques of ancient Greece and Rome)

* **baptistery** building where baptisms are performed

See color plate 3, vol. 1

their late twenties. To make a successful marriage, a girl needed a sizable dowry*. The money spent on dowries was exempt from taxes, leading many fathers to overstate the size of their daughters' dowries.

Jews made up a significant community in Florence. Most trade guilds did not admit Jews, effectively barring them from city politics. By the 1400s they were limited to a small number of professions, such as pawn-broking. In general, Jews in Florence fared better under Medici rule than they did when the city was a republic. In 1495 city leaders attempted to drive the Jews out of Florence, but a crisis in the economy caused them to think twice about losing an important source of income within the city.

**Culture.** Florence played a major role in shaping Renaissance culture. A staggering number of the age's great artists and humanists* worked in Florence. During the 1300s the city was home to the writers Dante Aligheri, PETRARCH, and Giovanni BOCCACCIO. Noted humanists, including Leonardo BRUNI and Coluccio SALUTATI, served as chancellors of Florence. Many famous sculptors and painters—including RAPHAEL, DONATELLO, MICHELANGELO BUONARROTI, and LEONARDO DA VINCI—were active in the city during the 1400s and early 1500s.

Scholars do not know exactly why Florence became the focus of Renaissance culture, but clearly one factor was the many sources of patronage in the city. Florence's guilds, churches, wealthy families, and city government commissioned a considerable amount of public and private art. At the same time, artists such as Leon Battista ALBERTI and Giorgio Vasari also promoted their city's reputation as an artistic center through their writings on painting, sculpture, and architecture. These works remain one of the most important sources of information about Renaissance art.

Architects in Florence produced some of the most notable buildings of the Renaissance. The cathedral, with its famous dome designed by Filippo BRUNELLESCHI, dominated the city. The neighboring baptistery* featured immense bronze doors with scenes from the New and Old Testaments by Lorenzo GHIBERTI. Other well-known examples of Florentine architecture include the palaces built by prominent families such as the Medici and Rucellai.

Churches and palaces were not only works of art in themselves; they also provided a place to display paintings, sculpture, and other forms of art. Even commercial buildings were used to showcase art. For example, the city's grain storehouses, Orsanmichele, featured niches containing sculptures of the patron saints of the city's various craft guilds. Several of the statues were by leading artists such as Ghiberti and Donatello. Brunelleschi designed the gallery of the city's home for orphans, the Ospedale degli Innocenti. Thus, even in the everyday world of business, outstanding art and architecture were hallmarks of Renaissance Florence. (*See also* **Architecture; Art; Art in Italy; Cities and Urban Life; Factions; Government, Forms of; Guilds; Medici, Cosimo de'; Medici, Lorenzo de'; Money and Banking; Naples; Palaces and Townhouses; Patronage; Popes and Papacy; Representative Institutions; Sculpture; Wars of Italy.**)

Most of the foods and beverages available to Europeans of the Renaissance would be familiar to anyone today. However, the ideas people had about food and nutrition differed considerably from modern thinking. Renaissance eating and drinking habits depended partly on what was available in a certain region or at a particular time of year. But they were also based on religious rules and on the medical ideas of the ancient Greeks. Class differences also played a role. The elegant banquets and expensive delicacies enjoyed by the upper classes set them apart from the common people.

**The Renaissance Diet.** For people of all classes, bread was the mainstay of the diet. Bread was more than a food: before the introduction of tableware, people used it as a plate or bowl, placing other foods on top of it. Wealthier Europeans preferred fine white bread made from processed flour, while poorer folk ate less refined brown bread containing more wheat bran. Coarser bread could also contain barley, rye, or even beans or chestnuts when times were hard. The diet also included cooked grains, which were easier and cheaper to prepare than bread because they did not require an oven. Southern Europeans ate porridge of cooked barley or millet. In the north, grains such as spelt and oats were more common. Rice, a relative newcomer to Europe, grew mainly in the Lombardy region of Italy.

Beverages also varied by region. Wine was the most important drink in the south, which had whole regions devoted to producing and trading it. Beer and ale were the most common beverages in the north, where many households brewed their own. Apple-growing regions in England and France favored cider as their chief drink. People rarely drank water by itself, probably for fear that it would make them sick, but they did mix it with wine. Southern and northern Europe also differed in their use of fat. Olive oil dominated in the south, butter in the north.

Renaissance cooks saw meat as the most desirable part of the diet. In fact, physicians warned against eating too many fruits or vegetables. The poorer a family, the greater role vegetables and grains played in its diet. Beans, cabbage, garlic, and onions were particularly associated with the lower classes. Peaches and melons, by contrast, became popular in the courts.

People raised cows, sheep, and goats both for their meat and for their milk, which could be made into cheese. Pigs were also an important source of meat throughout Europe. Preserving pork in such forms as sausages and hams allowed food from the fall slaughter to be eaten throughout the year. Families raised chickens, ducks, geese, and pigeons for food, and the practice of hunting wild birds or other game was common throughout Europe.

Fish also played an extremely important role in the diet. People in the Mediterranean region and on the Atlantic and Baltic seacoasts consumed local fish and preserved it for export to other regions. The main preserved fish were herring, cod, sardines, anchovies, and botargo (salted belly of tuna). Rivers produced salmon and trout, and some communities had fishponds. Whale and porpoise meat were among the most expensive and fashionable foods of the era.

Members of the upper classes tended to avoid eating many fruits and vegetables, which they viewed as less nourishing fare than meat. However, these foods formed a major part of the diet of the poor. In this wall paintng dating from the early Renaissance, vendors display fruit in a market stall.

To flavor their food, Renaissance cooks used native European herbs such as parsley, dill, sage, oregano, and mustard as well as spices imported from Asia and Africa, including pepper, cinnamon, cloves, nutmeg, and ginger. They also valued sugar as a "spice." The highly prized spices were a major trade item, and the search for better routes to their sources was one reason for the voyages of pioneering explorers such as Christopher COLUMBUS and Vasco da GAMA. However, it is unlikely that Europeans used spices to hide the odor of spoiled meat, as some have suggested. Anyone who could afford costly spices could also afford fresh meat. Instead, the rich used spices heavily to show off their wealth.

**Eating Patterns.** For the average European, the calendar of Christian holidays determined patterns of fasting and feasting. For example, during Lent—the 40-day period of strict religious observance leading up to Easter—good Christians were not supposed to eat meat, butter, or eggs. People could and did bend these rules, and the wealthy turned to rare and exotic fish and lavish displays of fruit to ease the hardships of Lent. Shorter periods of fasting occurred throughout the year.

Immediately before Lent came a holiday period called Carnival, during which people consumed the meat that they could not eat during Lent. In contrast to Lent, Carnival was a time of self-indulgence and gluttony. Some Carnival festivals included a skit in which the spirit of Carnival, a fat man carrying sausages, battled the spirit of Lent, an old thin woman carrying a herring.

Other Christian holidays also provided occasions for feasting throughout the year. In addition, many towns and cities held lavish feasts in honor of their patron saints. Popular stories or artworks some-

* **medieval**    referring to the Middle Ages, a period that began around A.D. 400 and ended around 1400 in Italy and 1500 in the rest of Europe

times defined happiness as a magical land of plenty or an eternal feast, where people could eat as much as they wished without labor and where rivers of wine flowed endlessly. Italian writer Giovanni BOCCACCIO, for example, wrote of a mountain of Parmesan cheese.

Theories about nutrition also influenced eating patterns during the Renaissance. Renaissance medical thought was based on the theory of humors, inherited from ancient Greek and Arab physicians. According to this theory, human health required a balance among four fluids in the body: blood, phlegm, bile, and choler. Too much or too little of any of these fluids led to disease. Physicians believed that specific qualities of food could increase the production of certain humors. For example, they thought that spicy and salty foods promoted choler, the hot and dry humor. Renaissance cooks sometimes combined different foods to balance their various qualities. For instance, they might serve pork (cold and moist) with mustard (hot and dry) or sweet dishes (hot and moist) with sour sauces or condiments (cold and dry).

In addition to their humors, foods were believed to have certain effects on the body, such as aiding digestion or promoting sleep. For this reason people felt that it was important to eat foods in a certain order. However, medical authorities disagreed on the details, producing many contradictory lists of rules for serving different foods. Although Renaissance theories of nutrition are long out of date, they reflect a very modern concern with the connection between food and health.

**The Art of Cookery.**   The cuisine of the early Renaissance did not differ very much from that of the Middle Ages. The first printed cookbook, *On Right Pleasure,* included several recipes borrowed from an older collection. Published in 1475, *On Right Pleasure* was the best-selling Renaissance book on the subject of food. The one major change that occurred at this time was the appearance of distinct regional styles of cooking. Unlike medieval* cuisine, which had been much the same throughout Europe, these new cooking styles reflected the ingredients and preferred flavor combinations of specific areas. Several cookbooks featuring the foods of different countries appeared, including the German *Kuchenmeystery* (1485), the English *Boke of Cokery* (1500), and the Italian *Cookbook* (1525).

The most massive Renaissance cookbook, *Opera (Works),* appeared in 1570. Its author, Bartolomeo Scappi, was chef to Pope Pius V. Scappi's position at one of Europe's leading courts gave him access to all the latest kitchen equipment, which he illustrated in his book. One of the new devices he mentioned was the fork, recently introduced as standard tableware. Scappi's hundreds of recipes show a clear break with medieval cuisine, and some recipes—especially for pastas and stews—approach their modern form.

Guides to managing kitchens and carving cooked meats became popular at European courts. One such book, published in 1581, explains how to present every dish from tiny fowl to exotic fruits. A 1549 book called *Banquets,* published by a member of the court of the ESTE family at Ferrara in Italy, reveals how elaborate Renaissance court meals could

be. It describes feasts of hundreds of courses designed to dazzle guests with many textures and tastes. The great majority of Renaissance Europeans, however, would never experience such a meal. Although there is much less information available about the eating habits of the lower classes, it is clear that a glaring gap existed between upper- and lower-class meals, and this gap widened during the late Renaissance. (*See also* **Agriculture; Americas; Court; Fairs and Festivals; Medicine.**)

## Forgeries

As the arts flourished during the Renaissance, so did the art of forgery. Some forgers copied the style of famous Renaissance artists, while others created fake artworks and other objects from ancient cultures. The increasing public demand for art, combined with the growing fascination with the ancient world, produced an ideal environment for forgery in all forms of art.

**Forgery Types and Techniques.** The invention of printing expanded opportunities for forgery in both art and literature. Some forgers published their own writings under the name of a famous author, while others passed off cheap copies of books as the work of respected printing houses. Authors had little power to stop fake versions of their work, since most societies at the time lacked copyright laws. Artists were also the victims of forgery. For example, adding the initials of master artist Albrecht DÜRER to a print practically guaranteed that it would sell, even if the forgery was fairly obvious. The blossoming of forgery led critics to develop better standards for telling real art from fake.

Perhaps the most popular type of forgery was the creation of fake "ancient" works of art. The revival of classical* styles during the Renaissance taught writers and artists to imitate ancient models and produce new works in the same style. In some cases, the line between imitation and forgery could grow blurry. One of the greatest artists of the Renaissance, MICHELANGELO BUONARROTI, supposedly created a statue of an ancient Roman god, treated it so that it looked like an antique, and buried it. When the statue's discoverers hailed their find as an antique, Michelangelo revealed his joke—proving, in the process, that he had truly mastered the classical style.

**Famous Forgeries and Forgers.** Perhaps the most famous forgery to be unmasked during the Renaissance was a document called the Donation of Constantine. This document, supposedly written by the Roman emperor Constantine in the 300s, transferred power over the empire to Pope Sylvester I. Popes had historically claimed that this document gave the church the right to involve itself in the politics of other states. In the mid-1400s, humanist* Lorenzo VALLA took a closer look at the Donation of Constantine. An expert in ancient Latin literature, Valla studied the document's style and proved that it had actually been written about 400 years after Constantine's death. Valla not only exposed the document as a fake but also produced a "corrected" version of the

* **classical** in the tradition of ancient Greece and Rome

* **humanist** Renaissance expert in the humanities (the languages, literature, history, and speech and writing techniques of ancient Greece and Rome)

text, showing how it would have appeared in the Latin of Constantine's day.

The most successful forger of the Renaissance was Giovanni Nanni, a preacher from the Italian city of Viterbo. Viterbo stood on the site of an ancient city of the Etruscans, who predated the Romans. Nanni became a student of the Etruscans, the first to make serious progress toward translating their language. He then used his knowledge to create an entire false history of the Etruscans, based on objects he had unearthed around Viterbo. He claimed that the biblical figure Noah had traveled to Italy and established a kingdom on the site of Viterbo. Later, he offered "proof" that Noah was an ancient forerunner of the papacy*. This story won great favor with the popes, which may explain why Noah figures so prominently in Michelangelo's paintings in the Sistine Chapel. Interestingly, Nanni was also a great critic who developed strict standards for distinguishing ancient texts from forgeries. (*See also* **Art; Classical Antiquity; Humanism; Printing and Publishing.**)

* **papacy**    office and authority of the pope

## Fortifications

The development of new types of fortification during the Renaissance had far-reaching effects on military strategy and on political power. The new fortifications slowed down the pace of war by enabling cities to withstand attacks by gunpowder artillery and to use artillery in a defensive role. States on the offensive required large standing armies to carry out sieges and assaults against the fortifications. Supporting such armies may have contributed to the development of the centralized nation-state.

* **medieval**    referring to the Middle Ages, a period that began around A.D. 400 and ended around 1400 in Italy and 1500 in the rest of Europe

**Evolution of Fortifications.** Medieval* fortifications consisted of high walls and towers from which defenders shot missiles or dropped objects on attackers. The three traditional methods of attack against medieval walls all had distinct disadvantages. The first method, tunneling under the walls to collapse them from below ground, took a great deal of time. A second method, using battering rams to knock a hole in the wall, exposed attackers to arrows and stones from the defenders. The third method of attack involved building a wooden siege tower as high as the wall and moving it next to the fortification. However, siege towers could be damaged by fire or heavy stones hurled by catapults. Moreover, moving them into place required considerable effort and engineering work. These circumstances gave defenders the edge, and they could often hold out until help arrived or winter forced the attackers to leave.

The invention of mobile gunpowder artillery in the 1450s shifted the odds in favor of the attacker for a brief period. Cannons could easily punch through the high and relatively thin medieval walls. In addition, those defending the fortifications rarely used modern gun power because the older walls could not hold cannons. However, cities responded to the new weapons by making existing walls and towers lower and thicker. They also began to build platforms in front of the walls to hold defensive guns. Fortifications in northern and central

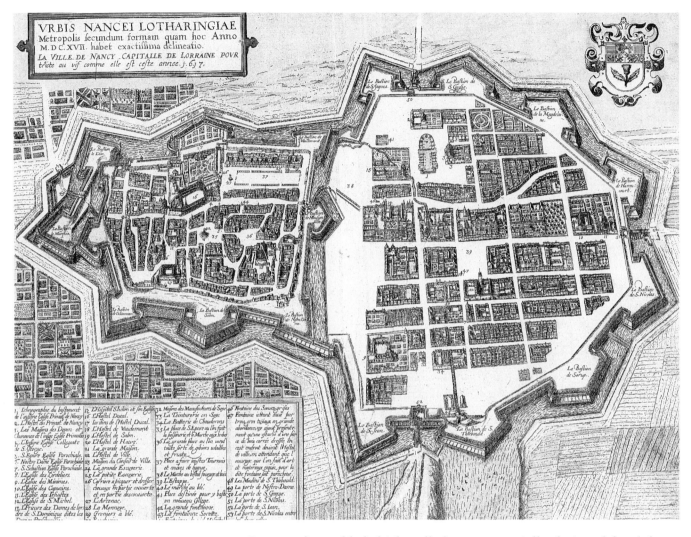

This view of the French city of Nancy in 1617 shows the three-sided bastions typical of the later Renaissance. Guns mounted in these areas enabled defenders to fire at attackers anywhere along the city wall.

Europe often added thick-walled towers specially designed for defense artillery.

The true revolution in fortifications occurred in Italy. Large, low gun platforms called bastions were built at the same height and thickness as the walls that connected them. This allowed defenders to mount heavy guns in the bastions and to move them quickly around on the walls as needed. Early bastions were circular, but by the late 1400s they assumed triangular or multisided pointed shapes. The pointed bastion eliminated the unavoidable blind spots of round towers and enabled defenders to shoot at attackers anywhere along the wall. Furthermore, the bastions and their connecting walls were set in deep ditches, making them lower and harder to hit. The pointed bastion was the key element in the new system of fortification, known as "the Italian trace."

The earliest pointed fortifications were not part of city walls but detached buildings defending city gates. They also appeared as "pillboxes" attached to the bases of round medieval towers. In the late 1400s some fortifications had round medieval towers combined with the newer thick, low walls and gun platforms. The first fortifications to

include all the Renaissance elements were not built until the early 1500s. By the late 1500s bastions and their connecting walls had grown much larger and thicker, and they were set in wider ditches.

**Complete Renaissance Systems.** The first complete system of Renaissance fortifications was built in Italy between 1516 and 1520 at the papal* naval base of Civitavecchia. In 1544 Antwerp became the first northern European city with bastions around its entire city wall. During the Eighty Years' War between Spain and the Netherlands (1568–1648), both sides built bastions in many towns in the Low Countries*. Milan was the largest Italian city to be completely fortified by bastions, and various Mediterranean cities exposed to Turkish attack also rebuilt their defenses.

The best examples of complete Renaissance systems appeared in small or recently built towns because refortification presented difficulties in large, established cities. Rebuilding thicker walls around a city was extremely costly and often required taking over or destroying existing property. Some cities were simply too big to encircle with a new wall, which meant that sections of the city would remain unprotected. Plans for refortifying Rome collapsed in 1540 because of such problems. The size of the challenge is reflected by the fact that it took the city of Lucca over 100 years to complete its refortification.

A more practical solution to complete refortification was the construction of small citadels within the walls. In cities such as Paris and London, royal fortresses of this type provided defense and served as symbols of power. By the 1500s, the rulers of Italian city-states and cities began to build their own urban strongholds for the same reasons.

Some scholars suggest that the changes in warfare caused by the new fortifications changed the political organization of European countries. The new fortifications made it much harder to capture cities, allowing small powers to stand up to larger ones. In addition, states needed large standing armies to carry out long sieges. The planning and financing required to support such armies forced European governments to centralize and streamline their operations, leading to the rise of the nation-state during the 1600s. (*See also* **Arms and Armor; Cities and Urban Life; Nation-state; Warfare.**)

* **papal** referring to the office and authority of the pope

* **Low Countries** region bordering on the North Sea, made up of present-day Netherlands and Belgium

**France**

The Renaissance was a time of great upheaval in France, marked by wars and religious conflict. Throughout the period a strong monarchy ruled the country, and powerful nobles and church leaders dominated French society. The economy was based on agriculture, with most of the population living in rural areas. Nevertheless, French cities and towns grew significantly, and the activities of merchants and explorers expanded beyond the nation's borders. Meanwhile, increased contact with other countries encouraged the development of Renaissance culture in France.

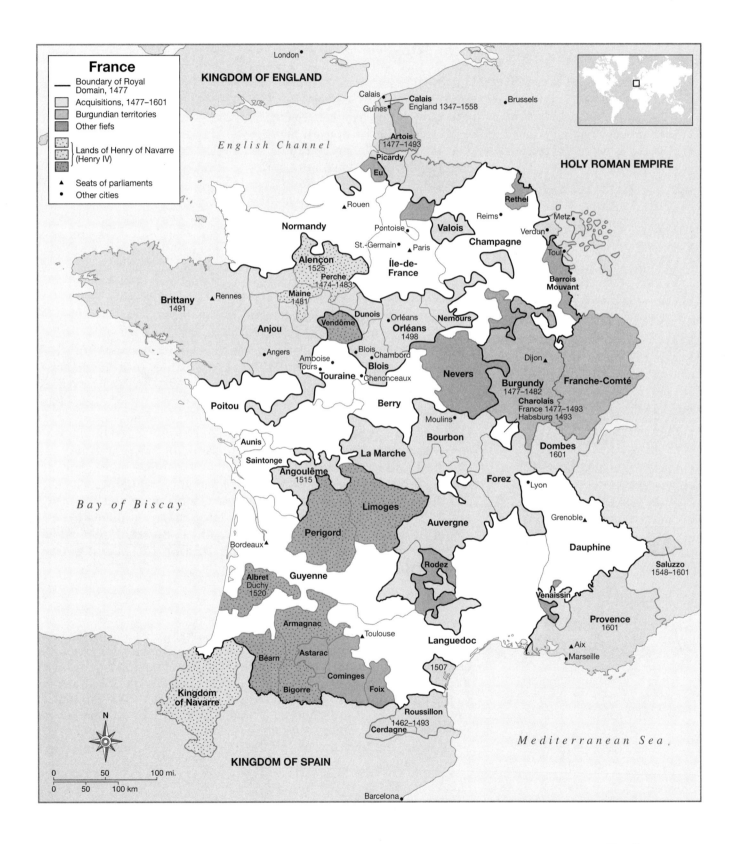

**France**

— Boundary of Royal Domain, 1477
☐ Acquisitions, 1477–1601
☐ Burgundian territories
☐ Other fiefs

☐ Lands of Henry of Navarre (Henry IV)

▲ Seats of parliaments
● Other cities

KINGDOM OF ENGLAND

London ●

*English Channel*

Calais
Guines
Calais England 1347–1558
Brussels ●

Artois 1477–1493

Picardy

Eu

Rethel

HOLY ROMAN EMPIRE

Reims ●
Metz ●
Verdun ●

Valois

Champagne

Barrois Mouvant

Toul

Rouen ▲
Pontoise ●
St.-Germain ●
Paris ▲

Normandy

Alençon 1525

Perche 1474–1483

Maine 1481

Île-de-France

Dunois
Orléans ●
Nemours

Brittany 1491

Rennes ▲

Vendôme

Orléans 1498

Dijon ▲

Anjou

Angers ●

Blois ●
Chambord ●
Amboise Tours ●
Touraine
Chenonceaux ●

Nevers

Burgundy 1477–1482

Franche-Comté

Blois

Berry

Charolais
France 1477–1493
Habsburg 1493

Poitou

Moulins ●

Bourbon

Dombes 1601

Aunis

Saintonge

La Marche

Forez

Lyon ●

Angoulême 1515

Limoges

Auvergne

Grenoble ▲

*Bay of Biscay*

Perigord

Dauphine

Saluzzo 1548–1601

Bordeaux ▲

Albret Duchy 1520

Guyenne

Rodez

Venaissin

Armagnac

Toulouse ▲

Provence 1601

Béarn

Astarac

Languedoc

Aix ▲
Marseille ●

Cominges

1507

Bigorre

Foix

Kingdom of Navarre

Roussillon 1462–1493

Cerdagne

*Mediterranean Sea*

N

KINGDOM OF SPAIN

0   50   100 mi.
0   50   100 km

Barcelona ●

# HISTORY

During the Renaissance a series of powerful monarchs from the VALOIS and BOURBON dynasties governed France. Notable rulers from this period include FRANCIS I, who promoted French Renaissance art and ideas in the early 1500s, and HENRY IV, who brought about a period of relative peace in the late 1500s. Although women of royal blood could not inherit the throne, several female members of the ruling family played influential roles as regents* or political advisers.

**The Valois Dynasty.** The Valois family ruled France from the late Middle Ages until 1589. Louis XI, who became king in 1461, helped break down the feudal* social structure by appointing people of relatively low rank to positions formerly held by members of the nobility. He also expanded the kingdom by gaining control of nearby lands. The death of Charles the Bold of BURGUNDY in 1477 allowed Louis to occupy Burgundy and Franche-Comté on France's eastern border and Artois on the north. The king was later forced to withdraw from Franche-Comté and Artois, but after the death of René, the duke of Anjou, he gained control of the provinces of Anjou and Maine on the west and Provence to the south.

When Louis XI died in 1483, his son Charles VIII inherited the throne. Because Charles was only about 13 years old, his older sister, Anne de Beaujeu, ruled as regent on his behalf. Between 1485 and 1488 opposition to Anne's regency erupted into civil war. In 1491 Charles took on the duties of the monarchy. Three years later, he marched into Italy to claim the kingdom of NAPLES, which had belonged to the dukes of Anjou. This mission failed, but Charles's invasion of Italy helped bring Italian Renaissance art and ideas to France.

Charles VIII died without heirs in 1498 and his cousin Louis XII took the throne. The new king gained control of MILAN and divided Naples with FERDINAND OF ARAGON, the king of Spain, who also had a claim to it. However, in the early 1500s a disagreement between France and Spain led to a conflict in which the French suffered defeat and withdrew from Naples.

In 1508 Louis XII joined the League of Cambrai, an alliance designed to stop the expansion of the republic of VENICE. Louis's troops forced the Venetians to give up some of their land, but Pope JULIUS II responded by forming the Holy League. The new alliance was established to drive the French out of Italy. The French king then tried to replace the pope at a church council. When this failed, Louis took military action and won a victory over the pope's army at Ravenna in 1512. However, the following year forces of the Holy League defeated the French, and Louis withdrew from Italy.

**Religious and Political Rivalries.** When Louis XII died in 1515, the throne passed to his cousin Francis I. The new king's reign (1515–1547) was troubled by religious conflict and international rivalries. Francis took a firm stand in defending the French Catholic church against the PROTESTANT REFORMATION. He also became involved in ongoing conflicts with HENRY VIII of England and CHARLES V, the Habsburg ruler of Spain and the Holy Roman Empire*. Despite Francis's opposition

* **regent**  person who acts on behalf of a monarch who is too young or unable to rule

* **feudal**  relating to an economic and political system in which individuals gave services to a lord in return for protection and the use of the land

* **Holy Roman Empire**  political body in central Europe composed of several states; existed until 1806

* **Ottoman Turks**   Turkish followers of Islam who founded the Ottoman Empire in the 1300s; the empire eventually included large areas of eastern Europe, the Middle East, and northern Africa

* **humanism**   Renaissance cultural movement promoting the study of the humanities (the languages, literature, and history of ancient Greece and Rome) as a guide to living

to Protestantism, he formed alliances with German Protestant princes against Charles V. He even reached an agreement with SÜLEYMAN I, the leader of the Ottoman Turks*, to challenge Charles in eastern Europe and the Mediterranean region.

At home, Francis actively encouraged art, architecture, and humanism*. He invited scholars and artists from Italy to work in France. He also undertook major projects, such as the renovation of the château of Fontainebleau near Paris in a style that incorporated many Renaissance elements.

Francis's son took the throne in 1547 as Henry II. The new king carried on his father's rivalries with England and the Habsburgs. He sent French troops to aid MARY STUART, queen of Scotland, against the English. Mary was the niece of the duke of Guise, a leading French nobleman. Henry also invaded Lorraine, in the western part of the Holy Roman Empire, and captured the towns of Metz, Toul, and Verdun. Meanwhile, Henry's government was torn by intense rivalry among the MONTMORENCY, Guise, and Saint-André families. The Guise family gained prominence when Henry's eldest son, Francis, married Mary Stuart. The king died in 1559 while participating in a tournament celebrating the marriage of his daughter Elisabeth to PHILIP II of Spain.

Francis II was only 15 years old when his father died. Two of his wife's uncles from the Guise family assumed control of the government. These men, both fervent Catholics, pursued a policy of repressing Protestants, even executing some who took part in demonstrations. In 1560 a group of Protestants organized a plot to remove the young king from the influence of his advisers, but the plan failed. Months later, Francis died and his ten-year-old brother, Charles IX, became king. The boys' mother, CATHERINE DE MÉDICIS, stepped in as regent.

Catherine tried to provide freedom of worship for the French Protestants, who were known as Huguenots, but high-ranking members of the Montmorency, Guise, and Saint-André families opposed her efforts. In 1562 the duke of Guise and a group of his followers broke into a Protestant service and massacred more than 60 of the worshipers.

During the next several years the conflict over granting rights to Protestants led to a series of civil wars. In 1572 a marriage was arranged between Catherine's daughter, Margaret of Valois, and a Protestant prince, Henry of Navarre, to help unite the warring groups. However, as the wedding drew near tensions remained high. On St. Bartholomew's Day (August 24) the Protestant nobles who had gathered in Paris for the wedding were murdered. The killing of Protestants spread to other parts of the country and continued for several weeks. An estimated 2,000 Huguenots were killed in Paris, and a few thousand more in the rest of France. The deadly attacks heightened the religious tension engulfing the kingdom.

When Charles IX died in 1574, his brother Henry succeeded him. The new king, Henry III, attempted to calm the religious turmoil with a peace agreement granting favorable terms to the Protestants. However, the Catholic League, a group of Catholic nobles and others, forced him to revoke the agreement. Henry's court was troubled by political

The French king Francis I was an important patron of art, architecture, and humanism in France. In this painting, members of Francis's court gather around him to listen to a translation of a work by a Greek historian.

intrigues among his followers and rivalry between the powerful Guise and Bourbon families. Nevertheless, the king managed to introduce some government reforms and encourage an atmosphere of learning through the Palace Academy.

In 1584 the death of Henry III's younger brother left Henry of Navarre, a Protestant, next in line to the throne. The prospect of a Protestant monarch led members of the Catholic League to drive Henry III from Paris and attempt to depose* him. The league hoped to replace Henry with a ruler less sympathetic to the Protestants. In 1589 the king joined forces with Henry of Navarre and marched toward Paris. On the

* **depose**   to remove from high office, often by force

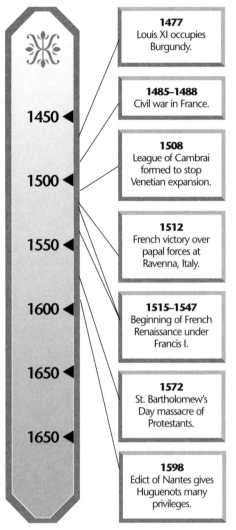

**1477**
Louis XI occupies Burgundy.

**1485–1488**
Civil war in France.

**1508**
League of Cambrai formed to stop Venetian expansion.

**1512**
French victory over papal forces at Ravenna, Italy.

**1515–1547**
Beginning of French Renaissance under Francis I.

**1572**
St. Bartholomew's Day massacre of Protestants.

**1598**
Edict of Nantes gives Huguenots many privileges.

1450
1500
1550
1600
1650
1650

way, Henry III, the last ruler of the Valois dynasty, was assassinated by a supporter of the Catholic League.

**The Bourbon Dynasty.** Henry of Navarre, who became Henry IV in 1589, was the first Bourbon king of France. As a Protestant, he stepped into the midst of the country's religious conflict. Some Catholics refused to support him, while others put pressure on him to return to Catholicism. Meanwhile, many Protestants mistrusted the new king because he had promised to maintain the special privileges granted to the Catholic Church in France.

While the religious dispute smoldered, the Spanish invaded France from their stronghold in the Netherlands. Henry IV, an able military leader, managed to defend his territory while attempting to strengthen his political base in France. In 1593 he returned to Catholicism. During the next few years, the war with Spain continued and Spanish forces advanced into BRITTANY. Finally, in April 1598, Henry issued the Edict of Nantes, a document that gave many rights to the Huguenots and relieved some of the religious tension. The following month Henry negotiated a treaty bringing the war with Spain to an end.

After decades of warfare and religious strife, the Edict of Nantes and the treaty with Spain ushered in a period of relative peace. Yet Henry IV still faced problems, including political plots, a tax revolt, and an uprising among the nobility. In foreign affairs, relations between France and Germany grew strained. In May 1610, while organizing an army to help the German Protestant princes fight the Habsburgs, Henry was assassinated by a fanatical follower of the former Catholic League.

Henry IV's nine-year-old son inherited the throne of France as Louis XIII. The boy's mother, MARIE DE MÉDICIS, ruled as regent. Although Marie's authority was repeatedly challenged, she managed to govern the kingdom and put down a series of revolts with help from her late husband's advisers. In 1617, however, one of Marie's principal advisers was killed, and Louis exiled his mother and established his own rule.

## ECONOMY, GOVERNMENT, AND SOCIETY

The population of France rose dramatically from the late 1400s until about 1570 and then leveled out at about 19 million. The economy and government also expanded to meet the needs of the growing population. The nobility dominated French society, playing major roles in the government, the church, and the military under the leadership of the king.

**Agriculture and Trade.** During the Hundred Years' War (1337–1453) between England and France, much farmland in France had been abandoned. After the war farmers returned to the land, and agricultural production revived. The typical estate, known as a seigneury, was divided into sections. The landowner planted crops on some of the land and rented the rest out to peasants. In addition to paying a fee for the right to work the land, peasants also had to pay taxes

**French Monarchs, with dates of reign**

Louis XI (1461–1483)
Charles VIII (1483–1498)
Louis XII (1498–1515)
Francis I (1515–1547)
Henry II (1547–1559)
Francis II (1559–1560)
Charles IX (1560–1574)
Henry III (1574–1589)
Henry IV (1589–1610)
Louis XIII (1610–1643)

to the crown and make contributions to the church. In the early 1500s new laws allowed individuals to obtain loans to purchase land. As a result, pieces of property began to change hands more frequently. In southern France laws authorizing heirs to divide estates led to the creation of many small farms. Elsewhere, however, estates generally became larger. The countryside was dotted with villages, which served as centers of rural society.

Renaissance France also contained many towns and cities. These gradually expanded as a result of population growth and migration from rural areas. By the mid-1500s, Paris had about 250,000 inhabitants. Louis XI encouraged urban growth and economic activity by granting special privileges to towns and by establishing local trading fairs. Francis I expanded commercial opportunities by sponsoring French expeditions to the Americas in search of trade. During the late 1500s, civil wars in France brought urban growth to a temporary halt, but the process resumed again during the reign of Henry IV.

**Government.** During the Renaissance, the power of the French monarchs was held in check by various forces, including the national assembly, the high courts, and the church. The center of the government was the royal council, which made major policy decisions. It consisted of various advisers, including princes, cardinals, and other influential individuals. Assistants known as secretaries of the finances recorded decisions and prepared correspondence for the king's signature. These officials often married into each other's families, establishing a network that barred outsiders from gaining positions at court.

The Estates General, the national assembly, brought together representatives from the clergy, the nobility, and the towns. At meetings of the Estates General, the king consulted with his subjects and listened to their grievances. After the meetings, the royal council might enact needed measures. A number of provinces had their own assemblies, which negotiated taxes with the crown and controlled provincial finances.

At the top of the French judicial system was the high court of the Parlement of Paris. The court consisted of an upper chamber, staffed by 30 judges, and a lower chamber that dealt with minor cases and the preparation of lawsuits. A president and two deputies supervised the Parlement. There were also several provincial Parlements under the direct authority of the crown, as well as various local courts. The judicial system expanded greatly in the mid-1500s, partly because Francis I allowed qualified individuals to purchase offices and transfer them to their heirs.

**The Military.** Because of its involvement in numerous wars, France needed a strong and reliable army. The core of the army was a heavily armored cavalry, which had been created toward the end of the Hundred Years' War in the mid-1400s. The cavalry companies were made up of rural nobles commanded by provincial governors. During the religious wars, these troops often followed their commanders rather than the king.

In the 1400s, the French infantry consisted primarily of archers. Later, infantry troops used firearms and long, pointed spears. The French army included many hired soldiers from other countries, particularly Switzerland and Germany. In the early religious wars about one-third of France's 72,000 soldiers were foreigners.

**The Church.** Beginning in the early Middle Ages, the monarchy took an active role in the administration of the Catholic Church in France. In 1438 the French church gained the right to elect its own bishops, thus winning some independence from the king and the pope. However, under the Concordat of Bologna (1516), the monarchy regained the right to name bishops. Kings rewarded members of the nobility by nominating them for high church positions. Because there were many such positions in France, the crown wielded considerable power in church affairs. In addition, monarchs often seized church property to finance their campaigns in the religious wars.

**The Nobility.** Though few in number—less than 2 percent of the population—the French nobility possessed a great deal of power. It had a hierarchy*, with princes at the top, and lower levels that included dukes, marquesses, counts, viscounts, barons, chevaliers, and squires. During the Middle Ages, the ranks of the nobility were relatively fixed. In the 1500s, however, the upper ranks of society became more fluid, with some opportunities to advance in rank.

* **hierarchy** organization of a group into higher and lower levels

Families could become part of the nobility by paying a fee—called the *franc-fief*—and not engaging in commerce or manual labor for three generations. Individuals could also gain noble titles by purchasing a special license or by receiving a knighthood for extraordinary achievements in battle.

Members of the top ranks of the government received noble titles, which they could pass on to their heirs. The titles of middle-level officials did not become hereditary until they had been in the family for three generations. As the government expanded, more individuals were able to join the nobility. Nobles flocked to the royal court in search of sponsors and other benefits. They also sought to ensure their wealth and position by marrying their children to members of other noble families.

The power of the nobility in French government and society created problems for many monarchs. The upper nobility, in particular, continued to challenge royal leadership until the reign of Louis XIV in the late 1600s and early 1700s. Nevertheless, the authority of the French monarchy gradually increased during the Renaissance, leading to greater centralization, a stronger military force, and a growing sense of national unity. (*See also* **Aristocracy; Art in France; Drama, French; Dynastic Rivalry; French Language and Literature; Guise-Lorraine Family; Habsburg Dynasty; Wars of Religion.**)

## France, Art in

**See** *Art in France.*

---

## Francesco di Giorgio Martini

**1439–1501**
**Italian painter, sculptor, architect, and engineer**

* **illuminated** having pages ornamented with hand-painted color decorations and illustrations

* **treatise** long, detailed essay

Francesco di Giorgio Martini is best known for his contributions to architecture and engineering. Italian rulers of his day valued him above all for his expertise on military fortifications. However, Francesco was involved in numerous forms of art, and his workshop in SIENA produced everything from sculptures and paintings to illuminated* manuscripts.

Francesco probably received his early training in his native Siena. Scholars know little of the first years of his career, but some believe that he worked as a military architect in southern Italy. The most notable work of the young artist is a larger-than-life-sized wooden sculpture of John the Baptist, which he carved for a religious society in Siena. In the 1470s, Francesco entered the service of the Duke of URBINO. He worked on several parts of the duke's palace and also designed a cathedral, monastery, and convent for the city of Urbino.

During the later years of Francesco's life, the leading courts of Italy competed for his services. He worked in MILAN, Pavia, Abruzzo, and NAPLES before returning to Siena in 1489. He became the city's chief architect and engineer and resumed his activities as a painter and sculptor. He also served twice on Siena's chief governing body.

Francesco's reputation in modern times rests mostly on a pair of architectural treatises* he wrote in the late 1400s. Richly illustrated, they contain a wealth of information on the theory and practice of architecture, engineering, and the military arts. In the second of these works, Francesco emphasized the importance of drawing, tying the practice of architecture to other forms of art. These two treatises had a great influence on artists and architects of the following century. (*See also* **Architecture; Fortifications; Illumination.**)

---

## Francis I

**1494–1547**
**King of France**

* **humanist** Renaissance expert in the humanities (the languages, literature, history, and speech and writing techniques of ancient Greece and Rome)

* **Holy Roman Emperor** ruler of the Holy Roman Empire, a political body in central Europe composed of several states that existed until 1806

Francis I of France spent much of his reign on the battlefield, but he is primarily remembered for his contributions to the cultural life of the nation. The king played a major role in the development of the French Renaissance. He supported artists, assembled an impressive collection of paintings, built Italian-style palaces, and encouraged humanist* learning. During the 1500s he was commonly referred to as "the great king Francis."

A member of the VALOIS DYNASTY, Francis I was the son of Charles, count of Angoulême. He took the French throne on January 1, 1515, after the death of his cousin Louis XII. The year before, Francis had wed Louis's daughter, Claude. Francis was married a second time, in 1530, to Eleanor of Portugal, the sister of CHARLES V, the Holy Roman Emperor*.

Primarily a man of action, Francis excelled in various sports and spent much of his time hunting. He and his royal court often traveled from town to town, enjoying various festivities given in his honor by local

---

townspeople. Francis displayed a similar restlessness in his personal relationships. Unfaithful in marriage, he enjoyed the company of many mistresses.

**War and Politics.** Francis, the "knight-king," spent much of his reign fighting. In 1515 he invaded the Italian duchy* of MILAN, which he claimed through a line of descent from the daughter of a Milanese duke. After defeating the army of the ruling duke, Maximilian Sforza, Francis took over the duchy. In 1519 he put himself forward as a candidate for Holy Roman Emperor. However, the German rulers and church officials who elected the emperor chose Charles of Habsburg, who already ruled Spain and the Netherlands.

As emperor, Charles V became the most powerful ruler in Christian Europe and a lifelong enemy of the French king. War broke out between the two rulers in 1521. It ended with the king's loss of Milan and his defeat and capture at the Italian town of Pavia in 1525. Francis remained a prisoner in Spain until 1526, when he agreed to surrender the duchy of BURGUNDY to the emperor. However, the French king did not fulfill his pledge. This resulted in a new round of hostilities that lasted until the end of his reign.

Francis tried to find allies in his struggle against the emperor. He met with English king HENRY VIII, but Henry eventually sided with the emperor. Francis also sought help from the papacy* and plotted with German Protestant princes and the Ottoman Turks*. Many Christians in Europe were shocked when a combined French-Turkish fleet attacked the port of Nice, and the French king allowed the Turkish pirate Barbarossa to use the port of Toulouse in France as a base.

Francis I wanted to control the nation's political and religious affairs. In 1516 he came to an agreement with the pope, the Concordat of Bologna, that allowed the crown to make all major appointments to ecclesiastical* offices in France. Both the Parlement of Paris, the highest court of law, and the University of Paris opposed this arrangement, which put too much power in the king's hands. Francis overruled their objections. Although the king generally respected local privileges and customs handed down from the Middle Ages, he made most decisions himself, assisted by an advisory council.

Two major weaknesses of Francis's reign were the country's tax system and its financial administration, both plagued by corruption and inefficiency. Revenue fell far short of the king's ever-growing military needs, and Francis had to borrow from foreign bankers to pay for his wars and other projects. He tried to improve the financial system by creating a central treasury and prosecuting corrupt bankers. Another domestic problem that Francis faced was the growth of Protestant heresy*. After 1534, the king supported repressive measures against Protestants, including a massacre of heretics in 1545.

**The Renaissance King.** Francis I was a great patron* of Renaissance architecture and art. During his reign, he built or rebuilt numerous châteaus, including the Louvre in Paris and the magnificent royal resi-

* **duchy**   territory ruled by a duke or duchess

* **papacy**   office and authority of the pope

* **Ottoman Turks**   Turkish followers of Islam who founded the Ottoman Empire in the 1300s; the empire eventually included large areas of eastern Europe, the Middle East, and northern Africa

* **ecclesiastical**   relating to a church

* **heresy**   belief that is contrary to the doctrine of an established church

* **patron**   supporter or financial sponsor of an artist or writer

dence at Fontainebleau. The king invited the Italian master LEONARDO DA VINCI to settle in France, and the artist spent his last years there. Francis also collected art works by Renaissance masters such as RAPHAEL, MICHELANGELO, TITIAN, and Benvenuto CELLINI. His collection of art, including a famous portrait of the king by Titian, became the core of the Louvre museum.

Francis I also was an important patron of humanist scholarship. He had great respect for scholars and writers and included some in his royal court. In 1530 he created the foundation of what later became the Collège de France, a school in Paris for humanistic studies. A lover of books, Francis enlarged the libraries of his royal residences at Blois and Fontainebleau and hired agents in Italy and elsewhere to obtain precious manuscripts of ancient Greece and Rome. The combined libraries of the king eventually formed the basis of the present National Library in Paris. (*See also* **Art in France; Châteaus and Villas; France; Libraries; Ottoman Empire.**)

## French Language and Literature

* **epic** long poem about the adventures of a hero

The Renaissance period both transformed and renewed French literature. Centuries-old traditions of poetry, fiction, and drama gave way to new forms that lasted into the twenty-first century. The period produced some of the greatest literary works ever written in French, including François RABELAIS's mock epics* *Gargantua* and *Pantagruel* and Michel de MONTAIGNE's *Essays*.

## THE FRENCH LANGUAGE

The French language grew out of the common Latin tongue of ancient Rome. Over the course of the Middle Ages, it developed into a distinct language with many dialects. The two most important were the *langue d'oïl* of northern France and the *langue d'oc* of southern France. Because the area around Paris (in northern France) served as the political and intellectual center of the kingdom, the northern dialect came to dominate the language. Most people used this version of French, but scholars, the clergy, and members of the legal and medical professions also used Latin for many forms of communication.

The French language took a great step forward in 1539, when FRANCIS I decreed that judicial documents must be written in French. This decree made French the official language of the kingdom, although it took some time to put it into practice. French continued to change throughout the Renaissance, enriched by hundreds of words adopted from other languages. As the language developed, French literature developed as well. Writers promoted the use of French, rather than Latin, in poetry and prose. They saw the French language as the key to building a truly great French culture, one that would rival the glory of the ancient world.

## INFLUENCES ON FRENCH LITERATURE

Modern scholars disagree as to the precise period of the Renaissance in France. Many use the term to refer to the years between the coronation of Francis I (1515) and the death of Louis XIII (1643). Others argue that the French Renaissance really began in the late 1400s, when the Italian writers Petrarch and Giovanni Boccaccio first began to have an influence on French literature. In either case, France's Renaissance began much later than Italy's, and as a result, it was shaped by very different forces.

**Humanism and Religious Wars.** While the Italian Renaissance focused on reviving classical* culture, the French Renaissance began mainly as a religious movement. France was a major center of theology*, and French thinkers had a stronger interest in recovering the texts of early Christianity than in the pagan* literature of ancient Greece and Rome.

Trends and ideas from northern Europe played a major role in the French Renaissance. The Dutch humanist* Desiderius Erasmus, who tried to return the church to its early Christian roots, inspired the first wave of French Renaissance writers. Clément Marot translated several pieces by Erasmus and composed allegorical* poems about the rebirth of pure Christianity. In addition, he translated nearly 50 psalms into French verse that ordinary people could sing as they worked. Erasmus's literary techniques also had a great influence on François Rabelais, who produced works of biting satire* attacking the Christianity of his day.

Religious reformer Martin Luther also had a strong influence on French writers, especially Margaret of Navarre. Her poems, plays, and other works combined elements of Luther's theology with the mysticism* of the late Middle Ages. Many of her pieces portrayed humble souls who were saved by the mystery of God's grace. Through Margaret, Luther's views influenced the circle of young writers she supported and promoted, which included the young John Calvin.

The Protestant Reformation* in France set off a bloody civil war between Protestants and Catholics. Many writers took sides in the religious conflict. The Catholic author Pierre de Ronsard attacked Protestant beliefs and practices, while the Protestant Henri Estienne mocked what he saw as the superstitions of the Catholic Church.

**Classical Literature and Philosophy.** By the time the French turned to the classics for inspiration, they had access to a great number of ancient Greek and Roman works that had not been available to earlier writers. New advances in printing made these literary works easier to find and read than ever before. French writers also had an advantage in trying to understand these works. Italian scholars had made great advances in the study of Greek in the previous 200 years, and many Greek scholars had moved to western Europe in the 1400s, bringing their learning and libraries with them. By the time of the French Renaissance, writers could study the Greek language or read Greek works in Latin translation.

* **classical** in the tradition of ancient Greece and Rome

* **theology** study of the nature of God and of religion

* **pagan** referring to ancient religions that worshiped many gods, or more generally, to any non-Christian religion

* **humanist** referring to a Renaissance cultural movement promoting the study of the humanities (the languages, literature, and history of ancient Greece and Rome) as a guide to living

* **allegorical** referring to a literary or artistic device in which characters, events, and settings represent abstract qualities and in which the author intends a different meaning to be read beneath the surface

* **satire** literary or artistic work ridiculing human wickedness and foolishness

* **mysticism** belief in the idea of a direct, personal union with the divine

* **Protestant Reformation** religious movement that began in the 1500s as a protest against certain practices of the Roman Catholic Church and eventually led to the establishment of a variety of Protestant churches

These advances in classical studies had a decided influence on French writers. Rabelais, for example, knew enough Greek to lecture and write commentaries on the works of the ancient physicians GALEN and HIPPOCRATES. Poets of the mid-1500s, such as Ronsard and Joachim du Bellay, studied the works of ancient Greek and Roman poets, such as VIRGIL, Horace, Pindar, and Homer. Enthusiasm for these ancient writers inspired them to compose their own poetry in French. Many writers also admired the works of classical philosophers, such as PLATO, Lucretius, and Seneca.

**Italian Literature.** French writers studied Italian literature to find new ways of writing in the vernacular*. French art and literary works of the late 1400s already show distinct Italian influences. In the 1530s, a major phase of Italian influence began in the city of Lyon, in southern France. A large number of Italians lived in Lyon, and many Italian books were published there. One of them, Petrarch's *Canzoniere* (Book of Songs), became the model for a new kind of French poetry. Clément Marot translated several poems from the *Canzoniere* and composed what may have been the first original sonnet in French. Maurice Scève published the first French *"canzoniere"* in direct imitation of Petrarch. The Italian sonnet replaced all French lyric* forms as the standard for love poetry. French poets composed collections of sonnets devoted to a single lady, just as Petrarch had done.

French writers also imitated other Italian works, such as the *Decameron* by Giovanni Boccaccio and *The Book of the Courtier* by Baldassare CASTIGLIONE. *Orlando Furioso* (Mad Roland), a long poem by Ludovico ARIOSTO, inspired French writers in a less direct way. It provided a stock of well-known characters, situations, and speeches that appeared in all forms of literature. Italian influences on French literature remained strong until the late 1500s, when writers turned against the Italian style—largely because of anti–Roman Catholic religious feelings.

## STAGES OF DEVELOPMENT

Literature of the French Renaissance passed through four fairly distinct phases. Each new generation of writers developed its own set of ideas and styles. Many important works of this period are difficult to place within specific genres, or literary forms. Writers often created new forms by combining elements of various older traditions.

**Old Forms, New Ideas.** The first generation included Clément Marot, Margaret of Navarre, and François Rabelais. These writers borrowed the forms and customs of medieval* literature, but used them to express anti-medieval ideas and beliefs. Marot's earliest poems are allegories in the tradition of the *Roman de la Rose* (Romance of the Rose), a long French poem about courtly love. Margaret of Navarre wrote several plays similar in style and form to medieval farces*, but with a new emphasis on religious themes. She also copied the short, humorous, and often obscene stories of the Middle Ages in her *Cent Nouvelles* (One Hundred

* **vernacular**   native language or dialect of a region or country

* **lyric**   refers to a type of verse that expresses feelings and thoughts rather than telling a story

* **medieval**   referring to the Middle Ages, a period that began around A.D. 400 and ended around 1400 in Italy and 1500 in the rest of Europe

* **farce**   light dramatic piece that features broad comedy, improbable situations, stereotyped characters, and exaggerated physical action

FRENCH LANGUAGE AND LITERATURE

Michel de Montaigne was one of the leading French writers of the Renaissance. His influential *Essays* introduced a new form of writing that contrasted with earlier works in a classical style.

* **narrative**   story

* **ode**   poem with a lofty style and complex structure

* **Baroque**   artistic style of the 1600s characterized by movement, drama, and grandness of scale

Stories). However, this collection of tales also reflects the influence of Boccaccio's *Decameron,* leading some scholars to call it the *Heptameron.* The work represents the finest body of short stories from the French Renaissance.

Rabelais was perhaps the most groundbreaking writer of this generation. In his long narrative* *Pantagruel,* he borrowed from the tradition of the medieval epic, but at the same time moved far beyond it. The result was an entirely new form of heroic fiction more in tune with the author's humanist views. Combining humor with impressive scholarship, Rabelais recounted the adventures of giant heroes who are saved from a life of ignorance and brutality by a humanist education. They eventually save the world from the flawed political, religious, and scholarly ideas of the Middle Ages. In later sections, Rabelais broke away from the epic tradition completely to explore the limits of human knowledge and the idea of the abuse of power.

**The Pléiade.**   In the mid-1500s, a group of poets known as the Pléiade (a name based on Greek mythology) set out to make a clean break from the literary traditions of the Middle Ages. They systematically rejected all forms and customs of the French literary tradition and sought to return to ancient Greek and Latin models. Their aim was to sweep away all traces of the Middle Ages, which they saw as a period of ignorance, and raise the French language and culture to the heights reached by ancient Greece and Rome.

Joachim du Bellay expressed this ambitious goal in his *Defense and Illustration of the French Language.* He saw this work as the most important turning point in the history of French literature. Along with the *Defense,* du Bellay published a collection of odes* modeled on those of Horace. Pierre de Ronsard, a close associate of du Bellay, published a longer collection of poems that re-created the structure and style of Pindar's odes. Étienne Jodelle, another member of the Pléiade, attempted to revive the forms of classical drama with his tragedy *Cleopatra in Prison* and his comedy *Eugène.*

**Classicism in Decline.**   The next generation of French writers came to find classical forms and styles too limiting. They also saw the glory of the ancient world as an unimportant idea in a country increasingly torn by religious wars. On August 24, 1572, religious tensions in France burst out in a wave of killings that came to be known as the St. Bartholomew's Day Massacre. This tragedy inspired a new generation of writers to create violent, intense, and passionate works with a focus on the inner life of the mind. They began combining different types of literary forms, creating works that do not fall into familiar categories. Their works led in the Baroque* period in literature.

Michel de Montaigne was perhaps the most important writer of this period. Although he admired the classical poems of du Bellay and Ronsard, he chose to write in a manner that was decidedly anticlassical in form, style, and purpose. His *Essays* are essentially exercises in which he tests his own judgment on a variety of topics. Through these tests,

**The Lady from Lyon**

Louise Labé (ca. 1520–1566) was the most important female poet of the French Renaissance. She belonged to a group of notable poets from the city of Lyon, sometimes called the École de Lyon, or Lyon School. Labé composed sonnets and long elegies, poems that express sorrow for one who has died. She also wrote dialogues, employing a form of debate used by philosophers since ancient times. One notable example is her *Debate Between Folly and Love,* a witty moral tale.

* **pastoral** relating to the countryside; often used to draw a contrast between the innocence and serenity of rural life and the corruption and extravagance of court life

* **libertine** one who rejects or ignores moral standards

* **brothel** house of prostitution

Montaigne revealed his own personality and his new vision of reality as uncertain and ever changing. Another great writer of this period was the poet Agrippa d'Aubigné. A student of classical literature, he kept some of the lyric forms created by the Pléiade, but he broke away from their style and filled his work with gruesome images of war, martyrdom, and destruction.

**The End of the Renaissance in France.** In the first decades of the 1600s, French writers continued the literary experiments of the previous generation, but in a different way. They returned to familiar literary forms and created new ones to express both the passions of the soul and the workings of the mind. Theater became the most popular form of literature during this period. Playwrights mixed genres to produce new types of drama, such as tragicomedy and the pastoral* play.

The so-called libertine* poets revived the poetic tradition with their spirited verses about the pleasures of the tavern and the brothel*, the wretchedness of poverty, and the sources of poetic inspiration. They used forms first invented by the Pléiade but also drew on the works of earlier writers, such as Marot. When this generation of poets died out, lyric poetry effectively ended in France for more than a century.

In the area of prose, autobiographies became popular. Perhaps the greatest of these was *Discourse on Method* by the noted scientist and philosopher René Descartes. The book traced the author's intellectual development and described his method of inquiry in a style that reflected the *Essays* of Montaigne. Montaigne's work also inspired author Charles Sorel, who drew on a great variety of literary forms to create the first authentic novel in French. In addition to Montaigne, his sources included French *nouvelles* (short stories), libertine poetry, and the Spanish picaresque novel (a story about the adventures of a rogue or rascal). (*See also* **Classical Scholarship; Drama, French; Literature; Philosophy; Poetry; Printing and Publishing; Wars of Religion.**)

---

**Froben Press**

**See** *Printing and Publishing.*

---

**Fugger Family**

* **Holy Roman Emperor** ruler of the Holy Roman Empire, a political body in central Europe composed of several states that existed until 1806

The Fuggers, one of the wealthiest families of the Renaissance, were German merchants and bankers with great political power. Hans Fugger was a weaver who settled in Augsburg, Germany, in 1367. He succeeded in the textile trade, and within 100 years, the Fuggers joined the ranks of the city's richest families.

Hans Fugger's grandson Jakob II became the most famous member of the family. Nicknamed "the Rich," Jakob acquired his wealth by loaning enormous sums of money to rulers, such as the Holy Roman Emperor* MAXIMILIAN I. In return, Jakob received control of valuable resources. The silver mines of Tyrol, in particular, generated huge profits for the Fuggers.

Jakob became deeply involved in the politics of his day and used his money to achieve the desired results. In 1519 he helped the Habsburg king of Spain win the office of Holy Roman Emperor as CHARLES V. Jakob bribed the German princes to vote for Charles, and Charles gave Jakob control of rich mercury and silver mines in Spain.

The Fuggers were patrons* of art and learning throughout the Renaissance. Jakob ordered portraits by a number of famous painters, including Hans Holbein the Elder and Albrecht DÜRER. His most original creation was the Fuggerei, a community of more than 50 homes built for the working class. The Fugger family also supported musicians and developed various collections, including books, ancient coins, and sculpture. More than 40 collections of printed music were dedicated to members of the family. (*See also* **Augsburg; Habsburg Dynasty; Holbeins, The; Holy Roman Empire; Patronage.**)

* **patron** supporter or financial sponsor of an artist or writer

See color plate 10, vol. 4

## Galen

### ca. A.D. 130–ca. 216
### Greek physician

* **apprentice** person bound by legal agreement to work for another for a specified period of time in return for instruction in a trade or craft

* **patron** supporter or financial sponsor of an artist or writer

* **dissect** to cut open a body to examine its inner parts

The ideas and writings of the Greek physician Galen influenced medicine for centuries after his death. His theories on subjects such as anatomy, disease, and patient care spread through translations in western Europe and the Middle East. His ideas formed the basis of European medicine during the Renaissance, when scholars studied and critiqued his work. Although many of his theories later turned out to be flawed, his ideas laid a strong foundation for further medical advances.

Galen grew up in the Greek colony of Pergamum in Asia Minor. As the son of a prosperous architect, he received an extensive education and became an apprentice* to a local physician. After completing his medical education, Galen served as a physician to gladiators, fighters who battled each other to the death as a form of public entertainment. In 161 Galen moved to Rome, where a member of the government became his patron* and recommended his services to wealthy patients. He also published two major works on anatomy, *On Anatomical Procedures* and *On the Usefulness of the Parts of the Body*. Galen soon became a well-known physician and writer, producing over 300 works. At the age of 40, he gained the post of court physician to the Roman emperor.

Galen based some of his medical theories on the ideas of HIPPOCRATES, another ancient Greek physician. For example, Hippocrates claimed that the body contained four fluids known as "humors"—blood, phlegm, yellow bile, and black bile. Hippocrates believed that a person was in good health if these fluids were in balance within the body. Galen adapted this idea, arguing that each part of the body had a unique mixture of humors, which he called temperament. He also upheld Hippocrates' belief that observation and experience were the keys to proper medical practice. In the course of his research, he dissected* apes, dogs, pigs, and one elephant.

Galen's work spread as Arabic translations of all of his writings appeared in the 800s. A monk in Italy later translated Galen's work into Latin in the 1000s. Hundreds of years later, his ideas thrived in Italy,

* **treatise**    long, detailed essay

with 590 editions of his works published there between 1500 and 1600. During the Renaissance, Galen's treatises* had a strong impact on Italian universities. They helped to influence the movement known as medical humanism, which aimed to practice medicine in the manner of the ancient physicians.

From Galen's writings, many Italian scholars learned how to dissect and describe different structures of the body. Interest in Galen's work helped to raise the status of anatomy from a minor part of medical education to an important field of study. As the study of anatomy expanded, scholars began to find flaws in Galen's work. Belgian anatomist Andreas VESALIUS revealed many errors in Galen's descriptions of human anatomy. However, he continued to support many of Galen's methods and medical ideas. (*See also* **Anatomy; Classical Scholarship; Medicine.**)

**1564–1642**
**Italian scientist**

* **classical**    in the tradition of ancient Greece and Rome

Galileo Galilei of Italy was the foremost scientist of the Renaissance. He made important contributions to the field of mechanics (the study of force and motion) and to the development of the SCIENTIFIC METHOD. He is chiefly remembered, however, for his work in ASTRONOMY. Galileo, as he is known, did much to promote the heliocentric view of the universe, which holds that the Earth revolves around the Sun. This idea met with opposition from the Roman Catholic Church and from some other scientists, who saw it as conflicting with the Bible and with earlier ideas on the nature of the universe. Galileo spent his final years under house arrest, but his ideas spread, influenced other thinkers, and became part of the foundation of modern science.

**Early Career.**   Galileo was born in Pisa, Italy. Eight years later his family moved to Florence, where Galileo received a classical* education at a nearby monastery. In 1581 Galileo enrolled as a medical student at Pisa's university, where he studied under several leading mathematicians of the day. After four years, Galileo left the university without a degree and began teaching mathematics privately in Florence. A few years later he became a professor of mathematics in Pisa. During his years there, Galileo wrote several volumes of notes on scientific subjects. One volume, which focused on topics such as gravity and bodies in motion, discussed a series of experiments that Galileo had performed in an effort to develop a set of laws of motion.

The death of Galileo's father in 1591 placed heavy financial burdens on the young scientist, who took a position at the University of Padua to improve his salary. He spent the next 18 years in Venice, a period that Galileo later described as the happiest of his life. During this time the scientist produced works on mechanics and kept notes and sketches of experiments he performed with pendulums, objects rolling on slanted surfaces, and thrown or falling objects.

**A New Look at the Universe.**   During his early career, Galileo taught astronomy according to the theories of the ancient scholar PTOLEMY. For

The most important scientist of the Renaissance, Galileo Galilei was known mainly for his work in the field of astronomy. His theories about the motion of the Earth brought him under attack from the Catholic Church.

centuries astronomers had relied on Ptolemy's model of the universe, which used an elaborate mathematical system to explain how the Sun, the Moon, and all the planets revolved around the Earth. A 1543 work by astronomer Nicolaus COPERNICUS, however, had presented a bold new view of the heavens, in which Earth and all the other planets revolved around the Sun. Galileo would come to be the leading champion of this new theory.

In 1609 Galileo heard that scientists in Holland had invented a new device called the telescope, which made it possible to view distant objects in greater detail than ever before. Galileo perfected the telescope for the study of heavenly bodies and turned his eyes toward the skies. He made startling discoveries, including new stars invisible to the naked eye, mountains on the surface of the Moon, and satellites orbiting the planet Jupiter. The following year he published these discoveries in a book called *Sidereal\* Messenger*, which quickly made him the most famous astronomer in Europe. Galileo's discoveries earned him the

* **sidereal**  relating to the stars

**\* patronage**   support or financial sponsorship

patronage\* of Cosimo II de' MEDICI, the grand duke of Tuscany (the region surrounding Florence). The scientist moved to Florence to serve as "mathematician and philosopher" to the grand duke. He also visited Rome, where he enjoyed the praise of fellow scientists.

Although Galileo had taught the theories of Ptolemy in Padua, his own observations and calculations convinced him that the Earth actually traveled around the Sun. He discussed this view with other scholars and referred to it in some of his writings. Although Galileo tried to argue that his evidence of the Earth's motion did not necessarily contradict the Bible, pressure against him began to mount. In early 1616 the church ordered Galileo not to "hold, teach, or defend" the view that the Earth moves and the Sun does not. Galileo agreed and avoided arrest. A few days later the church added Copernicus's revolutionary work to the INDEX OF PROHIBITED BOOKS.

In 1623 a new pope, Urban VIII, took office. At first, Urban VIII was sympathetic to Galileo, and most scholars believe that he granted the scientist some sort of permission to resume his studies of the Copernican system. By 1630 Galileo had finished his great work *Dialogue Concerning the Two Chief World Systems.* In this piece he compared the evidence for the systems of Ptolemy and Copernicus and came down heavily in favor of the Copernicans—in the process making those who held to the Ptolemaic system look rather foolish. Galileo argued that the Earth is similar to heavenly bodies in its motion and material. He disputed earlier proofs that the Earth is at rest and claimed that Earth was probably a planet that revolved around the Sun.

**Trial and Later Years.**   To get a church censor to approve the publication of the *Dialogue,* Galileo added a statement to the text claiming that he meant it as a mathematical exercise only, not a proof of a moving Earth or a stationary Sun. Despite this precaution, the book's publication in 1632 landed Galileo in deeper trouble than he could have imagined. Pope Urban VIII was furious, possibly feeling that Galileo had broken an earlier promise to write on the topic without taking sides. The pope also thought that Galileo had ridiculed his own answer to the problem of the two world systems, which was that human intellect could not solve it. The church banned all further publication and sales of the *Dialogue.* It then summoned Galileo to Rome to be tried for teaching a theory that the church had condemned as contrary to Scripture.

A committee of ten cardinals tried Galileo. They found that he had taught and defended the opinions of Copernicus, although they could not be certain that he actually believed them—a more serious charge. To bring the matter to a close, the head of the committee offered to let Galileo plead that he had become carried away while writing and had defended the Copernican theory without meaning to do so. Galileo agreed to this position, but the pope was not satisfied. He made Galileo swear that he did not believe in the Earth's motion and that his former teachings were wrong. The church then pardoned Galileo, but confined him to his home and forbade him to write any more on Copernicanism.

During his forced retirement, Galileo continued his research into the science of mechanics. He published his results in 1638 under the title

### Righting a Wrong

Centuries after Galileo's death, the Roman Catholic Church admitted that it had been wrong to put him on trial and ban his work. The process began in 1820, when the church withdrew its condemnation of the Copernican system. Fifteen years later it removed Galileo's *Dialogue* from its list of forbidden books. In 1981 Pope John Paul II established a special commission to reexamine Galileo's trial. Its report, released in 1992, officially declared that religious authorities had misunderstood Galileo's teachings.

* **villa** luxurious country home and the land surrounding it

*The Two New Sciences*—the manuscript had been smuggled to Holland for printing. After 11 years of quiet house arrest, the leading scientist of his age died peacefully at his villa* at Arcetri. He was buried in the church of Santa Croce in Florence, where his remains lie near those of such other celebrated Renaissance figures as the artist MICHELANGELO BUONARROTI and the author Niccolò MACHIAVELLI. (*See also* **Sciences, Physical; Scientific Instruments.**)

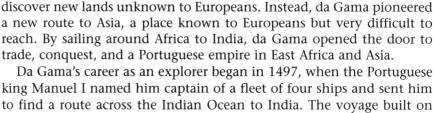

## Gama, Vasco da

ca. 1469–1524
**Portuguese explorer**

Vasco da Gama made one of the most important voyages of exploration in the Renaissance. Unlike Christopher COLUMBUS, he did not discover new lands unknown to Europeans. Instead, da Gama pioneered a new route to Asia, a place known to Europeans but very difficult to reach. By sailing around Africa to India, da Gama opened the door to trade, conquest, and a Portuguese empire in East Africa and Asia.

Da Gama's career as an explorer began in 1497, when the Portuguese king Manuel I named him captain of a fleet of four ships and sent him to find a route across the Indian Ocean to India. The voyage built on years of Portuguese exploration along Africa's coasts, including the voyage of Bartolomeu Dias nine years earlier around the Cape of Good Hope on the southern tip of Africa.

Da Gama headed south from Portugal, paused at the Cape Verde Islands off western Africa, and then moved out into the Atlantic. Although his exact route is unknown, da Gama sailed through the open ocean rather than inching his way along the coast. After 90 days at sea out of sight of land, the fleet arrived 100 miles north of the Cape of Good Hope. Da Gama rounded the cape in November 1497 and proceeded north along the eastern coast of Africa.

See color plate 2, vol. 4

After stopping at several ports, da Gama found an Indian sailor to guide him across the Indian Ocean. In May 1498 the Portuguese reached the Indian port of Calicut, where they spent more than three months trying to trade for spices and gems. Despite the hostility of Muslim traders and the local Hindu ruler, da Gama obtained a cargo of cinnamon and pepper. In 1499 he returned to Portugal. In some ways he had been less than successful, having wrecked two of his four ships and lost two-thirds of his crew. Yet he had proved that the sea route to India existed.

* **viceroy** someone who rules a territory on behalf of a king

King Manuel rewarded da Gama and promptly sent larger fleets along the new route. Da Gama made his second voyage to India in 1502 and another in 1524, this time as the viceroy* of India. (*See also* **Exploration; Portugal; Travel and Tourism.**)

## Gardens

The gardens of the Renaissance were art forms that, like the other arts of the era, took inspiration from the ancient world. The Renaissance garden emerged in Italy during the 1450s and reached a peak in the late 1500s with grand garden complexes featuring terraces and fountains. The style that developed in Italy influenced garden design throughout Europe.

The gardens of the Villa d'Este in Italy feature the symmetrical designs, low-lying compartments, and straight paths typical of Renaissance gardens.

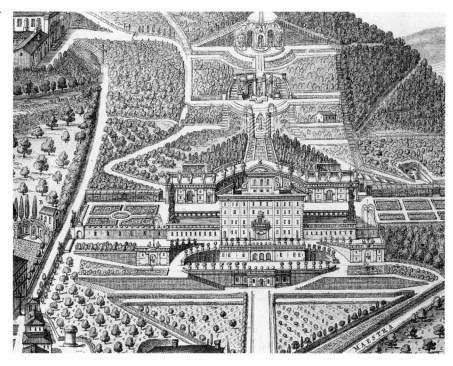

* **villa** luxurious country home and the land surrounding it

* **medieval** referring to the Middle Ages, a period that began around A.D. 400 and ended around 1400 in Italy and 1500 in the rest of Europe

* **antiquity** era of the ancient Mediterranean cultures of Greece and Rome, ending around A.D. 400

* **symmetrical** balanced with matching forms on opposite sides of a structure or piece of art

**Origins and Design.** The poet PETRARCH (1304–1374) had helped inspire an awareness of nature in Italy, and new translations of ancient writings about Roman villas* brought a renewed interest in elegant country living and garden making in the mid-1400s. The concept of *villeggiatura,* a retreat to the countryside, became fashionable.

Like medieval* gardens, the gardens that took shape in Italy at this time were enclosed by walls and planted with herbs and flowers both ornamental and medicinal. The new gardens, however, reflected the Renaissance fascination with antiquity*. Writing on architecture in 1452, Leon Battista ALBERTI emphasized the use of antiquity as a model, the role of geometry and order in the garden, and the importance of positioning the house and garden to create views of the landscape. Remains of ancient Roman gardens were few, so those who wanted to create gardens in the antique style relied on literary sources.

Despite regional variations in landscape and climate, the gardens of Renaissance Italy displayed a unity based on the design principles of order and geometry. Gardens were symmetrical*, with low-lying square or circular compartments separated by straight paths. This regularity was seen not as a sign of human control over nature but as a reflection of the divine harmony of the universe, the work of human hands revealing the order within nature. Trees and shrubs, carefully clipped, formed mazes and geometric shapes inspired by ancient Roman descriptions. Gardens designed on antique models also featured sculpture, fountains, and artificial caves.

The compartments of the geometric gardens were planted with herbs and flowers and bordered with hedges and fruit trees. The garden also featured orchards, orderly plantings of grapevines, and dense stands of trees arranged in rows. Although plants with medicinal uses remained

popular, the desire to include ornamental plants increased as the era's exploration and world trade brought rare and exotic specimens from Africa, Asia, and the Americas.

The garden reflected nature's orderly side. Nature's wild side found expression in the park, an area of irregular, unsymmetrical landscape and plantings. Grand villas had both gardens and parks, and some estates were designed as large parks, embracing both the tamed and the untamed. During the 1500s, steep hillsides became choice sites for villas and their gardens and parks because they offered the best views. Architects designed the gardens on large terraces that were supported by massive walls and connected by ramps and staircases.

**The Role of the Garden.** Gardens were considered both useful and recreational. They produced medicinal plants, fruit, and wine for their owners and also served as quiet retreats for strolling, conversation, and outdoor meals. People saw the garden as a healthful resort, a place where its owners could escape the foul air of the cities.

Like villas, gardens also provided opportunities for their owners to display their wealth, status, and culture. The finest gardens were companions to their owners' elegant and magnificent villas. Along with exotic plants and animals, they contained statues, either ancient or newly created, and elaborate waterworks such as fountains, waterfalls, and water-powered musical organs. Designed by leading architects for cardinals, popes, princes, and wealthy citizens, the gardens were built and maintained by enormous crews of laborers. In this way, the Renaissance garden reflected the divisions of society.

Architects, sculptors, gardeners, and travelers spread the ideas and designs of Italian gardens abroad. Italian-style gardens featuring grottoes, waterworks, and statuary appeared throughout central and northern Europe. Gardens such as that at Wilton House in England, laid out in 1630, drew on design principles developed in Italy nearly two centuries earlier. (*See also* **Architecture; Classical Antiquity.**)

| Gender |
| --- |

**See** *Sexuality and Gender.*

* **republican** refers to a form of Renaissance government dominated by leading merchants with limited participation by others

The coastal city of Genoa in northwestern Italy was a leading European port during the Renaissance. For many years, the city struggled for political stability as various powers inside and outside the city competed for control. However, after establishing a republican* government in 1528, Genoa entered a golden age of art and culture.

**A Troubled Period.** With rugged mountains on one side and the sea on the other, Genoa enjoyed significant natural advantages. It was easy to defend and had a natural harbor. During the Middle Ages, Genoa dominated trade in the eastern Mediterranean. In the mid-1300s, however, VENICE emerged as the region's leading commercial power after

conquering many of Genoa's bases in the Aegean Sea. Genoese traders then turned their attention to the Black Sea and the western Mediterranean, particularly Spain. Meanwhile, Genoese industries expanded, and wool and silk manufacturing became important elements in the city's economy.

Between 1339 and 1528, Genoa suffered from constant political conflict and civil war. Nobles and other wealthy families controlled the city's government and struggled to promote their own political and economic interests. The city had no system for restricting the activities of these warring factions*. This period of turmoil included 46 attempts to overthrow Genoa's government, 41 of them successful. Several times the city fell into the hands of foreign rulers, usually the king of France or the duke of MILAN. These continual conflicts eventually left the city in terrible debt.

In the early 1500s two powerful European families—the HABSBURGS, who dominated the Holy Roman Empire*, and the VALOIS, who ruled France—fought for control of Italy. Genoa's port became an important prize in this rivalry between the Habsburg and the Valois dynasties, and the city passed back and forth between the two powers.

**A New Era.** The combination of financial and political troubles stirred up a reform movement in Genoa. In 1528 a group of reformers, led by the admiral Andrea Doria, overthrew French rule and established an independent republic. This revolution benefited the city in two major ways. First, it created a stable government, which had never existed under the old system. Second, by overthrowing the French, Genoa established itself as an ally of the Habsburgs, who ruled Spain. As a result, the city received the protection of Spain without falling under its control.

Doria's personal strength and popularity helped hold together the new government and control the rivalries that had divided the city in the past. Although he never took a noble title, Doria effectively ruled Genoa as a prince* from 1528 until his death in 1560. But he also made a series of reforms in 1547 to ensure that all the noble families of Genoa would have a voice in government.

The arts flourished under the new regime. Doria's luxurious home by the sea is a striking example. Built in the style of ancient Rome, this impressive villa* reflected the city's new ties to Rome and Spain and its freedom from French rule. Decorated with formal gardens, sculptures, and tapestries, Doria's villa became a symbol of the new, glorious city Genoa had become. It also served as the cultural, military, political, and economic center of the Renaissance in Genoa.

Much of the art from this period focused on the heroic figure of Doria. Portraits and other works linked Doria with the ancient defenders of the Roman republic. A series of frescoes* in Doria's villa featured portraits of his ancestors, presenting Doria as the descendant of a long line of Roman-style military heroes. The leader also appeared in several pieces in the guise of a Roman god. (*See also* **Holy Roman Empire; Italy; Spain.**)

* **faction** party or interest group within a larger group

* **Holy Roman Empire** political body in central Europe composed of several states; existed until 1806

* **prince** Renaissance term for the ruler of an independent state

* **villa** luxurious country home and the land surrounding it

* **fresco** mural painted on a plaster wall

## Gentileschi, Artemisia

**1593–ca. 1653**
**Italian painter**

* **perspective**   artistic technique for creating the illusion of three-dimensional space on a flat surface

* **patron**   supporter or financial sponsor of an artist or writer

* **allegory**   literary or artistic device in which characters, events, and settings represent abstract qualities and in which the author intends a different meaning to be read beneath the surface

* **fresco**   mural painted on a plaster wall

Artemisia Gentileschi was one of the few female artists who gained an international reputation during the Renaissance. Her work stands out for its distinctive style and its expression of a woman's point of view. Many experts compare Artemisia to the Italian artist CARAVAGGIO because of the dramatic realism and use of chiaroscuro (contrasting light and dark) in her work.

Born in Rome, Artemisia learned to paint from her father, Orazio. Her favorite subjects were female characters from the Bible or from history, such as *Susanna and the Elders* (1610). Artemisia's artistic training included lessons in perspective* by the artist Agostino Tassi, who raped his student in 1612. Tassi's trial lasted seven months and resulted in a light sentence for the artist and an arranged marriage to a Florentine artist for Artemisia. In 1616 she became the first female member of Florence's prestigious art school, the Accademia del Disegno. While in Florence she became friends with the scientist Galileo GALILEI and made references to him in some of her paintings.

Artemisia returned to Rome around 1620 without her husband. She gained some important patrons* for her work but did not receive large commissions from the church. In 1628 she moved to Naples. There she painted a self-portrait (probably *Self-Portrait as the Allegory* of Painting) that combined the traditional female symbol of art with a concern about the status of the artist in society. She also gained commissions for religious paintings. In 1638 she joined her father in England at the court of CHARLES I. Together they worked on frescoes* for the ceiling in the Great Hall of the queen's house at Greenwich. In 1641 she returned to Naples, where she spent the last years of her life.

For many years scholars dismissed Artemisia's work by giving her father credit for her paintings. Despite the lack of appreciation in her lifetime, Artemisia influenced several outstanding artists, including the Dutch master Rembrandt. (*See also* **Art; Art in Italy; Women.**)

## Geography and Cartography

During the Renaissance, Europeans grew more interested in understanding their world, and the fields of geography and cartography gained new prominence. Geography involves the study of the places and peoples of the world, and cartography (mapmaking) is the visual representation of the world and its parts. Both played a part in furthering the economic and political ambitions of European states. In addition, the rediscovery of the work of an ancient scholar helped both geography and cartography take huge steps forward in the Renaissance.

**Geography.** Geography was closely linked to exploration and nation building, two important enterprises of the Renaissance. In earlier times geography had been part of cosmography, the study of the structure of the universe. During the 1500s and 1600s, geography emerged as a separate field that focused on Earth. Three related branches developed within geography—mathematical, descriptive, and chorographic—and each branch had special areas of study.

As explorers gathered information about distant lands during the Renaissance, mapmaking became more precise. This image of the Americas by the famous cartographer Gerhard Mercator appeared in a world atlas published in 1633.

Mathematical geography was most closely related to mapmaking. It provided mathematical tools for measuring Earth's surface, determining the exact position of points on it, and transferring real-world measurements to maps. Mathematical geography grew out of *Geographia,* a work of the ancient Greek scholar PTOLEMY, which was first translated into Latin in 1410. Ptolemy's key contribution was the notion of covering the Earth's surface with a grid of latitude and longitude lines, measurable through sightings of the sun and stars. These lines served as references for pinpointing the exact location of places. Many important Renaissance geographers, such as Peter Apian (1495–1552) and Sebastian Münster (1489–1552), published works based on Ptolemy's method, including world maps made with his system and measurements. By the mid-1500s, all major works on geography began with Ptolemy and used his framework.

Descriptive geography, the most familiar of the three branches, consisted of writings about physical and political structure of other lands and their inhabitants. Descriptive geography covered a wide range of

topics, from practical details about European road conditions and inns to outlandish tall tales of faraway places and people. Among the most popular books of the Renaissance were the collections of travel accounts written by Giovanni Battista Ramusio (1485–1557), Richard HAKLUYT (ca. 1552–1616), and Theodore de Bry (1528–1598).

Chorography involved the study of small areas or regions, focusing on histories of families, annals of events, landscapes, objects of antiquity*, and other points of interest. It combined a storyteller's interest in local sights, families, and wonders with demanding historical research. Two leading Renaissance chorographers were Joseph Justus Scaliger (1540–1609) and William Camden (1551–1623).

**Cartography.** Unlike geography, a field of scholarly learning, mapmaking was a more practical discipline connected with the guilds* and crafts such as printing. However, cartography also had close ties to mathematical geography, and developments in each field influenced the other.

During the Renaissance, mapmaking went through revolutionary changes. The introduction of the Ptolemaic system brought mathematical rules for representing the world on paper. Earlier maps of the known world had often been symbolic—for example, depicting the continents of Europe, Africa, and Asia in relation to the biblical Garden of Eden. Renaissance mapmakers, by contrast, sought to represent the world accurately and realistically. They wanted a measurable world, and Ptolemy offered them the perfect tools. In 1413, just three years after the first European publication of Ptolemy's work on geography, Pierre d'Ailly published Ptolemaic maps. Soon all cartographers were using Ptolemy's measurement-based approach, although some experimented with new forms of projection, the method of representing a spherical world on a flat map.

Although world maps before the Renaissance had not been created with realism in mind, another type of map had always stressed practical detail and accuracy. Sea charts, also known as portolans, were used for navigation in the Mediterranean and Red Seas and along the Atlantic coast. Based on observation, wind direction, and simple astronomical sightings, these charts represented firsthand geographic knowledge. Guarded jealously, passed from navigator to navigator, they were not published. During the 1500s, however, the information they contained began to appear in published maps and globes.

Part of the revolution in cartography was the explosion of interest in buying maps and globes. Martin Behaim of Germany made one of the first globes in 1493, and by the mid-1500s prosperous folk could purchase these symbols of worldly knowledge. The atlas, a set of maps bound into a book, appeared as a new and popular form of map ownership.

Two important mapmakers achieved considerable success. In 1569 Gerhard Mercator developed a new world map based on his own system of projection, which emphasized northern Europe and North America. Mercator's map was widely reprinted and copied, and his method of

* **antiquity** era of the ancient Mediterranean cultures of Greece and Rome, ending around A.D. 400

* **guild** association of craft or trade owners and workers that set standards for and represented the interests of its members

See color plate 4, vol. 4

projection remained in use for centuries. A year after Mercator's map appeared, Abraham Ortelius published the first world atlas. Called *Theatrum orbis terrarum* (Theater of the World), it set the style and standard for all later atlases.

The exploration of the world during the Renaissance fueled the rising interest in geography and cartography. By the end of the 1600s, Europeans had learned the value of maps not just to scholarship but also to trade, navigation, national pride and ambition, and overseas conquest. (*See also* **Americas; Exploration.**)

## German Language and Literature

* **bilingual**   speaking or using two different languages

The language and literature of Germany went through a transformation during the Middle Ages and Renaissance. Beginning in the mid-1200s, Latin—the language in which most official documents had been written—gradually gave way to German. This change produced a bilingual* literature in Germany that was both rich and diverse.

## THE EVOLUTION OF THE GERMAN LANGUAGE

Between 1350 and 1650, Germans spoke and wrote in a variety of regional dialects. The forms, spelling, and pronunciation of words all differed from place to place. "Standard" forms of German began to emerge during the 1500s, and by the end of the century a widely accepted written language had developed.

* **Holy Roman Emperor**   ruler of the Holy Roman Empire, a political body in central Europe composed of several states that existed until 1806

Several factors played a role in the standardization of German. The form of the language used at the court of the Holy Roman Emperor* had a significant influence on spoken and written German. Perhaps the most important figure at the imperial court was Johann von Neumarkt, chancellor to the emperor Charles IV in the mid-1300s. Neumarkt contributed to the development of both German and Latin. For international correspondence, he created a version of Latin modeled on that of the early Italian humanists*. At the same time, he combined two existing German dialects to produce a flexible and elegant form of German for everyday use.

* **humanist**   Renaissance expert in the humanities (the languages, literature, history, and speech and writing techniques of ancient Greece and Rome)

A second significant factor in the development of German was Johann GUTENBERG's printing press, invented around 1455. Some scholars believe that printers tried to reduce the use of regional dialects in their books in an effort to reach the widest possible audience. However, they did not create a single standard form of written German. Instead they developed several so-called printers' languages, all distinctly different.

The most important factor in the development of a standard German language was probably the German translation of the Bible that religious reformer Martin LUTHER produced in 1534. Widely distributed in German-speaking lands, this book spread its version of written German to thousands of readers. During Luther's lifetime, printers produced half a million copies of his Bible. This number is especially impressive considering that most Germans at the time could not read. Some writers have credited Luther with "creating" modern German, but this claim is

an exaggeration. However, he did contribute greatly to the development of the German that appeared in later literature. Luther's language was colorful and earthy. He had a good ear for rhythmic balances and a gift for meaningful phrases, and his writing abounded with images of everyday life.

Any history of the German language must include the linguistic societies that developed in the 1600s. The most important of these was the *Fruchtbringende Gesellschaft* (Fruit-Bearing Society). Modeled on an Italian ACADEMY, the group aimed to purify and preserve the German tongue. The society replaced numerous foreign words with newly coined German words, many of which are still in use.

## THE LITERATURE OF GERMANY

Various social and religious changes shaped German literature during the Renaissance. One major trend was the emergence of a middle class in European cities. Members of the new middle class demanded books that were both entertaining and instructive. At the same time, the development of printing made more books available, while the growing number of people able to read created a market for them. Most importantly of all, the Protestant Reformation* in the early 1500s challenged the authority of the Roman Catholic Church. Its influence touched every aspect of Renaissance life, including the types of literature that were produced.

**Religious Pamphlets.** In the wake of the Reformation, thousands of religious pamphlets flooded the German market. They took a variety of forms, including letters, sermons, parodies, songs, and fables. Often illustrated with woodcuts*, pamphlets urged readers to take a stand for or against the new religious ideas of the day. Aimed at average citizens, pamphlets were written in the vernacular* rather than in Latin, which until that time had always been used for religious writing.

Most pamphlets were published anonymously, but several major authors made their names public. Chief among these was Martin Luther. According to estimates, over 3 million copies of his works were sold between 1516 and 1546—not including the many editions of his German Bible. Another important writer of pamphlets was Hans Sachs, a shoemaker from NÜRNBERG. Both men also distinguished themselves in other literary forms, including lyric poetry*.

**Lyric Poetry.** The most important forms of lyric poetry during the German Renaissance were two types of religious songs. Church hymns, called *Kirchenlieder*, reflected the influence of Protestant ideas. Luther composed approximately 40 hymns, including the famous and still popular "A Mighty Fortress Is Our God." The Reformation also affected the songs of the *Meistersingers* (master singers) who met regularly after Sunday services to perform solo songs without instruments. Thousands of these songs, called *Meisterlieder* (master songs), were written and performed during the Renaissance, although few are remembered today.

* **Protestant Reformation** religious movement that began in the 1500s as a protest against certain practices of the Roman Catholic Church and eventually led to the establishment of a variety of Protestant churches

* **woodcut** print made from a block of wood with an image carved into it

* **vernacular** native language or dialect of a region or country

* **lyric poetry** verse that expresses feelings and thoughts rather than telling a story

Plate 1
Skilled craft workers produced most of the finished goods sold in Renaissance cities. Goldsmiths, for example, made jewelry and other fine metal objects, which were highly prized as status symbols. The painting *Precious Metal Workshop*, created by the School of Agnolo Bronzino, shows goldsmiths at their trade. Surrounding the workers are examples of their craft, including crowns, chains, and elaborate vessels.

**Plate 2: Left**
Renaissance women played a limited role in the workplace. The professions open to them—such as sewing, weaving, laundering clothes, or selling food and drink—were often of low status. This image of *Washerwomen* at work appeared in a German manuscript in 1589.

**Plate 3: Below**
Merchants occupied a fairly high position on the Renaissance social scale. As trade expanded during this period, many members of the merchant class gained great wealth and power, often rivaling that of the nobility. *Portrait of a Merchant*, painted in the early 1500s by artist Jan Gossaert of the Netherlands, shows one of these wealthy businessmen surrounded by the tools of his trade—pens and paper, coins and scales.

**Plate 4: Left**

The textile industry was a key part of the Renaissance economy, providing a variety of skilled and unskilled jobs. In this painting from the early 1570s by Mirabello Cavalori, laborers prepare wool to be made into cloth. The manufacture of woolen fabric was a complex process that involved shearing sheep, cleaning the wool, spinning it into yarn, and weaving the yarn into cloth.

**Plate 5: Below**

Peasants made up about 90 percent of Europe's population during the Renaissance. They earned their living by growing crops and raising animals on land that usually belonged to other people. Peasant women took part in many of these tasks, including harvesting crops and raising animals, such as sheep and chickens. The painting *Summer*, by Francesco Bassano, shows farm workers gathering crops and shearing sheep.

**Plate 6: Above**
Most Renaissance towns held a market day once a week. Vendors, such as the one shown in this painting by Bernardo Strozzi, set up stalls in the open air to sell their wares. Once a year, a town might expand its market into a larger, multi-day event called a fair. Though primarily economic in purpose, fairs broke up the routines of daily life and were social events. Sometimes traveling entertainers provided amusement.

**Plate 7: Below**
During the Renaissance, dividing lines began to emerge between the "high" culture of the upper classes and the popular, or "low," culture of the common people. Nonetheless, popular forms of entertainment provided some "high" artists with subject matter. Jan Mostaert of the Netherlands, for example, painted *The Egg Dance* in the early 1500s. The peasant in the picture is attempting to dance around the egg on the floor without breaking it.

**Plate 8: Above**
Michelangelo Merisi da Caravaggio of Italy was another artist whose works portrayed scenes from the lives of ordinary people. In *The Fortuneteller*, painted around 1592, a woman is reading the palm of a young gentleman. The artist's signature use of light and shadow hints at the "shady" nature of the fortuneteller's trade.

**Plate 9: Below**
*The Conjuror*, by Dutch painter Hieronymus Bosch, features an entertainer using his skills to cheat his customers. As the magician causes a toad to come out of an audience member's mouth, an assistant spirits away the victim's purse. The piece reflects Bosch's dark, yet humorous, view of human nature.

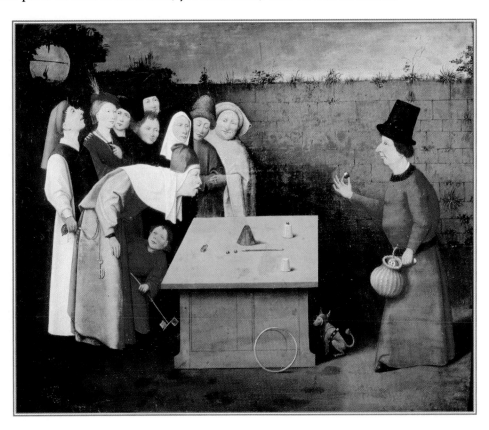

**Plate 10: Left**

The painting *Seven Sacraments*, by Flemish artist Rogier van der Weyden, portrayed the seven most important rituals of the Roman Catholic Church. The painting was a triptych, composed of three separate panels. The first panel, shown here, presents the baptism of infants, the confirmation of church members, and confession. Catholics also recognized four other sacraments that they believed Christ had established to help mortals reach salvation. Protestant leaders of the 1500s disputed this point, claiming that Christ had established only baptism and communion (the ritual sharing of bread and wine).

**Plate 11: Below**

The Protestant Reformation began in Germany and spread to many parts of western and central Europe. This painting by an anonymous artist shows a Protestant church in the French city of Lyon in 1564. A small-scale service, probably a baptism, is in progress. The minister delivering the sermon has one hand on the Bible and an hourglass beside him to remind him not to preach too long.

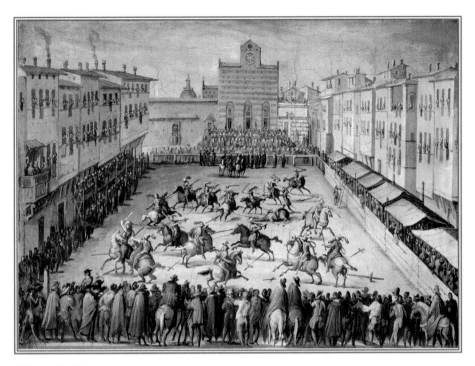

**Plate 12: Above**
Contests of military skill were popular forms of entertainment among the upper classes. Most such tournaments featured jousting, a sport in which two mounted knights would charge each other and attempt to knock the opponent from his horse with a long lance. Although Renaissance jousters used blunted weapons, they still risked injury and even death. Jan van der Straet created this wall painting of a joust in the Piazza Santa Croce in Florence in 1555.

**Plate 13: Below**
Real battles, like the mock battles of the jousting tournament, continued to involve armed knights on horseback. These mounted warriors were supported by foot soldiers armed with pikes (long poles topped by blades) and crossbows. Paolo Uccello's *Battle of San Romano*, painted around 1455, shows the prominent role of cavalry in Renaissance combat.

**Plate 14: Above**
Artist Sofonisba Anguissola of Italy created this painting of her sisters playing chess in 1555. By showing girls engaged in a game of mental skill, she challenged the traditional view of women as inferior to men. Questions about the role of women in society attracted the attention of many Renaissance intellectuals, male as well as female.

**Plate 15: Right**
Another family grouping appears in *Old Man and Boy*, painted in the 1480s by Domenico Ghirlandaio. Grandparents and other relatives often played an important role in the emotional life of young children, at least until they reached the age of seven. After that, they often began some sort of formal education outside the home.

Hans Sachs alone wrote more than 4,000 such pieces, making him the undisputed master of the master singers.

**Drama.** Drama in Germany in the 1500s fell into two categories. One type of play celebrated the festival called Carnival, a period of madcap celebration that preceded the serious season of Lent (several weeks before Easter). The other major dramatic form was modeled on Latin humanist drama, which drew on the styles of ancient Roman playwrights. At the time, Germany had no theaters and no professional actors. Amateurs performed plays in schools and universities, inns, public squares, and private homes.

Hans Sachs occupies a special place in German Renaissance drama. With little or no Latin and no firsthand knowledge of ancient or humanist drama, the shoemaker wrote about 130 plays. These pieces feature a collection of colorful stock characters—greedy merchants, simpleminded peasants, jealous spouses, lustful priests, cruel tyrants, and nosy neighbors. At a time of religious upheaval, Sachs's plays offered moral guidance and solid middle-class values, such as hard work, obedience, and thrift.

**Narrative Forms.** German narrative* forms of the Renaissance drew on sources from other parts of Europe. In the 1400s two women of noble birth, Elisabeth von Nassau-Saarbrücken and Eleonore of Austria, translated works from French into German. Early German humanists contributed translations from Italian and Latin, including the works of Giovanni BOCCACCIO, PETRARCH, and others. These translations introduced new ideas, themes, and stories into the German literary tradition.

The reading public enjoyed short humorous tales called *Schwänke*, written in prose or verse and often published in collections. One immensely popular work of this kind was *Till Eulenspiegel*. Modeled after a real person, Till is a prankster who constantly outwits the people he encounters. His name, which means "owl mirror," may come from an old saying that most people recognize their faults as little as an owl sees its ugliness in a mirror.

One of the most influential books of the time was *The History of Dr. Johann Faust*. It relates the legend of a scholar who turns from religious studies to magic and sells his soul to the devil in exchange for 24 years of riches, pleasure, and knowledge of all things. Intended as a cautionary tale against pride, it became a symbol for humankind's dangerous striving for knowledge at the expense of faith. Published anonymously in 1587, the story of Faust was immediately translated into several European languages and inspired novels, plays, and operas by many noted artists of later years. (*See also* **Art in Germany; Cities and Urban Life; Printing and Publishing; Religious Literature.**)

---

### The Legend of Dr. Faust

*The History of Dr. Johann Faust* was one of the most influential works in the German language. During the Renaissance, it inspired the play *Doctor Faustus* by the English dramatist Christopher Marlowe (a contemporary of Shakespeare). In the early 1800s, the great German writer Johann Wolfgang von Goethe turned it into a dramatic poem about a man who sold his soul for knowledge but was saved in the end. Author Thomas Mann used it as the basis for a novel in 1947, and many composers—including Charles Gounod of France and Franz Liszt of Hungary—based operas and other works on it.

---

* **narrative** storytelling

---

**Ghetto**

Italians first used the word *ghetto* in the 1500s. At the time, it referred to the enclosed areas of Italian cities where Jews were permitted to live. However, the segregation of Jews in European societies has a much

longer history than the word. Throughout the Middle Ages, Jews in Europe had chosen to live in their own communities, although they had many social contacts with their Christian neighbors. In 1179 the Catholic Church announced that Jews and Christians should not live together. However, few cities passed laws to enforce the church's policy, so the announcement had little effect.

The word *ghetto* had its origins in VENICE over 300 years later. Although Venice permitted individual Jews to reside in the city, Venetians disliked having Jews live wherever they wished. In 1516 the city's Senate required all Jews to move to a part of the city called *Ghetto Nuovo* (the New Ghetto). There they lived in a walled community that was locked from sunset to sunrise. The Venetian government later increased the size of the Jewish community by adding *Ghetto Vecchio* (the Old Ghetto), an area near *Ghetto Nuovo* that had previously been a foundry, a place for pouring and casting metals. Both places took their names from the Italian verb *gettare,* which means "to pour or to cast."

Separate, enclosed quarters for Jews became common in Italy during the Catholic Counter-Reformation*, a period when the Catholic Church became hostile toward Jews. In 1555 Pope Paul IV required Jews in the Papal States* to reside together in an enclosed quarter with only one entrance and one exit. Cities such as Florence, Siena, Padua, and Mantua followed this example, passing laws to force Jews into segregated districts. The laws used the Venetian term *ghetto* to describe these places. Soon, *ghetto* came to mean any segregated Jewish area. In later years, the meaning of the word became still broader. It referred to any area populated by many Jews, even if they chose to live there voluntarily. Today, the term *ghetto* often refers to any minority community.

Although many European Jews lived in ghettos, they maintained contacts on all levels with the outside world. The nature of the society surrounding the ghetto had a far stronger effect on Jewish life in Renaissance Europe than the fact that Jews lived apart from their neighbors. (*See also* **Anti-Semitism; Catholic Reformation and Counter-Reformation; Jews.**)

* **Counter-Reformation** actions taken by the Roman Catholic Church after 1540 to oppose Protestantism

* **Papal States** lands in central Italy under the authority of the pope

## Ghiberti, Lorenzo

### 1378–1455
### Italian artist

* **baptistery** building where baptisms are performed

* **relief** type of sculpture in which figures are raised slightly from a flat surface

Known primarily as a sculptor, Lorenzo Ghiberti achieved success in a variety of artistic fields. In the early 1400s he was the leading caster of bronze sculptures and statues in the city of Florence. He also worked as a goldsmith, architect, and writer. Many major artists of the age, including DONATELLO, assisted Ghiberti or spent time in his busy, well-organized workshop.

Trained as a goldsmith, Ghiberti entered a competition in the winter of 1400–1401 to design bronze doors for the Florence Baptistery*. The young artist received the commission to make the doors, and by 1424 he had produced 24 bronze panels illustrating saints and themes from the New Testament of the Bible. Ghiberti's style developed as he worked on the panels. The earlier ones reflect the artistic trends of Florence in the early 1400s, with graceful lines and elegantly posed figures. The later ones show more skillful use of relief* and greater appearance of depth in the backgrounds.

Between 1413 and 1429 Ghiberti created three bronze statues for the Orsanmichele, a public building that served as a center for Florence's guilds*. The first, *St. John the Baptist,* is notable for the rich draperies arranged in gracefully curving folds about the figure. The second, *St. Matthew,* reflects the styles of ancient art with its emphasis on the structure of the body. The final piece, *St. Stephen,* features a graceful pose and sweet expression that contrast with the classical* style of the second statue.

In 1425 Ghiberti returned to the Florence Baptistery to create a second bronze door. This project included ten panels on Old Testament subjects. The larger size of the panels on this door allowed Ghiberti to create greater illusions of depth and space and wider range of detail in the backgrounds. Other major works of Ghiberti's later career include bronze reliefs for the Baptistery in the nearby city of SIENA and a shrine to St. Zenobius for the cathedral of Florence. The artist also played a role in the planning of the cathedral, advising on the construction of the dome and designing the building's stained-glass windows.

Around 1447 Ghiberti began writing his *Commentaries,* a three-part work on art. The first part discusses ancient art, the second covers the art of his day (including his own works), and the third comments on the sciences a sculptor must master. However, Ghiberti's greatest legacy was his graceful sculpture, which influenced artists such as Benvenuto CELLINI. (*See also* **Art in Italy.**)

* **guild**  association of craft and trade owners and workers that set standards for and represented the interests of its members

* **classical**  in the tradition of ancient Greece and Rome

## Gilbert, William

**1544–1603**
**English physician and scientist**

The English physician William Gilbert earned fame for his studies in electricity and magnetism. His pioneering experiments in these fields marked the dawn of a new era in science.

Born in Colchester, England, Gilbert received his medical degree in 1569 and began practicing medicine in London. He served as a physician to many British nobles, including the monarchs ELIZABETH I and JAMES I. During this time, Gilbert also studied magnetism and electricity. In 1600 he published his most important work, *On the Lodestone; Magnetic Bodies; and the Great Magnet, the Earth.* A six-part review of magnetism, the work deals with the various forces produced by magnets and by the Earth's natural magnetism. In the final section, Gilbert argued that the rotation of the Earth itself depends on magnetic forces. He also distinguished between magnetism and another type of energy, which he called *electrica*—thereby introducing the word *electric* into the English language.

Gilbert's work had two major effects. First, his ideas influenced Johannes KEPLER, the German astronomer who wrote about the planets and their motion. Kepler was one of the first to discuss the force of the Sun on Earth. Second, Gilbert's writings inspired others to experiment with magnetism and electricity—especially Jesuit* scientists who made important advances in the field of magnetism throughout the 1600s. (*See also* **Astronomy; Medicine; Science.**)

* **Jesuit**  refers to a Roman Catholic religious order founded by St. Ignatius Loyola and approved in 1540

## Giocondo, Fra

ca. 1433–1515
Italian architect, engineer,
and humanist scholar

* **classical**   in the tradition of ancient
Greece and Rome

* **woodcut**   print made from a block of
wood with an image carved into it

* **humanist**   Renaissance expert in the
humanities (the languages, literature,
history, and speech and writing
techniques of ancient Greece and
Rome)

* **patron**   supporter or financial
sponsor of an artist or writer

* **Holy Roman Emperor**   ruler of the
Holy Roman Empire, a political body in
central Europe composed of several
states that existed until 1806

Fra Giocondo was an accomplished architect and engineer, renowned for his skill in designing complex structures and waterworks. He also had a great interest in classical* culture and created an illustrated edition of *On Architecture* (1511), by the ancient Roman architect Vitruvius. To accompany the text, Giocondo produced 136 woodcuts* illustrating fine points of ancient design and relating them to Renaissance building techniques. The work had a great influence on many architects of the time.

Born in Verona, Italy, Fra Giocondo joined a religious order and gained a reputation for his knowledge of structural design and the culture of ancient Greece and Rome. By 1489 he was working in the kingdom of NAPLES, where he met many humanists*, including the poet Jacopo SANNAZARO. In Naples, Fra Giocondo designed buildings, advised on military projects, and examined ancient Roman ruins for his patrons*. In about 1495, he went to the court of Charles VIII of France and became royal architect in charge of major buildings, bridges, and waterworks. While in Paris, Giocondo also acted as secretary to one of the diplomats who represented the Holy Roman Emperor* MAXIMILIAN I.

In 1506 Fra Giocondo accepted an appointment as architect to the government of Venice. He provided Venetians with technical expertise on projects concerning bridges, canals, and rivers, as well as the reclamation of land in the lagoon surrounding the city. Giocondo also worked as a military engineer, overseeing the construction of fortifications for territory controlled by Venice, both inland and on islands in the Mediterranean Sea.

In 1513 Pope LEO X appointed Fra Giocondo and Donato BRAMANTE as architects of the new church of St. Peter in Rome. When Bramante died the following year, the pope chose the artist RAPHAEL to replace him. Raphael and Fra Giocondo may have worked together on the initial designs for the church, but Fra Giocondo died before the project was completed. While Fra Giocondo's accomplishments as an architect and engineer were significant, his illustrated edition of Vitruvius's work is considered his greatest achievement. (*See also* **Architecture; Books and Manuscripts; Fortifications.**)

## Giorgione da Castelfranco

ca. 1477–1510
Italian painter

The Venetian painter known as Giorgione is one of the most mysterious figures in Renaissance art. The writer Baldassare CASTIGLIONE called him one of the greatest painters of the age, while artist and author Giorgio Vasari described Giorgione as the inventor of the "modern style" of Venetian painting. However, art historians have little information about Giorgione's career. They disagree over which pieces he painted because no works bearing his signature exist. In fact, they do not even know his full name.

Giorgione was born in the city of Castelfranco and, according to Vasari, studied under the artist Giovanni BELLINI. Most scholars believe that Giorgione began painting around 1500, but the absence of signed pieces makes tracing his early works difficult. He is known to have cre-

* **fresco**   mural painted on a plaster wall

* **patron**   supporter or financial sponsor of an artist or writer

* **classical**   in the tradition of ancient Greece and Rome

* **pastoral**   relating to the countryside; often used to draw a contrast between the innocence and serenity of rural life and the corruption and extravagance of court life

ated an altarpiece for the cathedral of Castelfranco. Records also show that he painted canvases and frescoes* for patrons* in Venice in 1507 and 1508.

Between 1521 and 1543 a Venetian nobleman named Marcantonio Michiel compiled a list of paintings that he claimed were by Giorgione. Scholars now accept three of these as the artist's works: *Bow with an Arrow, Three Philosophers in a Landscape,* and *The Tempest.* The last two feature extraordinarily beautiful landscapes. Michiel claimed that other artists, including the Venetian master TITIAN, finished some of these paintings. Most scholars agree on several other pieces as the work of Giorgione.

Giorgione's paintings reflect the classical* tastes of Renaissance Italy. They often feature sensual and pastoral* images. His exploration of landscape and mood led some critics to call his works "painted poems." In *The Tempest,* for example, the artist uses eerie lighting to add drama to the stormy scene.

Giorgione experimented with technique as well as subject matter. According to Vasari, Giorgione did not draw his subjects on the canvas before painting but sketched the outlines with his brush. His early paintings show smooth, even layers of color, typical of Bellini's technique. However, Giorgione soon moved away from this style toward a heavier, irregular layering of paint that emphasized the texture of the canvas and of the artist's brush strokes. A generation of artists adopted this technique, called impasto, which became a standard feature of Venetian painting in the 1500s. (*See also* **Art; Art in Italy.**)

**Giotto di Bondone**

**1267/75–1337**
**Italian painter and architect**

* **naturalistic**   realistic, showing the world as it is without idealization

* **patron**   supporter or financial sponsor of an artist or writer

Giotto di Bondone played a pivotal role in the history of Renaissance art. In his works, he attempted to show figures, space, color, and light in a realistic way. Giotto's naturalistic* approach set a new standard for painting that influenced many other artists and paved the way for the emergence of later Renaissance styles.

**Life and Career.**   Little is known for certain about Giotto's early life. According to tradition, he was born to a peasant family in a small village in Tuscany, near FLORENCE. Several writers say that, when Giotto was young, he met the painter Cimabue in the countryside. Cimabue noticed that the boy was drawing a picture of a sheep on a flat stone. Struck by the boy's artistic skills, Cimabue got permission from Giotto's father to take him on as a student. Eventually, Giotto surpassed his teacher as a painter.

Giotto worked in many of the major artistic centers of Italy, including Florence, Padua, and Naples. He completed projects for patrons* such as the king of Naples, wealthy business leaders, and the Dominican and Franciscan religious orders. In 1334 he was appointed to oversee the construction of the cathedral of Florence and to design its new tower. This important commission, late in his life, reflects the prestige Giotto had acquired as both an artist and an architect.

GIOTTO DI BONDONE

The fresco *Christ Entering Jerusalem,* by Italian painter Giotto di Bondone, displays the artist's naturalistic approach to painting. His style had a great influence on artists of the Renaissance.

* **fresco**   mural painted on a plaster wall

* **mosaic**   picture made up of many small colored stones or tiles

**Works.** Giotto worked in a variety of artistic media, including fresco*, tempera (egg-based paint), gold leaf, and mosaic*, and produced pieces ranging from panel paintings to large murals. Many of his murals, created for churches and chapels, depict scenes from the lives of major religious figures.

Giotto's work reveals his tremendous powers of observation and attention to detail. His fresco *St. Francis Preaching to the Birds* (Church of San Francesco, Assisi) includes minute elements of the foliage and the different types of birds. The painter used subtle contrasts in color and tone to create an impression of depth. In addition, the backgrounds for his scenes, such as rural settings or splendid palace interiors, often reflect the nature of the subject. Thus, *St. Francis Preaching to the Birds* is set in a country landscape that emphasizes the saint's life as a wandering spiritual leader.

In *St. Francis of Assisi Preaching before Pope Honorius III* (Church of San Francesco, Assisi), Giotto placed the figures in an elegant room. The pope, the supreme religious authority, dominates the center of the picture. However, he appears to be listening attentively to Francis's sermon, revealing his respect for the saint's faith and teaching.

Giotto's work also shows a realistic treatment of human emotions not found in earlier works of art. The people in his paintings display great emotion, from peaceful expressions to tension, turmoil, and suffering.

In *Kiss of Judas* (Scrovegni Chapel, Padua), Judas glares at Jesus, who remains calm while a group of angry soldiers bears down on them.

**Artistic Achievements.** Giotto gained fame in his own time as an accomplished artist. In the 1300s the poets Dante Alighieri and PETRARCH mentioned Giotto in their works. Giovanni BOCCACCIO, writing in the 1350s, said that Giotto had reintroduced a naturalistic style of art that had been lost since the time of ancient Greece and Rome. In the 1400s the sculptor Lorenzo GHIBERTI wrote about Giotto's importance in launching a new movement in Italian painting.

A century later, the art historian Giorgio Vasari praised Giotto in his *Lives of the Artists* (1550). Vasari, too, saw Giotto as having revived the high artistic traditions of the ancient world. In Vasari's view, Giotto was responsible for reestablishing nature as the highest model for artists to imitate. The historian traced the influence of this element of Giotto's work on the styles of painters of the 1500s, such as LEONARDO DA VINCI, RAPHAEL, and MICHELANGELO BUONARROTI. (*See also* **Architecture; Art; Art in Italy.**)

## Goes, Hugo van der

### ca. 1440–1482
### Netherlandish painter

* **guild** association of craft and trade owners and workers that set standards for and represented the interests of its members

* **Flemish** relating to Flanders, a region along the coasts of present-day Belgium, France, and the Netherlands

The religious paintings of Hugo van der Goes were very popular in his day and widely copied by other artists. In 1467 van der Goes became a master in the painter's guild* of the Flemish* city of Ghent. The following year he was among a group of artists asked to provide decorations for the marriage ceremony of Charles the Bold, the duke of BURGUNDY. In 1475 van der Goes joined a monastery, where he continued to paint. He suffered from depression and toward the end of his life had a mental breakdown.

Because van der Goes did not sign or date the few paintings of his that survived, scholars have used written records to connect him to certain works. For example, in the mid-1500s the writers Giorgio Vasari and Lodovico Guicciardini referred to a painting by "Hugo of Antwerp" that later scholars identified as van der Goes's 1475 work *Adoration of the Shepherds*. This huge triptych (three-panel painting) presents a richly colored and detailed scene of the Virgin, Joseph, angels, and shepherds around the Christ child. The highly original composition contains expressive figures, changes in scale, and a remarkable feeling of spatial depth. (*See also* **Art; Art in the Netherlands.**)

## Góngora y Argote, Luis de

### 1561–1627
### Spanish poet

* **classical** in the tradition of ancient Greece and Rome

* **genre** literary form

Luis de Góngora y Argote, one of Spain's greatest poets, was born in Córdoba, in southern Spain, to a noble but poor family. Although he studied classical* culture at the University of Salamanca, he never graduated. To support himself, Góngora joined the clergy. His position took him to Madrid, where he suffered financially. He returned to Córdoba in 1626 and died there in poverty in 1627.

Góngora saw poetry as an intellectual activity. Most of his works are complex, challenging the strict definitions of literary genres* and styles.

* **sonnet** poem of 14 lines with a fixed pattern of meter and rhyme

He wrote in a variety of forms. His sonnets* blend typical Renaissance ideas and themes with a distinctly personal style. He renewed the ballad, an oral poetic form, with sophisticated wordplay and wit. Other works, such as his *Solitudes,* do not fit neatly into any genre.

Like other Renaissance writers, Góngora drew inspiration from classical literature. In his last major poem, the ballad *The Fable of Pyramus and Thisbe* (1618), he parodies the writings of the ancient Roman poet Ovid. Góngora considered this to be his finest work.

Critics have come to see Góngora's style as completely unique. The name they gave it, *gongorismo,* came to mean poetry that is refined and intelligent. However, it also suggested—in an unflattering way—that the work defied conventional standards. Today, the term *gongoristic* refers to poetry that is knotty and difficult to understand. (*See also* **Spanish Language and Literature.**)

## Gonzaga, House of

* **Holy Roman Emperor** ruler of the Holy Roman Empire, a political body in central Europe composed of several states that existed until 1806

* **prince** Renaissance term for the ruler of an independent state

* **Papal States** lands in central Italy under the authority of the pope

The Gonzaga family ruled the Italian city-state of MANTUA throughout the Renaissance. Its first leader, Luigi I, seized power in the city in 1328. The Gonzaga were *signori* (lords) of Mantua until 1433, when the Holy Roman Emperor* gave them the title of marquis. By the 1470s, Gonzaga rulers had become powerful princes*, who defended their state from larger neighbors such as Venice and Milan. The family avoided potential conflicts by dividing its lands among numerous heirs. This practice helped maintain peace and gave rise to many small Gonzaga lordships.

The Gonzaga achieved their greatest success in the late 1400s and early 1500s under Francesco II and his wife, Isabella d'ESTE. Besides ruling Mantua, Francesco hired out as a military commander to Venice and the Papal States*. During the 1500s, when the HABSBURG DYNASTY and France competed for control of Italy, the Gonzaga sided with the Habsburgs. In return, Habsburg emperor CHARLES V conferred the title of Duke of Mantua on the leader of the family.

The last member of the original Gonzaga line died in 1627, and a war broke out over control of Mantua. The Habsburg emperor backed one heir, while the BOURBON family of France supported another. The Bourbons won the contest in 1631, placing a French relative of the Gonzaga in the duke's palace in Mantua. Gonzaga rule came to an end in 1707 with the exile of the last Gonzaga duke. Mantua then fell under the control of the Habsburgs.

* **humanism** Renaissance cultural movement promoting the study of the humanities (the languages, literature, and history of ancient Greece and Rome) as a guide to living

The Gonzaga made great contributions to Renaissance culture. Under their rule, Mantua became a center of humanism* and art. The family supported many famous artists, including Andrea MANTEGNA, Leon Battista ALBERTI, and Peter Paul RUBENS. The Gonzaga also played a prominent role in the Roman Catholic Church. Many members of the family held high church offices, and at least one was a noted reformer within the church. The Gonzaga family included several remarkable women, such as Isabella d'Este, a great supporter of the arts, and Cecilia Gonzaga, a female humanist. (*See also* **Catholic Reformation and**

Counter-Reformation; City-States; Italy; Princes and Princedoms; Thirty Years' War; Wars of Italy; Women.)

**Government, Forms of**

The forms of government adopted by various Renaissance states reflected their particular historical backgrounds and political dynamics. The most common form of government was MONARCHY—rule by a single powerful leader such as a king or queen. Most monarchs did not hold absolute power. Usually they worked together with representative assemblies that exercised some control over lawmaking and taxation.

Political systems such as oligarchy, despotism, and absolutism also appeared frequently in Renaissance states. Some systems were based on ancient political theories, while others emerged as a result of new developments. Over time, various European states switched from one form of government to another as political and social conditions changed.

## OLIGARCHY

The most complex form of government in the Renaissance was oligarchy—rule by a restricted number of men. Those in power, usually the leading merchants of the city, claimed to represent the interests of the people. Cities with oligarchies often called themselves republics* and looked to the cities of ancient Greece and Rome as models. These republics had laws that guaranteed some rights to all citizens and limited the power of members of the government.

Some cities were ruled by broad oligarchies, with many men sharing power; others were ruled by narrow oligarchies in which fewer men governed. In Italy, VENICE, FLORENCE, SIENA, Lucca, and GENOA had republican governments dominated by leading merchant families. But the number of men who held power varied considerably. In Florence and Siena, for example, 2,000 to 3,000 men (out of a total population of 20,000 to 50,000 men, women, and children) possessed the right to vote and to hold office. These republics had strict laws regarding the length of political terms, and this limited the power of individuals. In addition, some officials were chosen by lot, not by election. By contrast, Venice, the largest Italian republic, had a more narrow oligarchy. Only about 2,000 to 3,000 men (in a total population of about 175,000 men, women, and children) could vote and hold office. However, the rest of the citizens never tried to overthrow the government because it ruled Venice well.

Many northern European cities also had narrow oligarchies. Cities such as AUGSBURG, Frankfurt, Hamburg, Lübeck, and NÜRNBERG were ruled by oligarchies of 50 to 100 men. But even these oligarchies were not closed. Wealthy newcomers could become part of the oligarchy and participate in ruling the city. Some cities that were linked to larger states such as England or the Venetian republic also had oligarchies with considerable power. The Venetian government permitted city oligarchies to rule and decide local matters, as long as taxes were collected and the town did not rebel against Venice.

* **republic** form of Renaissance government dominated by leading merchants with limited participation by others

## Resistance to Tyranny

Political thinkers of the Renaissance debated how to get rid of tyrants. Some believed that citizens could resist tyrants who seized property, overturned the rule of law, or threatened religion. In the mid-1550s, English writer John Ponet argued that God grants authority to rulers through the consent of the people. If a ruler acts unjustly, the people may revoke that authority. Other writers stressed the need for formal procedures to unseat a tyrant. The most radical thinkers declared that an unjust ruler's violation of duties gave citizens the right to take any action, including killing the ruler, to defend the public good.

---

* **Holy Roman Emperor** ruler of the Holy Roman Empire, a political body in central Europe composed of several states that existed until 1806

* **tyranny** form of government in which an absolute ruler uses power unjustly or cruelly

City oligarchies were remarkably durable. Although some German cities turned from Catholicism to Lutheranism in the 1500s, the same individuals and families often continued to rule. During the Renaissance, oligarchies became smaller and more restrictive. By the late 1500s, many of them were hereditary, with sons and nephews of former council members following their fathers and uncles in office.

## DESPOTISM

The meaning of the term *despotism* has changed over time. Originally, the word referred to the relationship between a master and a slave. The ancient Greek philosopher ARISTOTLE used *despotism* to describe unlawful power exercised to advance the interests of the few against the will of the many. Later, some writers referred to lords who ruled Renaissance cities as *despots.*

In the late 1200s, rivalries between political FACTIONS threatened to tear apart communities in northern and central Italy. To restore order, many towns and cities gave power to the head of a prominent local family. The town councils chose these lords as rulers but kept certain privileges, such as the right to approve or reject the lord's choice of a successor. Over time, the lords acquired political, financial, and military power and often received a title from the pope or the Holy Roman Emperor*. This helped strengthen the lord's power. It also reduced or eliminated the people's control over succession, in effect creating a hereditary dynasty.

Scholars dispute whether the term *despotism* accurately describes the rule of Renaissance lords. Some have seen despotism as a form of government halfway between monarchy and tyranny*. Others have compared the rule of a despot to the authority of the head of a household over his slaves or the rights of a conqueror over the conquered.

Some scholars have regarded despotism as unlawful rule that destroys the legitimate organs of government. However, this view does not reflect the political reality of the Renaissance. Lords who rose to power during this period did not aim to eliminate traditional city government. Instead, they usually cooperated with existing organizations, and governments continued to function and often grew and prospered under their rule.

## ABSOLUTISM

*Absolutism* has two different, but related, meanings. It can signify a form of government in which the central authority has almost unlimited control over the citizens. It can also refer to the idea that legitimate heads of state answer to no one but God and may govern without the consent of the people.

**Concept and Theory.** During the 1500s various political theorists, such as French writer Jean BODIN, favored absolute monarchy. Bodin argued that the stability of the state depended on rule by a single indi-

French king Henry IV, shown here, expanded the authority of the monarchy in the late 1500s. Under his rule, the power of the king increased while that of representative bodies declined. He set France on a course toward absolute monarchy that would reach its peak in the late 1600s under Louis XIV.

vidual. He and other supporters of this form of government believed that rulers should respect the established rights of groups and individuals. But kings or queens should also have the powers needed to govern effectively, including the ability to act without restrictions in times of emergency. In Bodin's view, subjects should not actively resist the king, but they may disobey royal orders that violate divine law. In addition, the king should generally obtain the people's consent to raise taxes.

By the early 1600s, the theory of "the divine right of kings" emerged to support the claim that rulers received their power from God, not from the people. Some writers viewed the state as a family and compared the king's authority to that of a father over his wife and children. Based on

these views, many supporters of absolutism dropped the requirement that monarchs obtain the people's consent before raising taxes.

**Practice of Absolutism.** The period from the late 1500s to the mid-1700s is often seen as an age of absolutism, during which states increased their power at the expense of representative assemblies, local officials, and the church. As state power grew, central bureaucracies expanded, governments created large standing armies, and monarchs began to exercise greater authority over legislation and state finances.

France was one of the first countries to move toward an absolutist form of government. The turmoil caused by the religious wars between Catholics and Protestants in the late 1500s led to a demand for a stronger central government. France's king HENRY IV expanded the authority of the monarchy in the late 1500s and early 1600s. Royal power continued to grow under Henry's successors and peaked during the reign of Louis XIV in the late 1600s. Under Louis, the high court lost the right to challenge royal orders, and the clergy confirmed the king's right to control the French church.

Similar developments occurred during the 1600s in Prussia and Russia. In all these places the monarch's ability to direct public affairs had practical limits. Nevertheless, the power of kings in many countries was much stronger at the end of the 1600s than it had been a century earlier. (*See also* **City-States; Constitutionalism; Nation-state; Political Thought; Princes and Princedoms; Representative Institutions, Wars of Religion.**)

---

| **Grand Tour** |
| --- |

**See** *Travel and Tourism.*

---

During the Renaissance, western Europe became home to many Greek émigrés (a term that refers to people fleeing a country, usually for political reasons). These immigrants had a significant influence on the culture of the Renaissance. The Greek scholars who came to Italy not only translated ancient works into Latin but also taught Italians to read and translate the originals.

The most important teacher of Greek in the Renaissance was Manuel Chrysoloras, who came from Greece to teach in Florence in 1397. Chrysoloras taught his students a new theory of translation that focused on capturing the sense of a text and not simply its words. One of his students, Leonardo BRUNI, became the first major translator of Greek texts in the Renaissance. Bruni led other humanists* to begin translating the entire body of ancient Greek literature into Latin, a campaign that lasted for 200 years.

Another important teacher was George of Trebizond, an émigré who came to Italy as a Greek scribe*. Like many Greek émigrés in Italy, Trebizond was unable to support himself with only his knowledge of Greek. He quickly learned Latin and became a successful Latin teacher.

* **humanist** Renaissance expert in the humanities (the languages, literature, history, and speech and writing techniques of ancient Greece and Rome)

* **scribe** person who copies manuscripts

He also translated a number of Greek scientific and philosophical works into Latin.

The Council of Ferrara-Florence, which brought together leaders of the Roman Catholic and Orthodox Churches, brought many Greeks to Italy in 1438 and 1439. One of the most important participants was a bishop named Bessarion, who was one of the most learned men in the Greek Orthodox Church. In 1440 Bessarion settled in Italy permanently, and he made many contributions to Italian scholarship. He wrote on theology* and other topics, and he translated Greek works into Latin. His most important works included a defense of PLATO, an ancient Greek philosopher, and a translation of *Metaphysics,* a work by ARISTOTLE (another ancient thinker).

When the city of CONSTANTINOPLE fell to the Ottoman Turks* in 1453, many upper-class Greeks, including scholars, fled to western Europe. Bessarion helped many of the émigrés who came to Italy, but eventually they had to support themselves. Translating became an important source of income for some. Pope NICHOLAS V wanted Greek texts of every kind translated into Latin, and the new arrivals were a valuable asset to this project because they could tackle difficult texts on topics such as science and philosophy.

Translating, however, was not steady work. While some émigrés found careers in teaching, publishing, and the church, others were less fortunate. Their situation worsened after Bessarion's death in 1472. John Argyropoulos, a major figure in the intellectual life of the Renaissance, had to sell his library to survive in Italy. Other prominent émigrés died in exile, became wandering teachers, returned to Greece, or disappeared.

Western Europe received one of Bessarion's greatest contributions after his death. After the fall of Constantinople, Bessarion had devoted himself to preserving the Greek culture. Over the years, he had assembled the greatest collection of Greek books anywhere in western Europe. After his death, the city of Venice inherited his personal library and constructed a new building to house it. Bessarion's books became part of the Biblioteca Marciana, one of the great public libraries of the Renaissance. (*See also* **Councils; Libraries; Ottoman Empire.**)

* **theology**   study of the nature of God and of religion

* **Ottoman Turks**   Turkish followers of Islam who founded the Ottoman Empire in the 1300s; the empire eventually included large areas of eastern Europe, the Middle East, and northern Africa

### Grey, Jane

**1537–1554**
**Queen of England**

* **humanist**   referring to a Renaissance cultural movement promoting the study of the humanities (the languages, literature, and history of ancient Greece and Rome) as a guide to living

A reluctant queen, Jane Grey ruled England for nine days when she was 15 years of age. As a Protestant with some claim to the throne, she had been pushed forward as the successor to EDWARD VI. The king's Protestant advisers feared that if the crown passed to his sister Mary, a devout Catholic and the rightful heir, England would become Catholic again.

Jane did not come to the throne completely unprepared. She was related to HENRY VIII and had spent two years in the household of Katherine Parr, Henry's widow. When she returned home in 1549, she received a humanist* education, one of the few women of her generation to do so. Jane knew several languages and impressed people with her skills.

In 1553 John Dudley, the Duke of Northumberland and the chief adviser to Edward VI, arranged a marriage between Jane and his son Guildford. The duke also persuaded the king to name Jane rather than Mary as his successor. Jane became queen in July 1553, when Edward died. But Mary soon unseated Jane, with wide support from the people, and took the throne as MARY I. She had Jane and her husband imprisoned in the Tower of London and executed as traitors. (*See also* **England.**)

### Grotius, Hugo

#### 1583–1645
#### Dutch humanist

* **humanist**   Renaissance expert in the humanities (the languages, literature, history, and speech and writing techniques of ancient Greece and Rome)

* **classical**   in the tradition of ancient Greece and Rome

* **Calvinist**   member of a Protestant church founded by John Calvin

* **theology**   study of the nature of God and of religion

Dutch humanist* Hugo Grotius was skilled in matters of law, literature, history, and religion. An accomplished writer, he authored more than 120 works in Latin and Dutch and wrote around 7,800 letters. Though he held several official posts, his most enduring accomplishment was his work on law and religion.

Grotius's father, a humanist and well-connected official, greatly affected his son's education. At age 11 Grotius enrolled at the University of Leiden in southern Holland. He later traveled to France and earned a degree in law, but he returned to Holland to open a practice. By this time he was gaining a reputation as a Greek and Latin poet and editor of classical* texts. He gained employment based on his exceptional writing skills, first chronicling Holland's history, and later writing texts for the Dutch East India Company, which carried out Dutch trade.

In the early 1600s Grotius became a leader on one side of a bitter dispute among Dutch Calvinists* over theology* and the power of the state in church matters. When the other side won, Grotius was sentenced to life in prison, where he prepared a number of later books. After three years there, he made a famous escape by hiding in a book chest—a plan devised by his wife.

Soon after his escape, Grotius moved to Paris, where he received a regular yearly income from the king, Louis XIII. There he wrote his two most famous books. The first, *The Law of War and Peace* (1625), was an in-depth study of the law of conflicts. It quickly gained recognition, becoming a foundation of international law. His other work, *The Truth of Christian Religion* (1627), was a scholarly defense of Christianity. It remained popular into the 1900s, appearing in more than 150 Latin editions as well as translations in 12 languages. (*See also* **Law.**)

### Grünewald, Matthias

#### ca. 1475/80–1528
#### German painter

* **medieval**   referring to the Middle Ages, a period that began around A.D. 400 and ended around 1400 in Italy and 1500 in the rest of Europe

German painter Matthias Grünewald is best known for his highly emotional religious paintings. His style reflects the continuing influence of medieval* ideas and images on German art in the early 1500s.

Grünewald was probably born in Würzburg, Germany. Scholars know almost nothing about his training and early career. One of his earliest surviving works is a painting, the *Mocking of Christ,* which dates from around 1505. Records show that Grünewald was working as an engineer in 1510 and as a painter, stonecutter, and architect in 1511. The follow-

ing year he created a series of paintings with gruesome images of the dead Christ for a monastery in the region of Alsace. The expressive style of the paintings recalls religious images of the German Gothic* period.

From about 1516 to 1526, Grünewald worked for the archbishop of Mainz, Albrecht von Brandenburg. Scholars suggest that Albrecht dismissed Grünewald in 1526, either because the artist had embraced the Protestant ideas of Martin LUTHER or because he took part in the PEASANTS' WAR, a revolt that occurred in 1525. Grünewald moved to Frankfurt and later to the city of Halle, where he worked as an engineer until his death.

The German humanist* Philipp MELANCHTHON considered Grünewald to be nearly as great an artist as Albrecht DÜRER. Through his creativity, powerful symbolism, and skill with color and light, he conveyed the powerful emotions and spirituality of his religious subjects. Unlike Dürer, he drew little inspiration from the ancient world or the Italian Renaissance. Instead, he continued to work with the images, ideas, and styles of the Middle Ages. (*See also* **Art in Germany; Protestant Reformation.**)

* **Gothic** artistic style marked by bright colors, elongated proportions, and intricate detail

* **humanist** Renaissance expert in the humanities (the languages, literature, history, and speech and writing techniques of ancient Greece and Rome)

### 1374–1460
### Italian educator

* **humanist** referring to a Renaissance cultural movement promoting the study of the humanities (the languages, literature, and history of ancient Greece and Rome) as a guide to living

* **classical** in the tradition of ancient Greece and Rome

The Italian scholar Guarino Guarini had a great impact on the field of education. His schools used the language, history, and culture of the ancient world as the foundation for knowledge. These goals reflected his own education and upbringing.

Born in Verona, Italy, Guarini studied Latin as a boy. In the 1390s he traveled to Padua and Venice to pursue his studies. In Venice he came into contact with the Greek scholar Manuel Chrysolaras, whose lectures on the Greek language were sparking interest in the developing humanist* movement. Guarini followed Chrysolaras back to his home city of Constantinople (modern-day Istanbul) and spent five years there learning Greek. He returned to Italy around 1408. After several years of failed efforts in scholarly fields, Guarini opened a successful humanist boarding school in Verona. In 1429 he moved to Ferrara, where he served as a tutor at the court of the ruling ESTE family. He founded a school in Ferrara that soon became one of the most famous in Europe.

Guarini's challenging schools helped to invent a new style of education. He instructed boys in classical* studies with the goal of turning them into free—or "liberal"—thinkers and well-developed human beings. Their education began with the rules of Latin grammar. They learned advanced grammar from Guarini's own text, *The Rules of Grammar,* which was the first Latin grammar book of the Renaissance. In addition to speaking and reading classical Latin, students learned about the history, major figures, and mythology of the ancient world. They also developed a basic familiarity with Greek. Guarini's teaching methods came to dominate European education for centuries. The ideal he established of "liberal education" persists to this day.

Guarini also made a name for himself as a scholar and translator. He translated the works of several major Greek authors, including the historian Plutarch, into Latin. His work made these texts available to the

large number of early humanists who did not know Greek. Guarini also played a role in the rediscovery of many ancient Latin authors. (*See also* **Classical Scholarship; Education; Humanism.**)

---

## Guicciardini, Francesco

### 1483–1540
### Italian statesman
### and historian

* **humanist**   referring to a Renaissance cultural movement promoting the study of the humanities (the languages, literature, and history of ancient Greece and Rome) as a guide to living

* **Holy Roman Emperor**   ruler of the Holy Roman Empire, a political body in central Europe composed of several states that existed until 1806

* **sack**   to loot a captured city

* **republic**   form of Renaissance government dominated by leading merchants with limited participation by others

---

Francesco Guicciardini, a member of one of the leading families of Florence, gained distinction during the Renaissance both for his active role in the events of the day and for his written accounts of these events. Guicciardini's works, particularly the *History of Italy,* have earned him the reputation as the greatest historian of the Renaissance.

**Political Career.**   Guicciardini was educated in the humanist* tradition and entered public life at an early age. He served as an ambassador to Spain from 1511 until 1514. On his return to Florence, Guicciardini found favor with the powerful Medici family then in control in the city. He acted as governor of the cities of Modena and Reggio, and his success led to appointment as president of the turbulent province of Romagna.

In 1526 Guicciardini advised Pope Clement VII in negotiating an alliance known as the League of Cognac against Charles V, the Holy Roman Emperor*. He served as lieutenant general in the pope's army, fighting to expel the emperor's forces from Italy. The Italians suffered defeat, and though Guicciardini managed to save Florence from attack, the imperial forces turned south and sacked* Rome in 1527.

Meanwhile, in Florence, the republic* was restored. The new leaders banished Guicciardini for working for the Medici and took his possessions. When the Medici returned in 1530, Guicciardini took part in punishing the republican leaders who had expelled him. He served as an adviser to the Medici until dismissed in 1537. Guicciardini devoted the rest of his life to writing his masterpiece, the *History of Italy.*

**Writings.**   Among Guicciardini's historical and political works prior to the *History of Italy* were an unfinished history of Florence and a commentary on the city's government. In these works he argues that the best form of government is a republic led by a select group of wise citizens. He mistrusted rule by the people, seeing their proper role in government as ensuring that rulers did not become tyrants.

Guicciardini's *History of Italy* began as an attempt to explain his role in the war of the League of Cognac in 1526. However, he decided that readers needed more background to understand the events of that time. He researched Italian history back to 1494, relying on memoirs, chronicles, and histories of the day as sources. His use of diplomatic records and other government documents marked a important turning point in the development of historical research. Another innovative feature of the *History of Italy* was its focus on personal motives behind the actions of historical figures. Because the work criticized many political leaders, it was not published until 1561. However, it quickly became recognized as the best account of the Italian Wars (1494–1559). (*See also* **History, Writing of.**)

During the Renaissance, trade organizations called guilds played a major role in city life, particularly in Italy. Their chief function was regulating business practices. Guilds set standards for manufacturing and protected their members' interests, working to keep people who did not belong to guilds from working in any craft. Although their main role was economic, guilds also had a great influence on social, political, and religious life. They promoted community spirit and helped to establish ties among members of the same trade. In an era known for promoting the idea of the individual, guilds provided a way for people to find their identity within a group.

The earliest European guilds arose in the 1200s. Skilled crafts workers, known as ARTISANS, controlled most guilds, but merchants ran some of them. In some cities, such as Venice, a single guild represented the interests of all people involved in a particular field—from the wealthiest merchants to the poorest crafts workers. Each guild controlled its members' activities in several ways. It set standards of quality for their products and dictated the hours they could work and the materials they could use. It also oversaw the training of new members.

To join a guild, a young man (most guilds were closed to women) had to go through a period of apprenticeship*, usually lasting several years. During this period, he worked for an older, experienced guild member, observing and learning his trade. When his term of service was up, he gained the right to work in the craft. If he wished to become a master—a full-fledged member of the profession—he had to submit a "masterpiece" to be judged by the guild. In the late 1500s many guilds complained about sons of master craftsmen who were moving up in the trade without creating their masterpieces first.

Guilds contributed to society in a variety of ways. Through the apprenticeship system, they kept young, unattached males off the streets and provided them with food and lodging. Guilds also provided an early form of insurance for their members, aiding them in case of illness or accidents. If a member died, the guild provided a funeral for him, which all other members were required to attend. For many people who did not come from wealthy families, the guild may have acted as a kind of substitute family. Town authorities generally supported the guilds because they saw them as a useful guard against social unrest.

Guild members often engaged in social activities as a group. They met on a yearly basis to celebrate the festival of their patron saint (a saint who was believed to protect and aid its members). They also marched together in city parades, helping to promote a feeling of unity within the group. In many cities, guilds came to dominate political life. In Florence and London, for example, only guild members were eligible to hold public office. Guild membership took on such importance that wool workers in Florence staged a revolt in 1378, demanding the right to form their own guilds.

Another guild function was patronage* of the arts. Guilds played a major role in the artistic life of Florence, where a public building called Orsanmichele served as their headquarters. Each guild in Florence contributed a statue of its patron saint to decorate the building. Many guilds

* **apprenticeship** system under which a person is bound by legal agreement to work for another for a specified period of time in return for instruction in a trade or craft

* **patronage** support or financial sponsorship

hired master artists such as DONATELLO and Lorenzo GHIBERTI to create these figures as a way of increasing their glory and status within the city. (*See also* **Cities and Urban Life; Florence.**)

## Guise-Lorraine Family

* **duchy**   territory ruled by a duke or duchess

* **medieval**   referring to the Middle Ages, a period that began around A.D. 400 and ended around 1400 in Italy and 1500 in the rest of Europe

One of the most powerful families in Renaissance France, the house of Guise-Lorraine rose to prominence in the 1500s through military ability, political skill, and unswerving loyalty to the Catholic Church. The family's service to the French crown was rewarded with lands, titles, public offices, and positions in the church.

The house of Guise-Lorraine had its origins in the duchy* of Lorraine, known for independent rulers who traced their lineage from Charlemagne, the great medieval* ruler. When René II of Lorraine died in 1508, he left the duchy to his son Antoine and his territories in France, including Guise, to Antoine's younger brother. That brother, Claude, grew up at the French court and developed a close relationship with the future king of France, FRANCIS I. In 1527 Francis rewarded Claude for his loyalty and military service by naming him the first duke of Guise.

When Claude died in 1550, his title went to his son François, a friend and military companion of the French king Henry II. François married Anne d'Este, a member of the ruling ESTE family of Ferrara, Italy. Later that same year, François's brother Charles was named cardinal of Lorraine. As a political adviser to the French king, Charles led the French delegation at the Catholic Council of TRENT.

François, the lieutenant general of France, became a military hero. In 1558 he recaptured the French city of Calais, which had been under English control for more than 200 years. The prestige he gained with this victory enabled him to arrange a marriage between his niece Mary STUART (the daughter of James V of Scotland) and the heir to the French throne. When Mary's husband became Francis II, king of France, François and his brother Charles were in control of royal policy. The dominance of the Guise family at the French court created tensions and rivalry among the noble families of France.

Religion was another source of tension. Many members of the French nobility had converted to Protestantism during the 1500s. The Guise family, however, remained steadfastly Catholic and worked to preserve the Catholic faith. In 1562 troops under François's command massacred a congregation of Huguenots*, setting off a series of WARS OF RELIGION in France that lasted until 1598. A year after the massacre, François was assassinated and was seen as a Catholic martyr*.

* **Huguenot**   French Protestant of the 1500s and 1600s, follower of John Calvin

* **martyr**   someone who suffers or dies for the sake of a religion, cause, or principle

His son Henri, the third duke of Guise, continued the family role of defenders of the faith. In 1576 he became head of the Catholic League, a group committed to limiting Protestant influence. He opposed the choice of Henry of Navarre, a Huguenot, as heir to the French throne. In 1588 Henri seized power in Paris. To regain control, Henry III of France arranged the assassination of Henri and his brother Louis, the cardinal of Guise. In the 1600s the Guise-Lorraine family gradually lost political influence, although it held on to its wealth and its church

offices. The last duke of Guise, François Joseph, died in 1674, and by 1688 the entire house of Guise-Lorraine had come to an end. (*See also* **Aristocracy; France; Henry IV; Protestant Reformation.**)

## Gutenberg, Johann

ca. 1398–1468
German inventor

Johann Gutenberg of Germany invented a printing press that used movable type to print books. His invention enabled printers to produce hundreds and thousands of accurate copies of books far more efficiently and cheaply than in the past, greatly aiding the spread of information. The printing press had such a great impact on cultural and commercial development that some scholars see it as a turning point in the history of Western civilization.

Gutenberg spent most of his life in Mainz, Germany, where he borrowed large sums of money to set up his print shop and create his press. He developed a method of producing movable type that was suitable for printed books. His technique involved creating a separate metal piece for each letter of the alphabet. Many of the metals Gutenberg employed—including tin and lead—are still in use today. He also developed his ink, a mixture of oil, varnish, and finely ground black powder that worked well on the calfskin and paper used in printing at the time.

Gutenberg's print shop in Mainz may have held up to six printing presses. It was there that he printed his first book, a Latin version of the Bible. During 1454 and 1455 he printed more than 200 copies of this Bible, which contained 42 lines of print on each page. Gutenberg's Bibles are of extremely high quality. The type is sharp and clear and the right-hand margins are straight. Surprisingly, almost a quarter of the volumes in Gutenberg's original printing still exist. Many of these copies are illuminated* with capital letters and headings added by hand

* **illuminated** having pages ornamented with hand-painted color decorations and illustrations

Johann Gutenberg developed a printing press that used movable type, enabling printers to produce thousands of copies of books quickly and accurately. In this engraving, Gutenberg displays the first proofs made with his new invention.

in spaces the printer left for that purpose. The cost of printing these Bibles exceeded the profits, and by the time Gutenberg printed the last of them it was clear he would not have enough money to pay off his loans. He handed over his shop in place of payment and produced few other works.

At first, people used Gutenberg's invention mainly to reproduce existing texts. In the early 1500s, however, the printing of original works became common. As printing became more widely available, the handwritten manuscript and the oral tradition of the Middle Ages shifted to the world of the printed page. (*See also* **Bible; Books and Manuscripts; Printing and Publishing.**)

## Habsburg Dynasty

* **patronage** support or financial sponsorship

Rising from obscure origins, the Habsburgs became the dominant political family of Europe during the Renaissance. Through a series of advantageous marriages, the family managed to overcome territorial and language boundaries and gained control of much of Europe and of vast tracts of land in the AMERICAS. The Habsburgs also played a significant role in the cultural life of the Renaissance through their patronage* of major artists, literary figures, and scientists.

**The Rise of the Habsburgs.** The reign of the house of Habsburg began in 1246, when the family took control of Austria. At first, the Habsburgs seemed to be just another noble family with ambitions to expand its territory by waging war and making favorable alliances though marriage. But they were more successful than others, winning the throne of the Holy Roman Empire* for Rudolf I (ruled 1273–1291) and his son Albert I (ruled 1298–1308).

* **Holy Roman Empire** political body in central Europe composed of several states; existed until 1806

* **imperial** pertaining to an empire or emperor

Quarrels within the family, the ambitions of rival families, and the general political instability in Europe prevented the Habsburgs from regaining the imperial* throne until 1438, when Albert II seized power. Although Albert ruled for only about a year, he became the first of an unbroken line of Habsburg rulers that lasted until 1740.

**Father and Son.** Albert's cousin Duke Frederick of Styria succeeded him and ruled as Frederick III until 1493. During his reign, Frederick took several steps that strengthened the power and holdings of the Habsburg dynasty. He married Eleanor of Portugal, which allowed the Habsburgs to acquire that kingdom in the late 1500s. He also reached an agreement with Pope NICHOLAS V that gave the Holy Roman Emperor considerable authority over the appointment of church officials in Habsburg lands. Finally, he married his son, Maximilian, to Mary of Burgundy (daughter of the prosperous duke of BURGUNDY). He had less success in his role as Holy Roman Emperor, failing to establish a workable system of taxation in the empire and raiding the royal treasury. However, as a patron of the arts, he introduced humanist* learning to Germany.

* **humanist** referring to a Renaissance cultural movement promoting the study of the humanities (the languages, literature, and history of ancient Greece and Rome) as a guide to living

One of the most remarkable princes to emerge during the Renaissance, Frederick's son MAXIMILIAN I (1459–1519) had studied

## Habsburg Dynasty

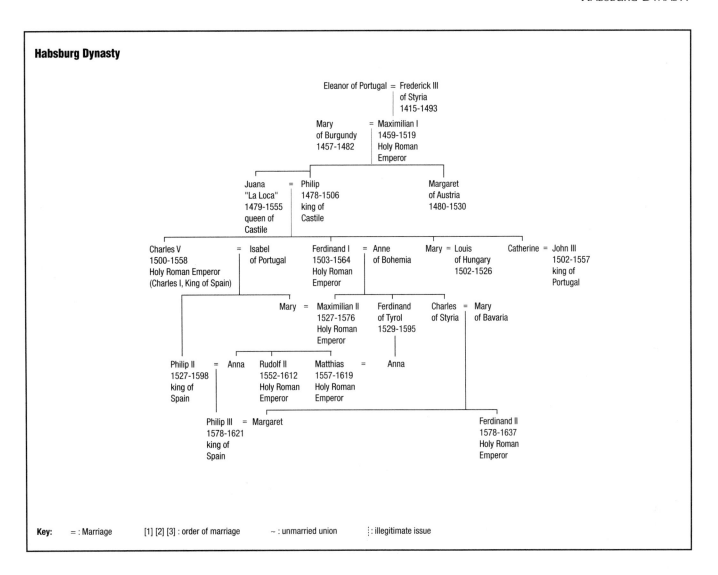

**Key:**    = : Marriage        [1] [2] [3] : order of marriage        ~ : unmarried union        ⋮ : illegitimate issue

---

* **multilingual**    referring to many languages

* **Ottoman Turks**    Turkish followers of Islam who founded the Ottoman Empire in the 1300s; the empire eventually included large areas of eastern Europe, the Middle East, and northern Africa

astrology, music, carpentry, mining, hunting, weaponry, and other subjects in his youth. He spoke seven languages, which greatly helped him rule his multilingual* empire. Maximilian defended the Burgundian inheritance in battle against two French kings and became king of the Romans in 1486, joining his father in managing the Holy Roman Empire.

When Frederick died in 1493, Maximilian became the sole ruler of the Holy Roman Empire and head of the house of Habsburg. The new emperor faced many problems, including a fierce rivalry with France over Italy and threats to the empire's eastern frontier by the Ottoman Turks*. He dealt with the efforts of reformers to alter the political structure of the realm and with disagreements over taxes. To advance his interests in Italy, Maximilian married Bianca Maria Sforza, daughter of the duke of Milan, in 1494. He made an unsuccessful expedition to Italy, but because of opposition from the Venetians, failed to reach Rome for his imperial coronation in 1508.

### While Others Wage War

As a matchmaker, Maximilian I had few equals. His greatest success was in arranging the marriage of his son Philip to Joan I of Castile, daughter of Ferdinand and Isabella of Spain. The result of this union was that his grandson Charles inherited the Spanish crown and a prominent place in the order of succession as Holy Roman Emperor. Some people said of the Habsburgs, "Others may wage war, but thou, happy Austria, marry!"

* **exploit**   to take advantage of; to make productive use of

On the positive side, Maximilian secured Austria by driving the Hungarians from Vienna. He also persuaded the king of BOHEMIA to pass the crowns of Bohemia and HUNGARY to the Habsburgs if he died without a male heir. Like his father, Maximilian supported the arts and literature. He employed such artists as Albrecht DÜRER for numerous projects, including illustrations for his own literary works.

**World Empire.** The grandson of Maximilian, CHARLES V held more than 60 royal and princely titles, including emperor, king of Castile and Aragon, and archduke of Austria. In addition to his titles, Charles inherited a multitude of problems. The Holy Roman Empire was facing a religious crisis sparked by Martin LUTHER, who called for church reform. Charles, a steadfast Roman Catholic, failed in his attempts to suppress Luther's movement and to eliminate Protestants from the empire. He did, however, manage to hold off the Ottoman Turks in central Europe and the French in Italy. Operating from Spain in 1535, he captured Tunis in North Africa. New rounds of fighting between the Valois, the French royal family, and the Habsburgs broke out in 1536 after the French king FRANCIS I forged an alliance with the Ottomans. These wars finally ended in 1544 when Francis signed the Peace of Crépy.

Under Charles's sponsorship, the Portuguese navigator Ferdinand MAGELLAN began his quest to sail around the world in 1519. Hernan Cortés completed his conquest of the Aztecs in Mexico (1521) and Francisco Pizarro vanquished the Inca in Peru (1533). Charles never fully realized the significance of his overseas possessions. He simply exploited* their resources and used them to enhance the image of Habsburg power. In the arts, Charles maintained the Habsburg tradition of patronage, supporting DÜRER and the great Italian painter TITIAN.

**Dividing the Habsburg Inheritance.** Wishing to keep the empire in the hands of one man, Charles announced in 1550 his intention to turn over the entire Habsburg inheritance to his talented son Philip. The plan received little support. To avoid the threat of civil war, Charles signed an agreement in 1551 that his brother FERDINAND I would succeed him as emperor. Ferdinand would be followed by Charles's son PHILIP II and then by Ferdinand's son MAXIMILIAN II. The arrangement pleased no one and led to suspicions that the Habsburgs intended to turn the elective emperorship into a hereditary monarchy. Worn out by conflict and troubled by illness, Charles turned over his imperial responsibilities to Ferdinand in 1555. The Netherlands, Spain, Italian lands, and the colonies went to Philip. Charles retired to his country house and died in 1558, the year Ferdinand was crowned emperor.

Ferdinand I spent much of his reign trying to settle religious conflicts in Germany and urging war against the Ottomans. He was an enthusiastic follower of the open-minded humanist scholar Desiderius ERASMUS. His tolerance for diversity, however, went only so far. Before he allowed his son Maximilian II to be crowned king of the Romans, Ferdinand forced him to renounce his Protestant beliefs.

When Ferdinand died in 1564, the Habsburg lands were divided among his three sons. Maximilian II succeeded his father as Holy

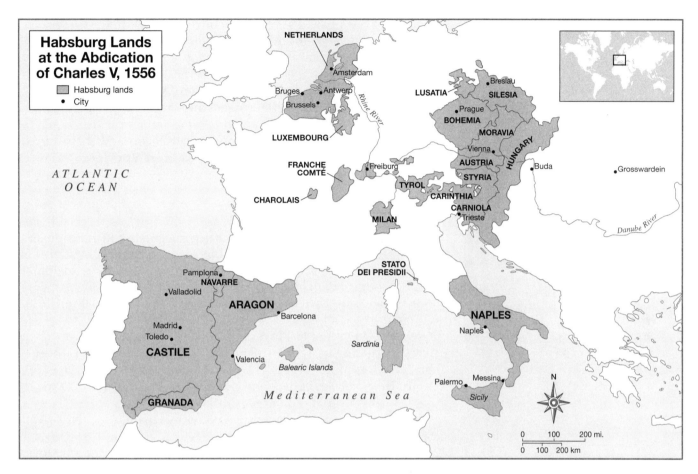

**Habsburg Lands at the Abdication of Charles V, 1556**

☐ Habsburg lands
• City

NETHERLANDS
Amsterdam
Bruges • Antwerp
Brussels
Rhine River
LUXEMBOURG
FRANCHE COMTÉ
Freiburg
CHAROLAIS
MILAN

LUSATIA
Breslau
SILESIA
Prague
BOHEMIA
MORAVIA
Vienna
AUSTRIA
HUNGARY
STYRIA
Buda
TYROL
CARINTHIA
CARNIOLA
Trieste
Grosswardein
Danube River

ATLANTIC OCEAN

Pamplona
NAVARRE
Valladolid
ARAGON
Barcelona
Madrid
Toledo
CASTILE
Valencia
Balearic Islands
GRANADA

STATO DEI PRESIDII

NAPLES
Naples

Sardinia

Mediterranean Sea

Palermo
Messina
Sicily

N

0    100    200 mi.
0    100    200 km

Roman Emperor and gained Bohemia, part of Hungary, and Upper and Lower Austria. His brother Charles acquired Inner Austria, while the third brother, Ferdinand, received lands in Germany. Their cousin Philip II of Spain, named head of the house of Habsburg in 1564, ruled over what became the world's leading military power. Philip had some success against the Ottoman Turks, winning significant battles in North Africa and in the waters off Lepanto, Greece.

Both Philip and Maximilian had broad intellectual interests and both men became great patrons of the arts and sciences. Determined to make Vienna the cultural center of Europe, Maximilian brought distinguished scientists and scholars to the city. Philip continued his father's patronage of the Italian artist Titian and also promoted the career of one of the leading female painters of the late Renaissance—Sofonisba ANGUISSOLA of Cremona. He also established academies to promote mathematics and science.

**The Later Habsburgs.** Despite numerous intermarriages, the Habsburg inheritance remained divided between its Austrian and Spanish branches. Philip III succeeded his father Philip II on the Spanish throne, ruling from 1598 to 1621. Maximilian II became the Holy Roman Emperor in 1564, followed by RUDOLF II in 1576. Already king of Bohemia and Hungary, Rudolf never married and is best known for his

patronage of the arts and sciences. He turned Prague (in the present-day Czech Republic) into a great cultural center by bringing the astronomers Tycho BRAHE, Johannes KEPLER, and others to his court. Rudolf's brother Matthias succeeded him. Lazy and in poor health, Matthias left government matters in the hands of Melchior Klesl, bishop of Vienna. Klesl's efforts to make peace between Catholics and Protestants were hampered by Matthias's cousin Ferdinand, who became emperor in 1619. By that time the THIRTY YEARS' WAR (1618–1648) had begun and the house of Habsburg was in decline. (*See also* **Holy Roman Empire; Ottoman Empire; Valois Dynasty.**)

## Hakluyt, Richard

### ca. 1552–1616
### English geographer

* **Flemish**   relating to Flanders, a region along the coasts of present-day Belgium, France, and the Netherlands

Although not a world traveler himself, geographer Richard Hakluyt played an important role in promoting English exploration and trade. His writings, based on explorers' accounts of voyages, highlighted and encouraged England's involvement in global affairs.

Born in London, Hakluyt was raised by his cousin, from whom he got his interest in geography and overseas travel. As an avid collector of geographical information, Hakluyt corresponded with great Flemish* mapmakers, including Gerardus Mercator. He also came to know such English navigators as Sir Francis DRAKE, Martin Frobisher, and Sir Walter Raleigh. He collected, edited, and often translated accounts of voyages undertaken by a variety of European travelers.

For all his interest in geography, Hakluyt was mainly concerned with promoting English expansion and trade. He argued for a bold English effort to challenge and counter Spanish power in the Americas. Hakluyt's most important work, *The Principal Navigations, Voyages, Traffiques, and Discoveries of the English Nation* (1589), attempted to give England a history of voyaging stretching back some 1,600 years. It had a lasting effect on the country's view of itself. (*See also* **Americas; Exploration; Geography and Cartography; Travel and Tourism.**)

## Harvey, William

### 1587–1657
### English physician

William Harvey is best known for his theory on the circulation of blood in the human body. Using only a magnifying glass, he overturned the most popular theory about blood flow at the time. He also discovered as much about the structure and function of the heart as one can see without a microscope.

Harvey received his medical degree from Italy's University of Padua in 1602. He returned to London to practice medicine and the following year married Elizabeth Browne, whose father was a court physician to JAMES I. In the years following, Harvey was elected to the College of Physicians, which oversaw professional medicine in London. He also served the college as a lecturer in surgery and anatomy. In 1618 he reached the peak of his career as a royal physician to James I and later to James's son, CHARLES I. Harvey supported Charles I against Parliament during the English Civil War (1642–1649). As a result, supporters of

Parliament attacked his house and destroyed most of his records. After the king's defeat, Harvey retired outside of London.

While working for the king, Harvey made his great discoveries on the circulation of the blood. His work contradicted the most popular theory of this time, which the ancient Roman physician GALEN had proposed hundreds of years earlier. According to Galen, food and drink combined in the stomach to produce a substance called chyle. The chyle then passed to the liver, where it became blood that flowed into the veins. Some of the blood went to the hands and feet and some went to the right side of the heart to be purified. Most of the pure blood then flowed into the veins, while a small portion went to the left side of the heart. There it mixed with a life-giving "vital spirit" before leaving through the arteries for various parts of the body.

* **dissect** to cut open a body to examine its inner parts

By dissecting* live animals and studying the movements of the heart, Harvey found several problems with Galen's theory. For example, too much blood left the heart at one time for the liver to absorb and replace with fresh blood made from chyle. Harvey also noted that in Galen's model, the amount of blood that the heart pumped in an hour exceeded the amount of blood in the entire animal. Therefore, Harvey stated that the body does not continually produce blood, but rather circulates the same blood around the body. He also proved that the veins carried blood to the heart, not away from it as Galen had taught.

In 1628 Harvey reported his findings in the book *On the Movement of the Heart*. In the Renaissance tradition, this work stressed the authority of personal observation over written sources that had no experiments to back them up. Although his theory met a mixed response at first, Harvey lived to see it accepted by the scientific world. (*See also* **Anatomy; Medicine; Science.**)

---

## Hebrew Language and Literature

**See** *Jewish Languages and Literature.*

---

### Henry IV

**1553–1610**
**King of France**

Henry IV was the first monarch in the BOURBON dynasty, which ruled France until the French Revolution of 1789. One of France's most popular leaders, Henry united the country after the WARS OF RELIGION in the late 1500s and helped bring peace between Catholics and Protestants in France.

Henry of Navarre was the son of Antoine de Bourbon, one of France's most powerful nobles, and JEANNE D'ALBRET, queen of the tiny country of Navarre, between France and Spain. As a descendant of the French king Louis IX, Henry held a distant claim to the French throne. His mother converted to Protestantism in 1555, a decision that would have a major impact on Henry and on France.

* **Huguenot** French Protestant of the 1500s and 1600s, follower of John Calvin

The Wars of Religion, a prolonged struggle between Catholics and Huguenots*, began in France in 1562. Ten years later CATHERINE DE MÉDICIS, mother of the French king Henry III, arranged a marriage between her Catholic daughter and Henry of Navarre, a Protestant. The

goal was to bring peace between the two faiths. Instead, the marriage set off a wave of violence that took the lives of thousands of Huguenots. Henry survived only by denying his Protestant faith.

Henry of Navarre was held prisoner at the French royal court until 1576, when he escaped and became a Huguenot leader. Eight years later the king's younger brother died, leaving Henry next in line to the throne of France. Catholics who strongly opposed Henry joined forces with the Catholic League, a militant group of Catholic leaders. To maintain order, the reigning king, Henry III, ordered the murder of the league's leaders. The plan backfired, however, and led to a general uprising in which the king was assassinated. On August 1, 1589, Henry of Navarre succeeded to the throne, but it would be five years before he fully controlled the kingdom.

Shortly after the assassination, Henry IV promised to consider converting to Catholicism. That pledge, along with military victories over Catholic opponents, increased his support among the people. Many Catholics continued to resist, however, and three years later Henry finally converted. He was crowned in 1594, and over the next few years he made generous peace offers to his former opponents. He also reassured Huguenots that they would not be persecuted, a promise that became law with the Edict of Nantes in 1598.

As king, Henry IV rebuilt France's treasury, which had been drained during the costly religious wars. He also named ministers to assume important government functions once handled by local assemblies. To win the support of the nobility he gave titles and pensions to his followers, but he dealt harshly with those who continued to oppose him. With France's finances restored and the kingdom unified, Henry planned to challenge the power of the HABSBURG DYNASTY, which dominated European politics. However, his plans were cut short by his assassination in 1610. (*See also* **France; Marie de Médicis.**)

### Henry VII

### 1457–1509
### King of England

* **patron** supporter or financial sponsor of an artist or writer

* **humanist** Renaissance expert in the humanities (the languages, literature, history, and speech and writing techniques of ancient Greece and Rome)

The founder of England's Tudor dynasty, Henry VII strengthened the English monarchy and brought peace and stability to his country. He helped bring Renaissance ideas to England from Italy and BURGUNDY and served as a patron* of poets and humanists*. His greatest architectural monument is his chapel at Westminster Abbey.

Henry's claim to the throne of England came from his mother, who was a great-granddaughter of John of Gaunt, the duke of Lancaster and fourth son of King Edward III. In the Wars of the Roses, an extended struggle between the houses of York and Lancaster for control of the English crown, the Lancasters supported Henry's claim to the throne. Forced to go into exile in Brittany and France in 1471, Henry became a serious threat to the Yorkists after the death of Edward IV in 1483. Two years later he gained the throne by defeating Edward's brother, Richard III, at the Battle of Bosworth.

King Henry used marriage as a tool to strengthen his hold on the English throne. In 1486 he wed Elizabeth of York, the daughter of Edward IV. However, he still faced opposition from the York family, and

he had to put down two Yorkist-led rebellions in the 1480s. In 1502 he averted the threat of a war with Scotland by marrying his daughter Margaret to the Scottish king James IV. He created ties with Spain by marrying his son Arthur to the Spanish princess CATHERINE OF ARAGON. Henry also tried to strengthen his connections with the HABSBURG DYNASTY through matrimony. He offered to take Margaret of Savoy, the daughter of Holy Roman Emperor* MAXIMILIAN I, as his second wife and arranged the marriage of his daughter Mary to Maximilian's grandson, the future emperor CHARLES V.

* **Holy Roman Emperor**   ruler of the Holy Roman Empire, a political body in central Europe composed of several states that existed until 1806

Henry showed great talent for government administration and finance. He ruled through committees of his governing council, which allowed him to bypass common-law courts and procedures. He also increased royal revenues by persuading Parliament to enact taxes on various imports and exports. This source of income grew steadily through his reign. In 1487 Henry tightened control over the collection and distribution of taxes as well. However, the high taxes imposed to finance a war in Scotland led to a rebellion in 1497.

* **gentry**   people of high birth or social status

Henry VII regarded most of the English nobility and gentry* with suspicion. He took steps to reduce their power within the judicial system by expanding the power of justices of the peace. He also tightened laws that regulated the relationships between lords and citizens. Such actions angered many members of the upper classes. Fearful of plots against him, Henry also employed a network of spies to keep watch on his subjects. As he grew older, Henry's rule became harsher. Despite his growing unpopularity, Henry survived politically and produced an heir, the future HENRY VIII, who carried the Tudor dynasty to great heights. (*See also* **Dynastic Rivalry; England; Holy Roman Empire; Scotland.**)

**1491–1547**
**King of England**

T he reign of Henry VIII marked the true beginning of the Renaissance in ENGLAND. During his younger years, Henry appeared to be the ideal Renaissance monarch—handsome and dashing, fond of sports and pageantry, well educated, and a supporter of the arts and learning. However, less attractive features appeared during the later years of his reign, when he faced increasing troubles in his married life and economic and social strains within his kingdom.

**Early Rule.** The second ruler of the Tudor dynasty, Henry was the younger son of HENRY VII. His brother Arthur, the heir to the throne, died in 1502, a year after marrying the Spanish princess CATHERINE OF ARAGON. Henry took the throne upon his father's death in 1509 and married his brother's widow in hopes of continuing friendly relations with Spain.

Henry and Catherine remained happily married for 18 years. During this time, Henry was devoted to the Roman Catholic Church and the papacy*. He joined the pope's Holy League, an alliance aimed at preventing France from gaining territory in Italy, and he supported the papacy against the Protestant ideas of Martin LUTHER. The pope gave Henry the title "Defender of the Faith" in thanks for his support.

* **papacy**   office and authority of the pope

Henry VIII, shown here in a painting by the famous German artist Hans Holbein the Younger, ruled England for much of the early 1500s. His support of the arts and humanist learning ushered in the Renaissance in England.

ANNO · ETATIS ·                 · SVÆ · XLIX ·

* **annulment**   formal declaration that a marriage is legally invalid

* **Holy Roman Emperor**   ruler of the Holy Roman Empire, a political body in central Europe composed of several states that existed until 1806

By 1527, however, Henry had become concerned about the lack of a male heir. Catherine's childbearing days were over, and their only surviving child was a daughter named Mary. The king feared that the English would not accept a female ruler. Determined to continue the Tudor dynasty, he tried to end his marriage to Catherine. He planned to take Anne Boleyn, one of Catherine's attendants, as his second wife.

The king and his chief minister Thomas WOLSEY asked the pope to grant Henry an annulment* and permission to remarry. Normally, such a request would not have posed a problem. However, Catherine opposed the divorce, as did her nephew CHARLES V, the king of Spain and Holy Roman Emperor*. The pope denied the divorce because he needed Charles's help in various political matters. In response, Henry summoned the so-called Reformation Parliament in 1529 and began taking steps to undermine the power of the Catholic Church in England.

**The English Reformation.** In 1533 Thomas CROMWELL, Henry's new chief minister, proposed that England should break its ties with Rome. This would allow the archbishop of Canterbury, head of the English church, to grant the divorce. Thomas CRANMER, the new archbishop, supported the plan. Henry married Anne Boleyn in January, and a few months later Parliament passed a law denying the papacy any authority in England. Cranmer then granted Henry his divorce and legalized his marriage to Anne. In September, Anne give birth to Henry's second daughter, Elizabeth.

Parliament continued to reshape the English church. It passed laws that named Henry VIII as Supreme Head of the Church, cut off all payments to the papacy, regulated church doctrine, and closed all the Catholic monasteries in England. Although many English people were unhappy about these actions, others welcomed the reform of a church they viewed as corrupt.

In 1536 Henry came to believe that Anne Boleyn had been unfaithful. She was charged with adultery and beheaded. Soon afterward, Henry took his third wife, Jane Seymour, who provided the king with his long-awaited son, Prince Edward. Jane died from complications of childbirth. Henry married three more times, but none of these wives bore him any children.

Troubles both at home and abroad marred the later years of Henry's reign. Following the break with Rome, Henry and his advisers feared that Catholic powers in Europe would wage war on England. The government spent vast sums of money on building up the nation's military defenses. In addition, after about 1536 the members of Henry's government were divided over the issues of further reforms in the church and in social policy. The country also faced economic and social strains. One major source of tension was the growing practice of enclosure, which involved converting open fields into pasture for sheep. This movement pushed many rural laborers from their homes and led to social unrest.

**Henry and the Renaissance.** Renaissance ideas had begun to trickle into England during the reign of Henry VII. Under Henry VIII, these ideas spread more rapidly and widely. Sir Thomas MORE, Henry's lord chancellor, led a group of humanists* at the court who promoted Renaissance learning. One of More's followers, Sir Thomas Elyot, wrote a treatise* that examined Renaissance ideas on political thought and education. Elyot also helped revive ancient medical teachings and produced the first English dictionary of classical* Latin. In addition, More's circle included the German artist Hans HOLBEIN the Younger, who painted several portraits of the king and some of his wives.

After Henry's break with Rome, religious debates and divisions drew public attention away from humanist studies. But Renaissance ideas had taken hold, and they grew in popularity and importance during the reign of Henry's daughter ELIZABETH I and her successor, JAMES I. (*See also* **Art in Britain; Edward VI; England; Mary I; Protestant Reformation; Scotland.**)

* **humanist**   Renaissance expert in the humanities (the languages, literature, history, and speech and writing techniques of ancient Greece and Rome)

* **treatise**   long, detailed essay

* **classical**   in the tradition of ancient Greece and Rome

<table>
Henry the Navigator
</table>

**Henry the Navigator**

See *Exploration.*

**Heraldry**

Heraldry is the practice of designing and describing emblems called coats of arms. During the Middle Ages, knights painted these emblems on their shields to make their identities known on the battlefield. After the mid-1100s families began passing down their coats of arms from generation to generation. Eventually these emblems lost their military function and became status symbols.

**Heraldic Rules and Terms.** In medieval* combat, being able to recognize the shields of friends and foes was a matter of life and death. To make their emblems distinctive, knights adopted strict rules, such as declaring that a shield must contain one dark and one light color. Acceptable dark colors included black, blue, green, purple, and red. Light colors resembled precious metals—yellow for gold or white for silver.

The arrangement of colors on a coat of arms was called a blazon, from the German word *blasen*—referring to the trumpet blast that announced the arrival of a competitor in a jousting tournament. The rules of heraldry required the use of specific terms to describe a blazon. The description began with the background color, or field, of the coat of arms. Each color had a special name. Several came from French words: *argent* for silver; *or* for gold; *vert* for green; and *purpure* for purple. Blue was *azure* (from the Arabic word *azraq*) and red was *gules* (from the Persian word *gûl,* or rose). The name for black was sable, after the black-furred animal. In addition to these basic colors, knights could paint their shields in ermine or vair—two patterns designed to resemble animal fur.

There were several ways to divide a shield to display two colors. One color could be shown on the left and one on the right, an arrangement known as *per pale*. A shield could also be divided *per fess* (horizontally), *per bend* (diagonally), or in a more complicated pattern. The description of a divided blazon began with the color on the top or on the right side (from the shield-bearer's point of view). The right and left sides of the shield were called *dexter* and *sinister,* from the Latin words for right and left. For example, a description of "per fess, gules and argent" would indicate a shield divided in half by a horizontal line, with the top red and the bottom silver.

On top of the background color, a shield could display one or more shapes, or charges. The simplest types of charges were basic geometric shapes called ordinaries. For example, a shield could have a vertical line down the center, called a *pale,* or a horizontal line, called a *fess.* More complex charges covered a wide ranges of shapes, including animals, human figures, heavenly bodies, and inanimate objects. Often, the charge on a shield involved some sort of puns or wordplay. For example, the arms of humanist* Johann Reuchlin featured an altar with curling wisps of smoke. The word *Räuchlein* in German means "a little smoke." Playwright William SHAKESPEARE had a coat of arms with a falcon holding a lance, hinting at the phrase "shake spear."

* **medieval**   referring to the Middle Ages, a period that began around A.D. 400 and ended around 1400 in Italy and 1500 in the rest of Europe

* **humanist**   Renaissance expert in the humanities (the languages, literature, history, and speech and writing techniques of ancient Greece and Rome)

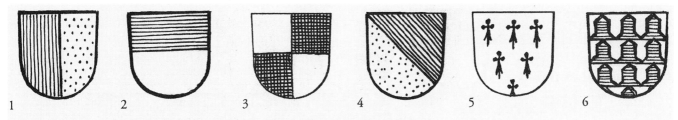

**Figure 1. Hatchments and Furs.** (1) Per pale, gules and or; (2) per fess, azure and argent; (3) quarterly, argent and sable; (4) per bend, vert and or; (5) ermine; (6) vair. COURTESY OF HELMUT NICKEL

This diagram illustrates some of the colors and patterns used in coats of arms. From left to right, the shields are divided (1) per pale, vertically, (2) per fess, horizontally, (3) quarterly, and (4) per fess, diagonally. The shields on the right show the two patterns known as "furs," (5) ermine and (6) vair.

* **woodcut**   print made from a block of wood with an image carved into it

* **Holy Roman Emperor**   ruler of the Holy Roman Empire, a political body in central Europe composed of several states that existed until 1806

In heraldry, individual colors and the order in which they appeared were very important. "A lion or in gules" indicated a completely different blazon from "a lion gules in or." This posed a problem because woodcuts*, engravings, and personal seals did not show color. However, in the late 1500s an engraver invented a system of hatching (drawing lines) to represent color: horizontal hatches for azure, vertical for gules, diagonal for vert, cross-hatched for sable, dotted for or, and blank for argent.

**Uses of Heraldry.** By the mid-1400s, advances in armor made the use of shields in combat unnecessary. But noble families continued to use their coats of arms as status symbols, and countries began establishing rules for their use. The English king Richard III established the College of Arms in 1484 for that purpose, and the Holy Roman Emperors* had officials who granted new arms and confirmed existing ones. Custom within the Holy Roman Empire allowed any free man to adopt a coat of arms. Middle-class workers often used basic designs that indicated their trade, while scholars and minor nobles tended to design their own blazons. Rules were established to distinguish the arms of noblemen from those of commoners.

Because shields now existed mainly to display the coat of arms, new shapes replaced the old-fashioned triangular battle shields. A U-shaped shield, which allowed for a more pleasing arrangement of charges, became common in many areas. Italians adopted an almond-shaped shield called a *chanfron,* which existed only for display purposes. The only shields that still served a military function were targes, the square shields used in tournaments. These included a cutout in the upper right corner to support the bearer's lance. Some targes had cutouts in both corners to make them look more balanced.

Some noble families used their coats of arms to show their heritage or the territories they owned. A shield could be divided into several parts to display the arms of several different territories. For example, when the kingdoms of Castile and Leon united in 1230, Spain developed a "quartered" coat of arms that combined the arms of the two kingdoms. Spanish arms also tended to include sayings, or mottoes, as part of the design. These elements eventually became popular throughout Europe. In the late 1400s and early 1500s, it became fashionable for coats of arms to include figures that supported the shield, such as lions or unicorns. Originally just decorations, these figures eventually became signs of rank with rules to govern their use. (*See also* **Arms and Armor; Chivalry; Tournaments.**)

## Hippocrates

ca. 450–ca. 370 B.C.
Greek physician

* **treatise** long, detailed essay

The ancient Greek physician Hippocrates is often called the father of Western medicine. Although historians know little about Hippocrates' life, his teachings had a great influence on Renaissance medical practices. Much of what scholars know about ancient Greek medicine comes from a group of about 60 treatises* called the Hippocratic Corpus. However, they can directly link only a few of these texts to Hippocrates himself.

Hippocrates became famous in his own lifetime for teaching medicine on the island of Cos, where he was born. One important aspect of Hippocrates' teaching was that he rejected magical and religious explanations of health and looked for rational ones. He also emphasized the need to observe a sick person's physical symptoms and base the course of treatment on them. The Corpus also contains the Hippocratic Oath, perhaps the earliest statement of medical ethics. Although Hippocrates probably did not write the oath, it reflects his ideas.

Hippocrates' ideas influenced medicine for many centuries. The Greek physician GALEN (ca. A.D. 130–ca. 216) included many of Hippocrates' concepts in his own works on the art and practice of medicine. By the 1100s, works by Hippocrates had become required texts at medical schools. Renaissance scholars such as the German physician PARACELSUS praised Hippocrates for relying on observation and experience rather than theory. The writings of Hippocrates remained part of standard medical training until the early 1800s. (*See also* **Medicine.**)

## History, Writing of

* **classical** in the tradition of ancient Greece and Rome

* **vernacular** native language or dialect of a region or country

* **humanist** Renaissance expert in the humanities (the languages, literature, history, and speech and writing techniques of ancient Greece and Rome)

The growth of classical* learning during the Renaissance had a great impact on the way Europeans wrote and thought about history. Works by ancient Greek and Roman authors, such as Plutarch, Livy, and Tacitus, provided models for historians to use in writing the histories of their own nations. Renaissance historians made substantial advances in the writing of history. They also used history to support political positions.

## CLASSICAL HISTORIANS

During the Renaissance, scholars unearthed many works of ancient history that had been lost during the Middle Ages. They also translated the texts of Greek and Roman historians into vernacular* languages, making these works available to the general public.

**Roman Historians.** Scholars of the Middle Ages were familiar with many history writers of ancient Rome, either directly or through excerpts and summaries of their works. The writers included Livy, Sallust, and Julius Caesar, the Roman general and statesman. In the 1300s scholars began to rediscover many long-forgotten Latin writings. The first great effort in this area was the reconstruction of Livy's *History of Rome* by the early Renaissance humanist* PETRARCH and a colleague. This work had existed only in fragments during the Middle Ages.

Later humanists studied and commented on ancient Roman writings such as the *Histories* of Sallust, the *Annals* of Tacitus, and the *Commentaries* of Julius Caesar. The study of Latin texts became a key part of a humanist education. During the early Renaissance, when republican* governments flourished in Italy, most scholars focused on histories of the Roman Republic. Later, as absolutist* forms of government took over in many places, works about the Roman Empire became more popular.

**Greek Historians.** Before 1400, most scholars knew the texts of Greek history only through Latin translations. In 1397 Manuel Chrysoloras, a Greek scholar, arrived in FLORENCE and began teaching Greek to young humanists. His work helped generate interest in reading and translating ancient Greek authors. Chrysoloras's students, such as Leonardo BRUNI and Guarino GUARINI, translated the works of Polybius, Plutarch, and other writers of ancient Greece. Plutarch's *Parallel Lives,* one of the most popular Greek texts of the early Renaissance, compared the lives of famous Greeks and Romans and discussed their character traits.

Pope NICHOLAS V gave these studies a tremendous boost in the mid-1400s by hiring scholars to translate several major works of Greek history. Under his patronage*, scholars such as Lorenzo VALLA produced Latin versions of texts by Herodotus, Thucydides, and other noted Greek authors.

## RENAISSANCE HISTORIANS

During the Middle Ages, most history writing took the form of chronicles, or "annals"—listings of the important events that took place in a given year. Renaissance historians took a more narrative* approach to the past. They placed more emphasis on the forces behind the events and on the human beings involved. Reflecting the ancient idea of history as "philosophy teaching by example," they used history to illustrate the strengths and weaknesses of various forms of government and to provide examples of virtuous behavior.

Leonardo Bruni of Italy was the first, and by many standards the greatest, humanist historian. His *History of the Florentine People,* written in the 1430s and 1440s and modeled on the work of Roman authors such as Livy, traced the rise of Florence to the status of a great power. Unlike many historians, Bruni viewed his sources with a critical eye and used only those that he found reliable. Many later Italian historians, including Niccolò MACHIAVELLI and Francesco GUICCIARDINI, focused on the reasons for the WARS OF ITALY, when foreign powers took control of the region. Machiavelli used the events of this time to draw general conclusions about human societies.

Humanist historians in France turned to legal texts, a new type of historical source, to explain many aspects of French history. Jean BODIN and his followers examined the civil laws of the Roman Empire and con-

---

* **republican** refers to a form of Renaissance government dominated by leading merchants with limited participation by others

* **absolutist** refers to complete control by a single ruler

* **patronage** support or financial sponsorship

* **narrative** storytelling

cluded that they reflected the concerns of an ancient people, not the universal needs of all human societies. Later humanists such as Jacques Cujas built on this idea to proclaim the laws and customs of France as unique, not descended from ancient Rome.

French humanists also challenged many myths of their country's history, such as the popular notion that their ancestors came from the ancient kingdom of Troy. Some historians used this new view of French history as distinct from Roman history to support their political views. For example, those who objected to the influence of the Roman Catholic Church in France used historical evidence to argue that the early French church was independent of Rome.

In Britain, the annals of the Middle Ages lost favor while new forms, such as political history and biography, enjoyed new prominence. In 1521 scholar John Major produced a complete national history of England. Five years later Hector Boece of Scotland followed up with a history of his country, which drew heavily on medieval* chronicles and legendary sources. In the early 1500s biographies of important figures became a major form of historical writing in Britain. Sir Thomas MORE wrote a biography of the English king Richard III that became an important source for later scholars. More's own life became the subject of at least three biographies during the 1500s. Sir Walter Raleigh's *History of the World* (1614) was a popular combination of history and biography. Written while Raleigh was in prison under a death sentence, it offered a dark vision of ancient history and tied the fall of mighty leaders to their faults.

German historians of the Renaissance worked to discredit the Italian image of Germans as "barbarians." Scholars such as Conrad CELTIS pointed to the glories of ancient Germany and the victories of older German peoples such as the Goths and Vandals. They also observed that the Roman writer Tacitus had praised the virtues of ancient Germans, notably their intelligence, nobility, courage, and love of truth. German historians continued to use medieval chronicles, even as they embraced humanist ideas. Like the French, German Protestants drew on history to attack the authority of the pope. They created a new view of European history, particularly of church history, that presented the Protestant Reformation* as a rebirth of the true Christian church.

In Spain, the monarchy used history as a tool to support its claims of supremacy. When ISABELLA OF CASTILE married FERDINAND OF ARAGON and united their two kingdoms, the new nation looked to history to help it establish an identity. In the early 1500s Ferdinand hired several humanist scholars to research the history of Spain, but no one managed to produce a complete Spanish history until 1592. While some scholars tried to reconstruct Spain's history, others worked to lay out its geography. In 1548 Pedro de Medina produced a Spanish geography text with a patriotic slant, *The Book of Great and Memorable Things of Spain.* (*See also* **Biography and Autobiography; Classical Scholarship; Education; Humanism; Translation.**)

* **medieval** referring to the Middle Ages, a period that began around A.D. 400 and ended around 1400 in Italy and 1500 in the rest of Europe

* **Protestant Reformation** religious movement that began in the 1500s as a protest against certain practices of the Roman Catholic Church and eventually led to the establishment of a variety of Protestant churches

## Holbeins, The

The Holbeins, a family of painters, had considerable influence on northern European art in the late 1400s to mid-1500s. Hans Holbein the Elder and his youngest son, Hans Holbein the Younger, were the two who enjoyed the most success. They came from the region around Augsburg, Germany, where the elder Holbein established his workshop. Hans the Younger traveled extensively, painting portraits of important public figures and learning about Renaissance artistic styles.

**Hans Holbein the Elder (ca. 1460–1534).** Scholars know nothing of the elder Holbein's artistic training. By about 1496 he had opened his workshop in Augsburg and had produced altarpieces for various churches in southern Germany. His early work has the bright coloring typical of late Gothic* art of the region, but his later pieces moved away from this style. For example, in a series of religious scenes completed in 1500, the artist used only shades of gray so as to resemble sculpture.

The 1516 altarpiece *St. Sebastian* marks another departure for the elder Holbein. In this picture, he focused attention on the central figure of the saint by clearing a space around him, and he unified the panels of the altarpiece with architectural elements that spill over onto the side panels. Hans the Elder also created portraits, designs for glass painting, and patterns for sculptors and goldsmiths. Among the artists of his day, only Albrecht DÜRER produced as many pieces and had as much influence.

**Hans Holbein the Younger (1497–1543).** Hans the Younger worked at his father's shop until 1516, when he moved to Basel, Switzerland. One of his first commissions was to illustrate a copy of *Praise of Folly* by the humanist* writer Desiderius ERASMUS. Later, Erasmus hired the younger Holbein to paint several portraits of him, which he gave to colleagues and patrons* as gifts. In religious paintings, the artist had a distinctive way of portraying spiritual figures. His *Body of the Dead Christ* (1521) shows a thin and decomposing human form, rather than the muscular figures often seen in religious works of the time.

In the late 1520s, Erasmus recommended Hans the Younger as a portrait painter to prominent people in England. As a result, the artist gained commissions from members of the court of HENRY VIII, including Sir Thomas MORE. The younger Holbein returned to Basel in 1529, but religious unrest between Catholics and Protestants led him to resettle in London. From 1532 to 1538 he served as court painter to Henry VIII, producing portraits, jewelry designs, miniatures, and murals. The portrait he painted of Henry VIII is one of the best-known images of the king. On several occasions, the artist traveled to other parts of Europe to paint portraits of Henry's potential brides. Hans the Younger had a significant influence on the next generation of English portrait painters, as well as on the Flemish* masters Peter Paul RUBENS and Anthony Van Dyck. (*See also* **Art; Art in Britain; Art in Germany.**)

* **Gothic** artistic style marked by bright colors, elongated proportions, and intricate detail

* **humanist** Renaissance expert in the humanities (the languages, literature, history, and speech and writing techniques of ancient Greece and Rome)

* **patron** supporter or financial sponsor of an artist or writer

* **Flemish** relating to Flanders, a region along the coasts of present-day Belgium, France, and the Netherlands

The Holy Roman Empire, a political organization made up of states in central Europe, existed from 962 until 1806. By the late 1400s, the empire covered an area that reached from France in the west to Denmark in the north and to Poland and Hungary in the east. This vast empire was one of the great powers of Europe during the Renaissance.

**Origins.** During the Middle Ages many viewed the Holy Roman Empire as the successor to the ancient Roman Empire. The pope had granted the title of emperor to Charlemagne, the king of the Franks, in A.D. 800. But the empire only took full shape in 962, when the pope crowned Otto I as emperor. Otto controlled the eastern lands of Charlemagne's old empire. In the 1100s and 1200s, the rulers began to refer to their realm as the Holy Roman Empire. The link between the empire and the Roman Catholic Church made the realm "holy."

The ruler of the Holy Roman Empire also held the title "king of the Romans." However, he received his two titles in different ways. Emperor Charles IV passed a law in 1356 decreeing that seven electors would have responsibility for choosing the king of the Romans. Four of these electors were secular* rulers and the other three were high church officials. This law, called the Golden Bull, laid out the exact procedure for choosing the king, up to and including his coronation.

* **secular** nonreligious; connected with everyday life

Originally, the king of the Romans became Holy Roman Emperor when the pope crowned him in a special ceremony in Rome. However, in 1508 MAXIMILIAN I assumed the title of "Elected Roman Emperor" without the aid of the pope because he was unable to pass through Italy to Rome. In 1530 Emperor CHARLES V became the last Holy Roman Emperor crowned in Italy. The emperors that followed were still elected and crowned king of the Romans. However, each took the title of emperor on the death of the old emperor without a separate coronation by the pope. Although the electors could choose any prince* as their emperor, between 1438 and 1740 the title always fell to a member of the HABSBURG DYNASTY.

* **prince** Renaissance term for the ruler of an independent state

**The Imperial Diet.** The Holy Roman Emperor did not hold absolute control over his realm. A legislative body known as the imperial diet had the power to approve or reject his decisions. The members of the diet were princes and representatives from imperial cities—that is, cities that fell directly under the control of the emperor, such as AUGSBURG, Frankfurt, Cologne, NÜRNBERG, Regensburg, STRASBOURG, and Ulm. In the early 1500s, the Holy Roman Empire included more than 70 imperial cities.

The members of the diet met only when the emperor summoned them. After 1489 the diet split into three separate groups, known as "colleges." The electors sat in one college, the imperial princes in another, and the representatives of imperial cities in a third. The college of imperial princes had two smaller divisions called "benches," one for secular princes and one for bishops and other church officials.

At the beginning of the session, the emperor presented various proposals for discussion. These often concerned the military, the justice system, or the collection of taxes. Representatives from each college dis-

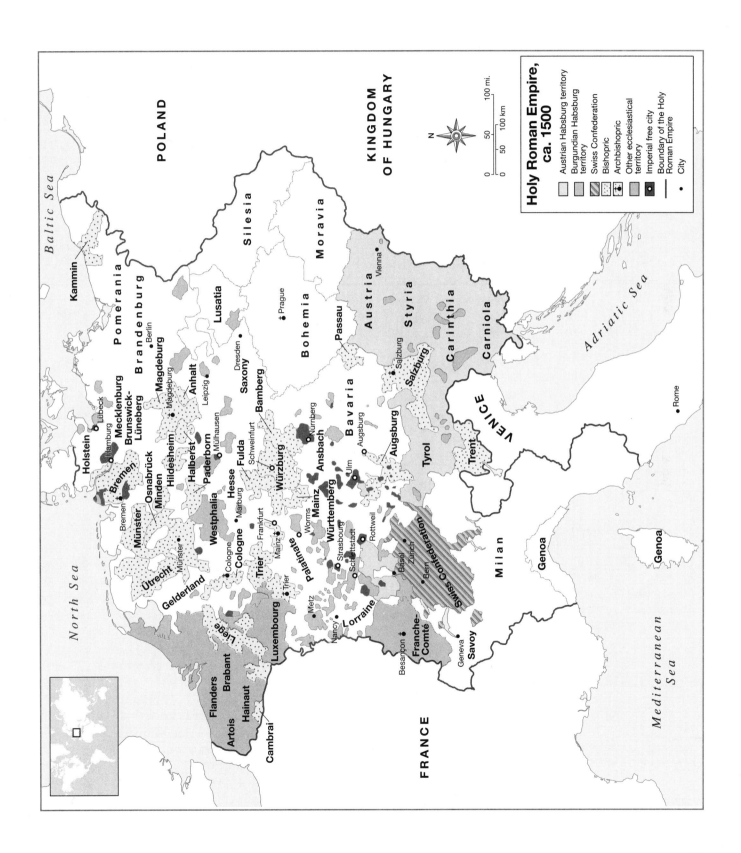

Holy Roman Empire, ca. 1500

Austrian Habsburg territory
Burgundian Habsburg territory
Swiss Confederation
Bishopric
Archbishopric
Other ecclesiastical territory
Imperial free city
Boundary of the Holy Roman Empire
City

100 mi.
100 km
50
50
0
0

Baltic Sea

POLAND

KINGDOM OF HUNGARY

Kammin

Pomerania

Brandenburg

Berlin

Magdeburg

Anhalt

Lusatia

Silesia

Moravia

Bohemia

Prague

Dresden

Saxony

Leipzig

Bamberg

Mülhausen

Schweinfurt

Passau

Austria

Vienna

Styria

Carinthia

Carniola

Salzburg

Salzburg

Adriatic Sea

Mecklenburg

Brunswick-Lüneberg

Lübeck

Hamburg

Holstein

Bremen

Bremen

Osnabrück

Minden

Hildesheim

Halberst

Paderborn

Fulda

Hesse

Würzburg

Nürnberg

Ansbach

Mainz

Bavaria

Augsburg

Augsburg

Ulm

Tyrol

Trent

VENICE

Rome

Münster

Münster

Westphalia

Marburg

Frankfurt

Cologne

Cologne

Worms

Mainz

Mainz

Palatinate

Württemberg

Württemberg

Strasbourg

Schlettstadt

Rottweil

Basel

Zürich

Bern

Swiss Confederation

Milan

Genoa

Genoa

Utrecht

Gelderland

Trier

Trier

Metz

Lorraine

Nancy

Besançon

Franche-Comté

Geneva

Savoy

Liège

Luxembourg

Flanders

Brabant

Hainaut

Artois

Cambrai

North Sea

Mediterranean Sea

FRANCE

This ink drawing by Joerg Breu the Elder is a tribute to the four men who ruled the Holy Roman Empire between 1438 and 1556—Albert II, Frederick III, Maximilian I, and Charles V.

cussed and revised the emperor's proposals. Only when all three colleges had hammered out a version that the emperor approved would the proposal become imperial law. Until the early 1600s, the diet met at irregular intervals. After 1663 it became a permanent governing body located in the imperial city of Regensburg.

**Reform and Reformation.** In the 1400s and 1500s, Holy Roman Emperors introduced a series of reforms to renew the Holy Roman Empire and give it greater security. For example, the imperial diet of 1495, which met in the city of Worms, proclaimed a permanent peace throughout the empire. This announcement aimed to restrict feuds within the realm.

In the early 1500s, the Protestant Reformation* swept across the Holy Roman Empire. Many imperial princes joined the new movement. In 1530 these Protestant princes presented a new declaration of faith at the imperial diet in Augsburg. From that time onward, disputes between Catholic and Protestant forces became more common in the empire.

Religious disputes interfered with the workings of the Chamber Court of Justice, the empire's highest court, which had been founded in 1495. In many cases, the court used religion as a basis for judging disputes, which led to calls for reform, especially from Protestants. Over time, another institution of justice, the imperial council, gained influence. In 1559 this council began to take over the function of a supreme court.

Protestant princes within the Holy Roman Empire formed an alliance against Catholics, known as the Schmalkaldic League. In 1446 they rose up in the Schmalkaldic War, but Charles V defeated them the following year. However, he could not wipe out the Protestant faith in his realm.

* **Protestant Reformation** religious movement that began in the 1500s as a protest against certain practices of the Roman Catholic Church and eventually let to the establishment of a variety of Protestant churches

**Renaissance Emperors**

Albert II (1438–1439)
Frederick III (1440–1493)
Maximilian I (1493–1519)
Charles V (1519–1556)
Ferdinand I (1558–1564)
Maximilian II (1564–1576)
Rudolf II (1576–1612)
Matthias (1612–1619)
Ferdinand II (1619–1637)

\* **serf** peasant who owes service and loyalty to a lord

In 1555 Protestant and Catholic princes reached a compromise called the Peace of Augsburg, which allowed each prince to choose the religion practiced in his realm. This agreement helped calm the religious aspects of the empire for the next 50 years.

However, religious issues continued to complicate the work of the diet. Members from Protestant areas often refused to discuss new taxes unless the diet also agreed to a debate on religious matters. In 1648 the diet finally settled on a method of treating religious and political issues separately.

**Social Unrest.** Like the rest of Europe, the Holy Roman Empire experienced a steady growth in population throughout the 1500s. Between 1500 and 1600 the population nearly doubled. This increase led to various problems, such as rising prices, falling wages, and shortages of agricultural products. These problems were most severe in towns, where about 10 percent of the population lived. Poverty increased, and with it came social unrest.

In the countryside, most peasants still lived as serfs\*. They depended on their lords and had to provide them with money, crops, or labor. The lords determined how peasants could use their land. They also controlled peasant marriages and had the power to prohibit peasants from moving from one place to another. Throughout the 1500s, lords in the Holy Roman Empire raised peasants' dues, making their living conditions still worse. In 1524 the serfs rose up in the PEASANTS' WAR, one of the greatest rural revolts in the history of the empire. Peasants demanded lower dues, an end to serfdom, and other changes. Although the princes crushed the revolt in 1525, local peasant uprisings continued during the 1500s and 1600s.

Despite problems and crises, the Holy Roman Empire was one of the strongest political systems in Europe during the Renaissance. It remained a major European power until the late 1600s. The Holy Roman Empire came to an end in 1806, when the last emperor, Francis II, gave up the imperial crown and the title of Holy Roman Emperor. (*See also* **Middle Ages.**)

## Homer

See *Translation.*

## Honor

The concept of honor played a key role in the societies of southern Europe during the Renaissance. Communities used the idea of honor to regulate behavior, social tensions, and conflict. The concept served to maintain social structures and to join different groups of people into a common culture that encouraged decency and respect.

A person might gain honor by being born into the right family or by achieving wealth, power, or fame. However, those who possessed honor had to behave in certain ways in order to maintain it. Codes of honor varied based on social position, power, and gender. The code of

* **medieval** referring to the Middle Ages, a period that began around A.D. 400 and ended around 1400 in Italy and 1500 in the rest of Europe

* **patronage** support or financial sponsorship

honor for nobles during the Renaissance drew largely on the code of medieval* knighthood, which stressed military ability, courtesy, and Christian virtue. Nobles of the 1400s and 1500s added manners and knowledge of the arts and humanities to this list. While noblemen continued to protect their honor through duels and war, they could also increase their glory through artistic patronage* and higher learning.

The concept of honor applied differently to women and men during the Renaissance. A woman's honor depended mostly on her sexual purity. Honorable women were good Christians, modest, and reserved. Women took care to protect their honor, as losing it could affect their chances for marriage in a society ruled by men. (*See also* **Chivalry; Duel; Women.**)

## Hospitals and Asylums

* **laypeople** those who are not members of the clergy

* **guild** association of craft and trade owners and workers that set standards for and represented the interests of its members

Renaissance hospitals and asylums provided spiritual and physical care, as well as limited medical care, to people with many different needs. The earlier "hospitals" of the Middle Ages were basically shelters for the poor and needy. They provided people with food and lodging, but they seldom offered specialized medical care. During the Renaissance, hospitals grew much larger and more advanced in their administration and use of medical treatment. This was particularly true in Italy, whose hospitals became the wonder of Europe.

**A Community of Care.** Traditional hospitals focused as much on spiritual care as on physical care. The earliest hospitals belonged to Roman Catholic monasteries, but during the 1300s laypeople* began to play a larger role in creating and running hospitals. Organizations such as guilds* and the religious groups called CONFRATERNITIES took charge, using members and their wives to perform such daily tasks as laundry and food preparation. They also hired a chief administrator to look after day-to-day business such as providing meals and supervising staff. A large part of the staff consisted of people staying in the hospital, who both gave and received care. A Catholic priest tended to the community's spiritual needs.

Despite the need for care, most communities had only one hospital for every thousand people. Of these hospitals, many were too small to serve the public adequately. Several had only one or two beds, while others had none at all. Some hospitals, however, received large monetary donations and became very wealthy. As a result, many even included banking among their services. As these hospitals gained wealth, political officials sought more control over them.

**The Changing Face of Care.** In the early 1400s governments began to merge, or consolidate, small hospitals to form larger ones. By creating one large hospital, authorities could pool resources to provide better care. In 1542, for example, Duke Cosimo I de' MEDICI merged hospitals in Tuscany (the region surrounding Florence) and placed them under the control of a group of government officials. These officials reviewed the hospitals' accounts and directed their excess funds to an orphanage in the capital.

As government authorities took greater control of hospitals, they developed a system to direct care more efficiently and to add more medical treatment. Small hospitals came into being to serve the needs of specific groups, such as people suffering from plague\* or syphilis (a sexually transmitted disease). Caretakers in these facilities had more knowledge about particular diseases and were more likely to be paid than those in earlier hospitals. Patients received a complete program of care that included food, rest, exercise, herbal remedies, and sometimes new forms of treatment.

In the 1500s nonmedical hospitals also began catering to specific groups of people. Asylums provided shelter for orphans, widows, battered women, former prostitutes, and Jews converting to Christianity. Confraternities played a large role in running them, though the clergy came to dominate the field over time. Asylums used a strict discipline of work, education, and spiritual exercises to reform troubled individuals and help prepare them to reenter society. At times this discipline became a form of punishment, and some hospitals for the poor became little more than prisons.

Hospital buildings also changed during the Renaissance. The earliest hospitals had been similar in design to monasteries, with separate quarters for men and women, a common dining room, and living areas for the staff. Hospitals of the Renaissance became larger and grander, partly as a way for towns to show off their wealth. They also included classical\* design elements, such as porticoes\*, which were both useful and beautiful. One of the most impressive Renaissance hospitals was the Maggiore Hospital in Milan, Italy. This large facility included a complex sanitation system; storage for food, water, ice, and drugs; and separate living areas for upper-class patients. (*See also* **Medicine; Poverty and Charity.**)

* **plague**   highly contagious and often fatal disease that wiped out much of Europe's population in the mid-1300s and reappeared periodically over the next three centuries; also known as the Black Death

* **classical**   in the tradition of ancient Greece and Rome

* **portico**   porch or walkway supported by regularly spaced columns

Humanism was a cultural movement that promoted the study of the humanities—the languages, literature, and history of ancient Greece and Rome. Humanist scholars used the works of ancient authors as models in writing, scholarship, and all aspects of life. The movement began in Italy in the 1300s and eventually spread throughout Europe. It had a great impact on many areas of Renaissance culture, including literature, education, law, and the arts. By the mid-1600s humanism began to fade as other intellectual movements emerged. All the same, it left a lasting impression on European culture and society.

## ORIGINS OF HUMANISM

The humanist movement was born in Italy. However, its roots lay partly in the work of French scholars of the late Middle Ages. Humanism blossomed in Italy as scholars became increasingly familiar with classical\* texts.

* **classical**   in the tradition of ancient Greece and Rome

* **antiquity** era of the ancient Mediterranean cultures of Greece and Rome, ending around A.D. 400

* **civic** related to a city, a community, or citizens

* **faction** party or interest group within a larger group

* **medieval** referring to the Middle Ages, a period that began around A.D. 400 and ended around 1400 in Italy and 1500 in the rest of Europe

* **papacy** office and authority of the pope

* **rhetoric** art of speaking or writing effectively

* **secular** nonreligious; connected with everyday life

**Early Italian Humanists.** During the 1100s, Latin grammar, literature, and history were widely studied in France. French poets produced books on these subjects as well as poetry in Latin. By comparison, Italian writers showed little interest in these subjects. However, after about 1180 Italian scholars began to read Latin works and to produce Latin poems and grammar manuals of their own.

Italians took an interest in antiquity* partly because they felt a close connection to ancient Rome. Writers of the 1200s, such as Brunetto Latini of Florence, saw Rome as a good model for the Italian city-states of their time. Latini and many other writers of his day encouraged Italians to return to the Roman values of civic* harmony and cooperation. They hoped that these values would help end the power struggles between rival factions* in the city-states. To promote the ideas of ancient Rome, many scholars in northern Italy began translating Latin works into their own language. Latini translated several texts by the Roman orator CICERO.

Around the same time, Italian poets began producing Latin verses in the style of the ancients. Lovato dei Lovati (ca. 1240–1309) was one of the first Italian writers to capture the style and rhythm of classical poetry. An expert on ancient literature, he considered the Roman style to be the highest form of verse. By the early 1300s, the interest in classical style had spread to prose writing. In 1315 Alberto Mussato published a work of history and a tragic drama based on ancient examples. Gradually, authors abandoned medieval* styles and adopted classical models for other forms of writing, such as letters and speeches.

**Petrarch.** Francesco Petrarca (1304–1374), known as PETRARCH, was one of the most influential Italian humanists. Born in central Italy, he grew up in the French city of Avignon, home to the papacy* at the time. Petrarch trained as a lawyer, but later abandoned the field to study classical literature. Impressed by the historical sites in Rome, he held ancient Roman culture in high regard. In Petrarch's view, Roman culture had fallen into a decline after the death of the emperor Constantine in the 300s. Europe had then entered a long "dark age," from which it was just beginning to emerge. In this way, Petrarch divided history into ancient, medieval, and modern eras.

Petrarch stressed the importance of rhetoric* as a form of argument. In his view, rhetoric had the power to convince people to make positive changes in their lives. Although scholars of the Middle Ages had placed more emphasis on logic in argument, Petrarch argued that simply knowing what goodness is would not make a person better. The stirring words of a skilled orator, however, could inspire people to become good.

Petrarch was also one of the first humanists to introduce religious ideas to the movement. Early humanists had been mainly secular* in their outlook and interests. Perhaps inspired by his years in the papal seat of Avignon, Petrarch added various Christian elements to humanism. This spiritual approach held particular appeal for religious scholars in northern Europe.

**The Growth of Italian Humanism.** Humanism first took hold in Florence and spread from there to the rest of Italy. Coluccio SALUTATI

(1331–1406), the chancellor of the city, promoted the movement. He invited other humanists, including Poggio Bracciolini and the Greek scholar Manuel Chrysoloras, to live in Florence. This generation of intellectuals unearthed a large number of ancient texts, including works on rhetoric that became the basis of humanist education.

The growth of humanism in Florence was closely tied to the artistic Renaissance of the 1400s. Artists such as DONATELLO studied classical principles of art and imitated ancient models. Leon Battista ALBERTI wrote a landmark book, *On Painting* (1436), in which he argued that painters should study history and poetry and associate with poets and orators. Alberti's book played a key role in elevating painting from a craft to one of the liberal arts.

Humanist ideas spread rapidly throughout Italy. In the early 1400s Manuel Chrysoloras traveled to the northern province of Lombardy to teach Greek. Other scholars brought humanism to Milan, Venice, Padua, and Verona. By the mid-1400s the movement had reached Rome, where Pope NICHOLAS V actively supported humanism by hiring humanist scholars to translate Greek texts into Latin. Alfonso I, the king of Naples, also encouraged the growth of humanism. The prominent humanist Lorenzo VALLA and the poet Jacopo SANNAZARO did their most important work in Naples.

**Humanist Literature and Education.** Humanists wrote in a variety of literary forms, including poetry, dialogue, letters, history, and biography. One of the more popular genres* was the personal letter, an idea revived by Petrarch. Later humanists, such as Salutati, used this form frequently. Some writers produced lengthy letters in which they explored and debated ideas in detail. Others kept their letters brief and examined more complex issues in dialogues. Humanist dialogues usually featured two characters arguing different sides of an issue, such as the nature of nobility or the relative merits of pleasure and virtue.

Humanists explored many of their ideas about culture and society in works of history. Humanists broke with the medieval view of history as a steady decline from a glorious past to the present. Instead, they saw their own era as a time of revival after the long dark age that had begun with the fall of Rome. They also believed that the lives of historical figures could serve as valuable examples of virtuous behavior. As a result, they became interested in biography, a form of writing unknown during the Middle Ages.

Humanists also introduced major changes to the educational system. They rejected the medieval curriculum, which had emphasized logic, religion, and writing according to strict rules. Instead, they favored a system based on five subjects—grammar, rhetoric, poetry, history, and moral philosophy—all based on the classics of ancient Greece and Rome. They argued that all civilized people needed this kind of education because it would teach them to speak and write well and to make sound moral decisions. This view came to dominate Italian, and later European, education for hundreds of years.

* **genre** literary form

The humanist movement began in Italy in the late Middle Ages. This detail from a painting by Domenico Ghirlandaio, painted in the late 1480s, features several famous humanists, including Marsilio Ficino and Angelo Poliziano.

## SPREAD OF HUMANISM

During the 1400s humanism spread throughout Europe. Scholars in many nations learned to read Latin and Greek, and classical learning became a basic part of education. As translations of ancient works became more widely available, writers continued to apply classical ideas to the important issues of their own day.

**Humanism in France.** In the mid-1300s, Italian scholars at the papal court in Avignon brought humanism to France. When the papacy returned to Rome in the early 1400s, the center of French humanism shifted to the College of Navarre in Paris. Known as the "cradle of French humanism," the school attracted scholars such as Jean de Gerson, Jean de Montreuil, and Nicolas de Clamanges. In the 1450s Guillaume Fichet introduced Italian humanism to the University of Paris. He also founded the first French printing press, which produced editions of classical works and books by Italian humanists.

French humanism reached its peak in the 1500s under Jacques Lefèvre d'Ètaples (ca. 1460–1536) and Guillaume Budé (1467–1540). Lefèvre first gained fame through his translations and commentaries on the works of the Greek philosopher ARISTOTLE. He later became a leader among Christian humanists with his translations of the Bible. Budé wrote books on literature, Roman law and coinage, and Greek grammar. At the same time, he served as a diplomat, secretary, and cultural adviser to the French king FRANCIS I. In 1530 Budé founded the Royal College, which provided free public instruction in Greek and Hebrew. The College gradually expanded its program to cover a wide range of academic subjects.

In the late 1500s a series of civil wars broke out in France over the issue of religious rights for Protestants. Prominent French humanists spoke out on various sides of the debate over religious reform.

Meanwhile, other humanists, such as Henri Estienne, continued to focus their efforts on the critical study of classical works. Through their influence, the works of the Roman authors Seneca and Tacitus came to public attention. These authors' writings eventually replaced those of Cicero as models for European writers. French scholars also exposed many forgeries, modern works created to resemble ancient ones.

**Humanism in Spain.** Humanist ideas reached Spain in the early 1400s. Spanish translations of classical texts and Italian humanist works spread throughout the country. By the mid-1400s educated Spaniards began to express an interest in the country's Roman heritage. They explored historical sites in Spain and studied the works of Spanish-born classical authors.

In the 1490s, Spanish humanism began to take on a more international flavor. The leading Spanish humanist of this period was Antonio de Nebrija (1444–1522). Nebrija promoted education reforms that emphasized classical studies. He also produced Latin and Spanish grammar texts. His Spanish grammar was the first such text in a modern language.

In 1516 the throne of Spain went to Charles I, who later went on to become Holy Roman Emperor* as CHARLES V. Leading Spanish humanists, such as Juan Luis VIVES and Diego Hurtado de Mendoza, helped promote the new king's political goals. In their writing they expressed support for eliminating abuses within the Roman Catholic Church, uniting the Christian world under the leadership of Spain, and converting the Turks and Moors* to Christianity. In Charles's court the ideas of the Dutch humanist Desiderius ERASMUS gained wide popularity. However, during the 1520s and 1530s some Catholic leaders came to see Erasmus as a supporter of Protestant ideas. Many of his supporters were jailed and his works were banned.

**Humanism in Portugal.** Humanism grew slowly in Portugal. Humanist ideas first began to have an impact there in the mid-1400s. Over the next 100 years, Portuguese monarchs such as Alfonso V, João II, Manuel I, and João III welcomed groups of humanists at the court. At the same time, Portuguese scholars studied abroad in Paris, Padua, Bologna, Louvain, and Salamanca, where they encountered humanist ideas. The Portuguese diplomat and historian Damião de Góis (1502–1574) worked closely with Erasmus and met the religious reformers Martin LUTHER and Philipp MELANCHTHON.

Humanist educational reforms, however, were slow to take root in Portugal. Not until the late 1530s did the university at Coimbra update its curriculum to place more emphasis on classical grammar and rhetoric. An independent school, known as the College of the Arts, opened in Coimbra in 1547. More than 800 students enrolled in the first year.

Beginning in the 1540s, religious forces in Portugal gradually suppressed the humanist works of Erasmus. Authorities banned his writings because they feared they would promote Protestant ideas. Eventually they banned all books in English, Flemish*, and German (the languages of Protestant Europe). Several humanists were jailed as heretics*. Under

* **Holy Roman Emperor** ruler of the Holy Roman Empire, a political body in central Europe composed of several states that existed until 1806

* **Moor** Muslim from North Africa; Moorish invaders conquered much of Spain during the Middle Ages

* **Flemish** relating to Flanders, a region along the coasts of present-day Belgium, France, and the Netherlands

* **heretic** person who rejects the doctrine of an established church

* **Jesuit** refers to a Roman Catholic religious order founded by St. Ignatius Loyola and approved in 1540

the influence of the Jesuits*, Portuguese education became solidly Catholic.

**Humanism in Germany and the Netherlands.** In northern Europe, humanism developed a distinct character that emphasized scholarship, religion, and national culture. Trade with Italy first brought humanist ideas to northern Europe. In addition, the major church councils held at Constance (in Germany) and Basel (in Switzerland) brought many well-known humanists to the region in the early 1400s. These humanists included Poggio Bracciolini and Pier Paolo VERGERIO, who later returned to northern Europe as visitors.

Debates arose about the merits of humanism as schools in northern Europe considered whether to adopt it. Humanist scholars spoke out in favor of the new learning and prepared the way for its acceptance. Writers such as Erasmus, Melanchthon, and Rudolf AGRICOLA produced textbooks that eventually replaced older texts from the Middle Ages. By the mid-1550s universities in Germany and the Netherlands had firmly embraced humanist ideas.

Humanism developed a strong religious element in northern Europe. Erasmus promoted the idea of learned piety, in which the goal of studying was "to become better no less than wiser." Both Erasmus and Melanchthon believed that a decline in learning had led to corruption in the church. In their view, a revival of sound learning would bring about a renewal of religious faith. Some people believed that humanist ideas, such as the importance of studying Scripture in its original languages, had played a role in starting the Protestant Reformation*.

The outbreak of the THIRTY YEARS' WAR in 1618 interrupted academic life in Germany and the Netherlands. By the time peace returned in 1648, humanism had lost much of its momentum. In the late 1600s the rise of modern science and the Baroque* movement in the arts replaced humanism as the main intellectual influences in northern Europe.

* **Protestant Reformation** religious movement that began in the 1500s as a protest against certain practices of the Roman Catholic Church and eventually led to the establishment of a variety of Protestant churches

* **Baroque** artistic style of the 1600s characterized by movement, drama, and grandness of scale

**Humanism in Britain.** In Britain, an interest in classical ideas blossomed in the late 1400s. Several British scholars traveled to Italy to study classical languages. The arrival of printing in Britain in 1475, which made books in Latin and Greek more available, contributed to the rise of classical learning.

Sir Thomas MORE (1478–1535), who served as chancellor to the English king HENRY VIII, was the greatest early British humanist. His home became a gathering place for humanist scholars such as Erasmus, who stayed there during his first visit to England. Two prominent medical scholars—Thomas Linacre and Thomas Elyot—were also members of More's circle. Linacre translated the works of the Greek physician GALEN into Latin (but not into English, since he did not want patients trying to diagnose themselves). Elyot, on the other hand, translated ancient medical texts into English. He also wrote on politics and education and compiled the first English dictionary of classical Latin.

English humanism reached its peak during the early 1500s under Henry VIII. After England broke away from the Roman Catholic Church in the 1530s, scholars began focusing more attention on religious ideas.

Sir Thomas More, shown here in a portrait by Hans Holbein the Younger, was a leading English humanist of the Renaissance. In addition to his scholarly work, More served as chancellor to the English king Henry VIII.

However, humanist ideas continued to influence Renaissance culture in England. During the 1600s, writers such as John MILTON and William SHAKESPEARE drew heavily on Greek and Roman history and literature in their works. British architects such as Inigo JONES used classical styles in their building designs.

Humanist ideas began to affect Scotland during the reign of James IV (1488–1513). King James, a well-educated man who spoke several languages, encouraged the founding of new universities in Scotland. He also passed a law in 1496 providing for the eldest sons of all major landowners to study Latin, law, and the arts. Throughout the 1500s and early 1600s, Renaissance humanism had an impact on Scottish education, law, religion, philosophy, literature, medicine, and astronomy.

The political turmoil of the English Civil War (1642–1648) brought an end to the British Renaissance. Even so, humanism and classical culture

## Equal Opportunity Humanism

Although men dominated Renaissance culture, a few women became noted humanist scholars. The most famous was Isotta Nogarola of Verona, a student of Latin and Greek, who was perhaps the most learned woman of the 1400s. Another outstanding female humanist was Cassandra Fedele of Venice. In the late 1480s Queen Isabella of Spain invited the 22-year-old Fedele to join her court. However, the Venetian senate prevented Fedele from accepting the offer, claiming that the state could not afford to lose her.

remained a powerful influence in Britain. During the 1700s and 1800s architects designed new buildings in the classical style, and education focused on Latin and Greek languages and literature.

**Legal Humanism.** At the beginning of the Renaissance, European law was based on the ancient Roman civil law, known as the *Corpus iuris civilis*. The Roman emperor Justinian had put together this code in the 500s. The work contained many contradictions and linguistic problems that medieval legal scholars had tried to resolve through logical analysis. These scholars believed that the *Corpus* presented a set of unchanging, universal laws that were as valid for their own time as they had been for the ancient Romans. They attempted to make the laws of the *Corpus* fit the circumstances of medieval Europe.

In the 1400s humanist scholars began to challenge this approach. Italian writer Lorenzo Valla criticized the use of logical analysis in addressing the problems of the *Corpus*. Valla pointed out that judges had used many of the Latin legal terms in the work in several different ways. He claimed that inconsistencies of this sort were impossible to avoid. He also argued that the law is not a fixed set of truths, but something that changes over time. Inspired by Valla's work, the French humanist Guillaume Budé set out to interpret the difficult passages in the *Corpus*. Drawing on his knowledge of Roman history and literature, he clarified the meanings of many contradictory terms in the text.

The work of Valla, Budé, François Hotman, and others weakened the authority of Roman law in northern Europe. These writers argued that legal scholars should study the laws of many lands, not just those of ancient Rome, and select the best legal traditions as a foundation for their nations' laws. They moved away from the heavy emphasis on classical thought found in early humanism and introduced a more sophisticated method of reading and criticizing sources. (*See also* **Biography and Autobiography; Catholic Reformation and Counter-Reformation; Classical Antiquity; Classical Scholarship; Councils; Education; Forgeries; History, Writing of; Ideas, Spread of; Individualism; Latin Language and Literature; Man, Dignity of; Popes and Papacy; Protestant Reformation; Translation; Wars of Religion.**)

*** rhetoric** art of speaking or writing effectively

It is difficult to make generalizations about humor during the Renaissance because the kinds of things that provoked laughter varied by country, language, and social class. In all parts of Europe, however, laughter was considered an important—even essential—part of life. Scholars often quoted the words of the ancient Greek philosopher ARISTOTLE, who described man as a being capable of laughter. Scholars of drama, medicine, and rhetoric* discussed the nature of humor and laughter. In the fields of drama and fiction, the Renaissance produced some of the greatest comic writers ever.

**Humor on the Stage.** Comedy played a major role in both formal and informal performances throughout the Renaissance. Renaissance festivals often featured comic performances that made a mockery of the established social order. The most important of these festivals was Carnival, a period of revelry before the sober days of Lent (the 40 weekdays leading up to Easter). Carnival festivities in all parts of Europe included comic plays. French celebrations involved "fools' plays," known as *sotties,* while Polish events included crude comedies in a realistic style. Songs with mocking or obscene lyrics also formed a part of some Carnival events.

Some early plays featured political humor. The French king Louis XII encouraged political comedies because they helped him to learn what was going on in the state. Other comedies based their humor on stock characters and themes, such as a cheating wife deceiving her dim-witted husband. Although most of these early farces* were penned by unnamed authors, a few well-known poets wrote in this style in France and England. In Italy, a kind of farce called COMMEDIA DELL'ARTE developed in the 1500s. Commedia dell'arte also involved standard character types caught in typical situations. This style of drama featured physical action and broad comedy, with plots ranging from the fairly realistic to the wildly fantastic. Humanist* comedies provided a more intellectual alternative to farce. Humanists of the Renaissance imitated the comedies of the ancient Roman playwrights Plautus and Terence. This classical* style of comedy arose in Italy and spread across Europe. The Italian statesman and author Niccolò MACHIAVELLI produced an obscene comedy called *The Mandrake Root* that is widely viewed as a masterpiece. Another brilliant work in this style is *Ralph Roister Doister,* by the English playwright Nicolas Udall.

In addition to staged performances, humor had a regular place at royal and noble courts in the person of the fool, or jester. Dressed in a costume that featured a cap with bells on it, the fool was the one person at the court allowed to ridicule everyone and everything. Fools appeared often as characters in literary works, such as the plays of William SHAKESPEARE. However, the fool's function was not always strictly comical. In many works, he served more to instruct than to amuse.

**Humor on the Page.** Like the drama of the period, literature of the 1400s and 1500s was largely comic. Renaissance humanists frequently gathered humorous material from classical Greek and Roman literature. They particularly enjoyed collecting short Latin works called *facetiae,* which could be jokes, serious stories, riddles, or moral fables. Humanists usually did not explain why they chose particular stories for their joke collections. Some, including the Italian poet PETRARCH, drew heavily on the ideas of the ancient Roman writer CICERO about what was funny.

Humanists also enjoyed creating their own humor—especially for the purpose of satire*. The Dutch scholar Desiderius ERASMUS was particularly good at using humor in his satire. One of his funniest works, "The Abbot* and the Learned Lady," ends with the laughter of the witty, educated lady who has outsmarted the rude, ignorant churchman. German and French humanists of the 1500s produced some extremely funny works of satire by writing mock letters in deliberately bad Latin.

* **farce**   light dramatic piece that features broad comedy, improbable situations, stereotyped characters, and exaggerated physical action

* **humanist**   referring to a Renaissance cultural movement promoting the study of the humanities (the languages, literature, and history of ancient Greece and Rome) as a guide to living

* **classical**   in the tradition of ancient Greece and Rome

* **satire**   literary or artistic work ridiculing human wickedness and foolishness

* **abbot**   male head of an abbey or monastery

## A Feast for the Eyes

Humor was so important during the Renaissance that even cooks found ways to use it in their art. *Of Honorable Pleasure,* an Italian cookbook published in 1475, recommends serving a cooked peacock dressed in its own skin and feathers, so that it looks alive. It goes on to explain how to make the bird appear to breathe fire, a trick designed "to make the people laugh and wonder." A Roman feast in 1513 included rabbits served with their skins on, while live rabbits hopped around the room and on the tables, to the amusement of the guests.

* **epic**   long poem about the adventures of a hero

* **convention**   established practice, custom

* **Protestant Reformation**   religious movement that began in the 1500s as a protest against certain practices of the Roman Catholic Church and eventually led to the establishment of a variety of Protestant churches

Other Renaissance writers turned to verse for their comedy. One of the Italian comic writers' favorite forms was the mock epic*, a takeoff on a highly respected literary form. The famous poem *Orlando Furioso* (Mad Roland), by the Italian poet Ludovico ARIOSTO, contains elements of the mock epic style. Another well-known mock epic is *The Chess Game* by Jan Kochanowski, Poland's most famous Renaissance poet. Poets in England or France do not appear to have used this style, but they did mock the conventions* of other poetic forms. For example, Petrarch had set certain standards for love poetry that involved praising the beloved in extravagant terms. Later writers made fun of Petrarch's style, as in Shakespeare's well-known sonnet "My mistress' eyes are nothing like the sun."

Humor appeared in both long and short fiction works during the Renaissance. Miguel de CERVANTES of Spain and François RABELAIS of France incorporated humor in novels that are still widely read today. Most French comic authors wrote shorter stories, often inspired by Italian sources. For example, MARGARET OF NAVARRE based several comic stories in her *Heptameron* on the famous *Decameron* (1353) by Italian author Giovanni BOCCACCIO. Some French stories, such as the collection *How to Succeed,* by Béroalde de Verville (written around 1612), were highly obscene.

In England one popular form of humor was the "jest," a very short story with a punch line (much like a modern joke). Writers collected these comic stories into jestbooks, which were similar to the Italian collections of *facetiae.* Jestbooks also became popular in Germany in the late 1500s, and some examples appeared in Spain and Italy.

**Humor in the Visual Arts.** The comic elements found in Renaissance literature also appeared in the art of the period. Art often used humor to deliver moral or religious messages. During the Protestant Reformation*, Protestant leaders put out illustrated pamphlets that portrayed their enemies as animals or showed the devil playing a Catholic monk like a musical instrument. However, not all humorous art had a moral message. In the late 1520s artist Giulio Romano painted a room at a palace in Mantua with lifelike figures of giants who appear to be pulling down the walls and pillars of the room. This witty style of illusion, known as *trompe l'oeil* (fool the eye), was very popular at the time.

In the early 1500s, artists began painting in a style known as grotesque, based on ancient Roman wall paintings. Grotesques often portray humans and animals in a fantastic manner, with leaves, flowers, and curly lines where arms and legs should be. The famous Italian artist MICHELANGELO BUONARROTI created several works in this style. Many grotesques still exist on the walls of museums and Italian palaces. Humor also found its way into Renaissance sculpture. The Boboli Gardens of Florence, Italy, built in the 1500s, contain such comic statues as a fat dwarf sitting on a turtle. (*See also* **Art; Drama; Drama, English; Drama, French; English Language and Literature; French Language and Literature; Italian Language and Literature.**)

I n the 1400s the central European kingdom of Hungary experienced its own Renaissance. Learning, literature, and art flourished during these years, and Hungary's Renaissance attracted and produced some of Europe's leading scholars. This glorious period came to an end in 1526, when Hungarian forces suffered defeat by the Ottoman Turks* at the Battle of Mohács. After this defeat, ideas from northern Europe began to have a substantial impact on the culture of the newly divided kingdom.

**The Hungarian Renaissance.** The bishop of Várad, Johannes Vitéz of Zredna (1408–1472), played a key role in bringing about the Hungarian Renaissance. Vitéz, who later became an archbishop and the leader of the Hungarian church, was a major patron* of artists and scholars throughout Europe. He also founded a university in the city of Pozsony.

Vitéz had served under the Hungarian military hero Johannes Hunyadi, and he played a leading role in putting Hunyadi's son, Matthias Corvinus, on the throne of Hungary in 1458. He also helped form Corvinus's court, which became an important center of scholarship and the arts. Located in the city of Buda, the court boasted a new royal palace and a magnificent library. It became a haven for leading humanists* from around Europe. At one time the great Italian writer Marsilio FICINO even considered moving to the Hungarian court. Corvinus was a generous patron of the arts, and many foreign authors dedicated works to him.

Hungary had a long tradition of scholarship. For hundreds of years, Hungarian students had traveled to other parts of Europe to attend foreign schools. The first recorded undergraduate at England's Oxford University was Hungarian. The wealthy students attended the universities of Padua and Bologna in Italy, while most others studied in Vienna or Cracow. After completing their schooling, some Hungarians remained abroad as teachers. One of these was Janus Pannonius, whose fame as a poet and politician spread to many countries. However, most Hungarian students returned to their homeland to pursue careers in politics or in the church.

Latin was the main language of religious, political, and cultural life in Hungary. The kingdom's borders contained people of many ethnic backgrounds, all with different languages. Latin provided a common tongue for these various peoples. Most Hungarian literature was written in Latin until 1400, when some scholars and writers began to use their local languages. However, Latin remained the chief tongue for the leading humanists, who came from many different lands. Hungary was the last country in Europe to abandon the use of Latin as a second language.

The Hungarian Renaissance changed in 1526, when Turkish forces defeated the Hungarians at the Battle of Mohács. This battle split the kingdom into three parts. The Turks controlled one area, the Holy Roman Emperor* FERDINAND I ruled another, and the third was under the control of a rival king, Johannes Zápolya. Hungary's humanists scattered, taking positions at the courts of the emperor, the king, and various nobles in the region. After Zápolya died in 1540, the HABSBURG

* **Ottoman Turks**  Turkish followers of Islam who founded the Ottoman Empire in the 1300s; the empire eventually included large areas of eastern Europe, the Middle East, and northern Africa

* **patron**  supporter or financial sponsor of an artist or writer

* **humanist**  referring to a Renaissance cultural movement promoting the study of the humanities (the languages, literature, and history of ancient Greece and Rome) as a guide to living

* **Holy Roman Emperor**  ruler of the Holy Roman Empire, a political body in central Europe composed of several states that existed until 1806

An Italian artist created this marble carving of the head of Hungarian king Matthias Corvinus in the 1480s. Corvinus's court, located in the city of Buda, was an important center of scholarship and the arts.

* **Protestant Reformation**   religious movement that began in the 1500s as a protest against certain practices of the Roman Catholic Church and eventually led to the establishment of a variety of Protestant churches

* **vernacular**   native language or dialect of a region or country

* **Counter-Reformation**   actions taken by the Roman Catholic Church after 1540 to oppose Protestantism

DYNASTY assumed control of all the non-Turkish parts of Hungary. They would rule the kingdom for the next 400 years.

**Influence of the Protestant Reformation.** In the 1530s, new ideas promoted by the Protestant Reformation* began to take root in Hungary. Latin and Greek traditions came to play a smaller role in Hungarian culture. They slowly gave way to the ideas of northern humanists, such as Desiderius ERASMUS and Philipp MELANCHTHON. At the same time, the use of vernacular* languages, rather than Latin, increased. The publication of a Hungarian-Latin grammar in 1539 gave a further boost to the use of local languages.

One leading Hungarian scholar of the early 1500s, Antonius Verantius, spoke five languages and held an important position in the Hungarian church. He also served as a personal representative of the king and made several official visits to the Turkish court between 1555 and 1568. On one of these trips, Verantius was part of a group that discovered the Ankara monument, an ancient tribute to the Roman emperor Augustus.

Faustus Verantius, the nephew of Antonius, has been called the greatest inventor of his day after the famous LEONARDO DA VINCI. Faustus's book *New Machines,* published in 1596, featured 56 original designs for mills, bridges, boats, and other devices. One of his "machines" was an early parachute, which some scholars claim the inventor actually tested by jumping off a tower in Venice. Faustus was also the author of one of the most famous multilanguage dictionaries of the time.

The Counter-Reformation* of the mid-1500s helped reestablish ties between Hungary and Italian culture. However, Protestantism still grew rapidly in the eastern region of Transylvania, which enjoyed considerable independence because of an arrangement with the Turks. This progressive region allowed its citizens to choose their religion and recognized people of different nationalities as equal under the law. No other European country showed a similar degree of tolerance at this time.

Most Hungarian literature of the late 1500s served political or religious purposes. Protestants favored the use of drama as a tool for expressing their views. Most Hungarian plays of the time were written in prose, usually in a realistic style. The 1500s also saw great achievements in poetry, notably the work of Sebestyén Tinódi and Bálint Balassi. The two wrote many songs about battles, inspired by the recent war against the Turks. Because of a lack of printing presses in Hungary, most of these works were published in Italy, Poland, or Germany. Local presses later appeared in the kingdom to keep humanist scholarship alive in the divided land. (*See also* **Art in Central Europe; Catholic Reformation and Counter-Reformation; Humanism; Ottoman Empire; Protestant Reformation.**)

## Ideas, Spread of

The Renaissance was a time of new ideas. Scholars not only rediscovered the works of ancient artists and writers, they also promoted their own views on science, religion, and education. Through word

of mouth, personal letters, and scholarly writings, they passed their ideas on to others. Schools and libraries also helped promote knowledge, so that eventually Renaissance thought spread to all areas of Europe.

**Early Developments.** Most scholars credit the Italian poet PETRARCH with setting the new ideas of the Renaissance in motion. His studies of ancient writers, especially CICERO, led him to the conclusion that the glory of the ancient world had been lost during the Middle Ages and that scholars should work to revive it. He expressed this view in his personal letters, which he gathered in two collections. He also produced other works praising ancient Rome, including biographies of great men from the past. His works inspired a generation of scholars to study the knowledge of ancient cultures.

The educational system helped spread Petrarch's views across Italy and into the rest of Europe. Humanists* such as Guarino GUARINI and VITTORINO DA FELTRE founded schools throughout northern Italy that focused on the study of the humanities. In these schools, new ideas flourished. The new style of schooling was the biggest change to take place in education in more than 1,000 years—and it lasted until well into the 1900s.

The revival of classical* studies occurred alongside an artistic revival in the Italian city of Florence. As a result, the enthusiasm for the ancient world spread to artists. In the early 1400s artists such as DONATELLO and Filippo BRUNELLESCHI began to study and copy the styles of classical art and architecture. Although most of these artists were not scholars themselves, many of them associated with humanists who taught them about ancient cultures. The new knowledge they acquired raised the status of art as a profession. Artists came to be viewed as part of the humanist tradition, not as mere crafts workers. Throughout the 1400s, humanists continued to pass classical knowledge on to artists by word of mouth. For example, the Italian painter BOTTICELLI learned about classical mythology from his humanist friends and made it the basis for several of his paintings.

The development of research libraries also helped promote classical knowledge. Cosimo de' MEDICI, the leader of Florence, funded a library in his home city where humanist scholars could read rare books. It housed both Latin and Greek works. Over the course of the 1400s, increasing numbers of scholars learned the Greek language and began discussing and debating ideas from ancient Greek culture.

**Changes After 1450.** The spread of Renaissance ideas accelerated after 1450. One factor was the conquest of the eastern city of CONSTANTINOPLE by the Ottoman Turks* in 1453. This event brought many Greek scholars from the east to Italy, following in the steps of other important scholars who had moved to the west earlier. Their knowledge of the language, and the books they brought with them, greatly expanded Greek studies. The invention of the printing press around 1455 also played a major role in the spread of ideas. Printing created identical copies of ancient texts, making it easier for humanists to correct errors in existing versions.

* **humanist**    Renaissance expert in the humanities (the languages, literature, history, and speech and writing techniques of ancient Greece and Rome)

* **classical**    in the tradition of ancient Greece and Rome

* **Ottoman Turks**    Turkish followers of Islam who founded the Ottoman Empire in the 1300s; the empire eventually included large areas of eastern Europe, the Middle East, and northern Africa

**\* vernacular**   native language or dialect of a region or country

Scholars also translated Greek works into Latin and both Greek and Latin works into vernacular\* tongues. Translations made the works of ancient writers available to the general reading public. In the 1460s, the Italian scholar Marsilio FICINO translated the complete writings of the Greek philosopher PLATO into Latin. For the first time in more than 1,000 years, readers could know Plato firsthand. The ideas of Plato influenced Western writers in many areas, including poetry and philosophy.

Humanists also promoted their ideas through oratory, the art of public speaking. Speeches were a part of all kinds of occasions, including visits from important foreign figures to a city or court, the opening of a new school year, and church sermons. For example, the philosopher Heinrich AGRIPPA of Nettesheim opened the school year at a French university with a speech arguing that women were superior to men. The Dutch scholar Desiderius ERASMUS wrote a speech against war for a character called Peace.

Humanists frequently argued with each other about their ideas and character. For example, Erasmus engaged in a famous war of words with critics of his biblical scholarship. In the 1500s, Protestants and Catholics frequently attacked each other's religious views in public. Arguments such as these became a powerful means of spreading new ideas. The printing press turned private debates into "pamphlet wars," which enabled people on all sides of religious, political, and scientific debates to air their views. (*See also* **Books and Manuscripts; Classical Antiquity; Classical Scholarship; Greek Émigrés; Gutenberg, Johann; Printing and Publishing; Protestant Reformation.**)

## Ignatius Loyola

**1491–1556**
**Saint and founder of the Jesuit order**

**\* papacy**   office and authority of the pope

**\* humanist**   referring to a Renaissance cultural movement promoting the study of the humanities (the languages, literature, and history of ancient Greece and Rome) as a guide to living

Ignatius Loyola founded the Roman Catholic religious order known as the Society of Jesus, or Jesuits. Born into a Spanish noble family, Ignatius had a brief military career before suffering a wound in battle. While recovering at the castle of Loyola, he experienced a religious awakening. He felt the desire to help people understand their own spiritual nature. Over the next year he collected his thoughts on paper for what would evolve into *Spiritual Exercises,* his most important work. The piece took him 20 years to complete.

Ignatius had received little formal education. He decided that he needed to expand his knowledge in order to help people effectively. He studied Latin in Spain before moving to Paris, where he received a degree in philosophy in 1533. In Paris he attracted a group of six followers whom he guided through his spiritual teachings. This group became the foundation for the Society of Jesus. In 1540 a larger group of followers formed the order in Rome and named Ignatius their leader.

Ignatius established the Society of Jesus as a way to strengthen the papacy\* and the Catholic Church. It quickly gained popularity, with over 1,000 members from western Europe and overseas during Ignatius's lifetime. The group committed itself to missionary work and acted as a promoter of humanist\* learning, becoming the first teaching order in the church. In fact, a high level of education with an emphasis on humanism was typical for Jesuits. The church recognized Ignatius' work

in 1622 by naming him a saint. (*See also* **Education; Religious Orders.**)

* **medieval** referring to the Middle Ages, a period that began around A.D. 400 and ended around 1400 in Italy and 1500 in the rest of Europe

* **humanist** referring to a Renaissance cultural movement promoting the study of the humanities (the languages, literature, and history of ancient Greece and Rome) as a guide to living

* **scribe** person who copies manuscripts

* **patron** supporter or financial sponsor of an artist or writer

* **Gothic** artistic style marked by bright colors, elongated proportions, and intricate detail

The art of illumination—embellishing pages of manuscripts with hand-painted decorations and illustrations—arose during the Middle Ages. Illuminated books often featured large elaborate capital letters at the beginning of each section and colorful illustrations in the margins. Artists of the Renaissance built on medieval* traditions of illumination and also created new styles. Various cities in Italy and other parts of Europe developed their own distinct styles of illumination.

**New Developments and Old Traditions.** One of the main changes that occurred in the Renaissance involved a new style of script. In the early 1400s scholars in Florence, including Poggio Bracciolini and Coluccio SALUTATI, developed a form of writing consisting of both capital and lowercase letters. The new script spread quickly among humanist* scholars. One of its distinctive characteristics was an initial capital letter known as white vine, which featured vines twining through and around the letter against a colored background.

At the same time, illumination artists remained faithful to many of the traditions of the Middle Ages. They worked mostly on Bibles and other religious texts. They followed medieval examples in their choice of subject, placement of illustrations, and decorative style. For example, they continued to show an image of Christ on the cross on missals (books with the text of the Roman Catholic Mass) and to use popular decorative elements of the Middle Ages, such as leaves, flowers, and fruit.

Throughout the Middle Ages, religious institutions such as monasteries had played a major role in manuscript production. This continued during the Renaissance, and many scribes* and some illuminators were members of the clergy. However, in many cities a network of people outside the church became involved in producing manuscripts and books. These included entrepreneurs who paid for the materials, commissioned the work, and sold the finished products, as well as the scribes, illuminators, and binders who worked on the manuscripts. Well-to-do nobles and merchants provided a growing market for these manuscripts as they sought to build their libraries. Religious houses also supported the book trade by buying manuscripts.

**Italian Illumination.** Florence was the most important center of illumination in the 1400s. Wealthy patrons* such as the MEDICI family promoted the enterprise. Lorenzo de' Medici even ordered a series of illuminated prayer books for the weddings of his daughters. The development of the university and the growth of humanist studies also helped boost the local book trade. In addition, some of Florence's leading artists, such as Fra ANGELICO, worked as illuminators.

Milan became a major center of illumination around 1400. Many of the best illustrators in the region continued to work in the Gothic* style

The first books printed in Venice in the late 1400s contained blank areas where illuminations could be added by hand. This copy of a work by Aristotle, for example, contains illustrations added by artist Girolamo da Cremona.

of the Middle Ages. Members of Milan's ruling Visconti family were important patrons and eventually collected a magnificent library. But after France conquered Lombardy (the region around Milan) in 1499, the library fell into French hands.

In Venice, state papers were often illuminated. Artist Leonardo Bellini decorated many of these documents, using some of the new artistic styles favored by his uncle, the painter Jacopo Bellini. However, the most innovative artists of the mid-1400s worked anonymously. The first

**\* woodcut** print made from a block of wood with an image carved into it

books printed in Venice contained blank areas where illuminations could be added by hand. Many of the artists who illustrated these books later produced woodcuts\* for printed works.

In Rome, popes and other church leaders provided patronage for many illuminators. This support reached a peak in the mid-1400s under Pope Nicholas V, who promoted the arts and learning. Popes and cardinals often hired illuminators from their home cities. Some of the most splendid illuminated manuscripts produced in Rome in the latter part of the 1400s were made for Pope Sixtus IV.

Many towns in Italy provided work for illuminators, and important nobles, such as members of the Gonzaga family in Mantua, were major patrons. In Urbino, Duke Federico da Montefeltro spent 30,000 ducats of his personal fortune on manuscripts for his library. Wealthy monasteries also commissioned illuminated works, particularly sets of choir books. In northeastern Italy, the dukes of Ferrara were the leading patrons. The most famous of all Italian Renaissance manuscripts, a great Bible, was created for Duke Borso d'Este between 1455 and 1462. It featured an illuminated opening for each book of the Bible.

**Later Developments.** In the late 1400s patrons in Spain and northern Europe began buying illuminated Italian manuscripts or receiving them as gifts. Italian works circulated as far away as England. The king of Hungary, Matthias Corvinus, even persuaded Italian illuminators to move to his court to produce their work. Northern European artists who traveled to Italy to study brought home new styles, such as the white vine initial. However, most illuminators in northern Europe continued to favor late Gothic, rather than Italian, styles.

The growth of printing in the 1500s severely weakened the market for illuminated manuscripts. However, the art form was still used for state documents in Venice and for missals in Rome. One of the greatest illuminators of the Renaissance, Giulio Clovino, worked in Rome during this period. The art historian Giorgio Vasari called him the "Michelangelo of small works." In fact, Clovino was a friend and admirer of Michelangelo. He also had a high regard for the work of German artist Albrecht Dürer, whose prints influenced many later illuminators. Although the production of illuminated books declined, they continued to be highly valued into the late 1500s. (*See also* **Art; Art in Italy; Books and Manuscripts; Libraries.**)

## Index of Prohibited Books

**\* Protestant Reformation** religious movement that began in the 1500s as a protest against certain practices of the Roman Catholic Church and eventually led to the establishment of a variety of Protestant churches

Since ancient times, churches and governments have attempted to ban books that they considered dangerous. During the Protestant Reformation\* the Roman Catholic Church took a special interest in stopping the sale, printing, and reading of books that promoted Protestant ideas. Church officials such as popes and archbishops created lists of forbidden books. Some Catholic rulers, such as the Holy Roman Emperor\* Charles V, also outlawed Protestant texts.

In 1544 professors of religion at the University of Paris issued the first Index of Prohibited Books to appear in print. This list contained 230

* **Holy Roman Emperor** ruler of the Holy Roman Empire, a political body in central Europe composed of several states that existed until 1806

* **humanist** Renaissance expert in the humanities (the languages, literature, history, and speech and writing techniques of ancient Greece and Rome)

* **Spanish Inquisition** court established by the Spanish monarchs that investigated Christians accused of straying from the official doctrine of the Roman Catholic Church, particularly during the period 1480–1530

* **papacy** office and authority of the pope

titles in Latin and French. Over the next 12 years, the number of banned works grew to 528. Most of these were works by Protestant authors or by humanists* such as the Dutch scholar Desiderius ERASMUS and the French writer François RABELAIS.

The Spanish Inquisition* published its own catalog of banned books in 1551. This list focused on religious texts. However, in response to pleas from scholars, printers, and booksellers, Spanish authorities allowed some of the forbidden books to appear in print with their offending passages removed. The papacy* issued lists of prohibited books as well. Pope Paul IV (ruled 1555–1559) became the first pope to create such a list, banning more than 1,000 works—including 45 editions of the BIBLE.

Throughout the 1500s, the different Indexes of Prohibited Books condemned works by about 2,000 authors. Three-fourths of these authors had all their works banned. It is not clear, however, how effective these restrictions actually were at stopping the spread of Protestant ideas. The Index of Prohibited Books was finally abolished in 1966. (*See also* **Books and Manuscripts; Catholic Reformation and Counter-Reformation; Censorship; Ideas, Spread of; Inquisition; Protestant Reformation.**)

## Individualism

Some historians, such as Jakob BURCKHARDT, have seen the Renaissance as a period when people became much more aware of themselves as individuals. Burckhardt thought that in the Middle Ages, people had tended to view themselves mainly in terms of their connection to other people—as members of a nation, a race, a family, or some other group. During the Renaissance they focused more on their personal identities and goals. Burckhardt saw this as one of the central developments of the Renaissance.

**The Individual's Place in Society.** The Renaissance movement toward individualism probably began with the Italian poet and scholar PETRARCH. In works such as *Familiar Letters* and *Life of Solitude,* Petrarch expressed the idea that individuals must struggle to achieve the kind of life best suited to their own moral sense and character. The poet combined his individualism with a concern for others, saying "whoever is secure in himself ... sins against the law of nature if he does not bring aid to the suffering when he can."

Later scholars echoed Petrarch's views on balancing personal needs and desires with helping others. The Italian humanist* Leon Battista ALBERTI addressed this idea in *On Governing a Household* (1470), a book on how to live a useful and satisfying life. Alberti urged his readers to be "active in some honorable task," arguing that "Man is born to be useful to himself and no less to others."

* **humanist** Renaissance expert in the humanities (the languages, literature, history, and speech and writing techniques of ancient Greece and Rome)

**God and the Individual.** Later scholars focused on the relationship between the individual and God. The German philosopher NICHOLAS OF CUSA argued in *On Learned Ignorance* (1440) that God is infinite and

human beings are limited. In order for humans to begin to grasp the nature of God, they first had to understand their place as individuals in the universe.

Other writers focused on the conflict between individual human will and the will of God. During the Middle Ages, people firmly believed in divine power as the ruling force in the world. Renaissance thinkers tried to blend this notion with their belief in human free will. Coluccio SALUTATI, a follower of Petrarch, wrote about this issue in *On Fate, Fortune, and Chance* (1399). He argued that God "moves" human will without forcing it, so that individuals are always capable of doing the right thing. Therefore, those who fall into sin do so of their own free will.

Two later scholars, Marsilio FICINO and Giovanni PICO DELLA MIRANDOLA, emphasized the power of humans to affect the world around them. Ficino, for example, placed great importance on the ability of humans to create various kinds of art. He wrote that this ability made them "seem not to be servants of nature but competitors." Pico, in *Oration on the Dignity of Man* (1486), argued that God had created people so that there would be someone capable of recognizing and appreciating the glory of God's creation. He claimed that God had placed human beings "in the middle of the world" and given them the potential to live anywhere and do anything on earth. Modern philosophers and historians still admire Pico's thoughts on the many possibilities of individual achievement. (*See also* **Man, Dignity of.**)

The production of goods changed in some ways during the Renaissance, but industry in the modern sense did not emerge until much later. The term *industria,* as used at the time, simply meant hard work. For the most part, items were made by hand in workshops rather than produced on a large scale in factories. Still, several aspects of the modern industrial world had their roots in the Renaissance.

**Urbanism, Capitalism, and Production.** During the Middle Ages, small-scale trade and manufacturing began to take root in towns from Flanders* to southern Germany and northern Italy. The Black Death* and later outbreaks of plague halted this development until the mid-1400s. Then as Europe began to recover from its population losses, new urban centers emerged. Though small and widely scattered, these cities encouraged a new attitude toward business and promoted capitalism*. However, this capitalism was fueled by commerce rather than by industry. Trade and commerce were still more important than manufacturing, which depended on the skill and effort of individual crafts workers. Moreover, trade involved raw materials rather than large quantities of finished goods.

The production of goods was a fairly simple affair during the Renaissance. It usually occurred on a small scale, even in major industries such as textiles. For example, an important group of cloth manufacturers in Florence employed no more than 15 workers. However, as

* **Flanders** region along the coasts of present-day Belgium, France, and the Netherlands

* **Black Death** epidemic of the plague, a highly contagious and often fatal disease, which spread throughout Europe from 1348 to 1350

* **capitalism** economic system in which individuals own property and businesses

the population of Europe began to grow again, the demand for goods increased. The urban expanding markets encouraged merchants to offer a greater variety of products, as well as luxury goods such as silk cloth.

**Large-Scale Activities.** While the production of most goods took place on a limited basis during the Renaissance, three industries—textiles, building construction, and mining—operated on a larger scale. Textiles were a source of new wealth for many cities. Florence had a reputation for its fine woolen cloth, but Florentine manufacturers did not raise their profits by increasing production. Instead, they used their contacts to bring the best materials and techniques to Florence so that they could produce less expensive cloth that more people could buy.

When the demand for cloth dropped sharply in the late 1300s, manufacturers began to invest in silk production. They could maintain their profits on luxury fabrics such as silk, brocade, and velvet even with a smaller market. In addition, the invention of a silk-throwing machine greatly simplified the process of making silk. When economic growth began again in the mid-1400s, the demand for luxury items expanded as well.

Building construction flourished in the Renaissance, as communities and princes* sought to erect ever more impressive structures. These projects employed large crews of workers for long periods of time. In Rome in the 1500s, more than 2,000 workers participated in the construction of St. Peter's church. In France and Spain, palaces became larger and more elaborate and incorporated many new luxuries such as glass windows.

The most remarkable building complex of the Renaissance was the shipyard known as the Venetian Arsenal. Several thousand people, including a significant number of women employed as sail makers, worked in what was the leading technological center of the age. In 1574 workers there outfitted a ship in the time it took for the visiting King Henry III of France to have dinner.

The major mining centers of Europe were located outside of Italy. Mining required many workers and enormous sums of money for the machinery needed to extract materials such as copper, silver, tin, and coal. At the beginning of the Renaissance, these mines produced most of the metals used for coins. However, in the late 1500s silver and gold from the Americas flooded Europe and greatly increased the number of coins in circulation. This increase, in turn, stimulated the demand for goods, which resulted in a widespread rise in prices.

The methods the Spanish used to extract gold and silver in the Americas formed a model for later industrial production. The Spanish assembled a large and dependent labor force, tightly controlled the means of production, and kept expenses to a minimum largely by ignoring labor conditions.

**War and Communication.** European countries at the time spent much of their wealth on military defenses and technology. The introduction of cannons had a profound impact on the nature of warfare.

* **prince** Renaissance term for the ruler of an independent state

City walls and fortresses had to be rebuilt to withstand the firepower of cannons. Knights on horseback gradually gave way to foot soldiers, and firearms came into general use. As a result of these changes, armies grew larger and wars became longer and much costlier. Few rulers could afford the steep increase in military expenditures, even the Spanish with their rich overseas resources.

Printing was another industry that developed quickly during the Renaissance and had far-reaching effects. A German invention, printing spread to Italy in the mid-1400s, and by 1500 Venice had become the leading book producer in Europe. However, printing remained a relatively small enterprise. Books were expensive and many people could not read. Nevertheless, printing was the beginning of a revolution in communications that made it possible to circulate new ideas and information rapidly throughout Europe. Printing helped spread the ideas of ERASMUS, the humanist* scholar, and of Martin LUTHER, the Protestant reformer. (*See also* **Cities and Urban Life; Mining and Metallurgy; Printing and Publishing; Warfare.**)

* **humanist** referring to a Renaissance cultural movement promoting the study of the humanities (the languages, literature, and history of ancient Greece and Rome) as a guide to living

## Inns of Court

London's four Inns of Court—Gray's Inn, Lincoln's Inn, the Inner Temple, and the Middle Temple—provided legal education to young men beginning in the 1300s. The Inns also became centers of intellectual and social activity in Renaissance England. Many of the men who attended them did not become practicing lawyers, but they used the Inns as a way to make connections with members of high society.

Beginning in the late 1400s, the Inns of Court became part of the growing humanist* movement. As in France and Italy, the lawyers of Renaissance England contributed to the growing interest in ancient cultures and history. By bringing together large numbers of students in the lively city of London, the Inns supported scholarship, creative writing, and patronage* of the arts and learning.

The Inns of Court also had a great impact on England's poetry and drama during the Renaissance. Life at the Inns included a steady diet of plays, dancing, and music. Many of England's finest Renaissance authors, including the poet John DONNE and the playwright John Ford, attended the Inns of Court. William SHAKESPEARE's plays *The Comedy of Errors* and *Twelfth Night* were also performed at the Inns. (*See also* **Drama, English.**)

* **humanist** Renaissance expert in the humanities (the languages, literature, history, and speech and writing techniques of ancient Greece and Rome)

* **patronage** support or financial sponsorship

## Inquisition

In the late 1400s and 1500s, the Roman Catholic Church and secular* governments set up several courts, or inquisitions, to investigate charges of heresy*. The popular image of these inquisitions consists of religious fanatics holding staged trials and burning thousands of innocent people at the stake. The reality, although unpleasant, was far different from these bloody legends.

* **secular** nonreligious; connected with everyday life

* **heresy** belief that is contrary to the doctrine of an established church

## THE ROMAN INQUISITION

During the Middle Ages individual members of the clergy had investigated cases of heresy in Rome. In 1542 Pope Paul III set up a formal inquisition in Rome to deal with charges of heresy. This court, established in response to the rising challenge of Protestantism, fell directly under the authority of the pope.

**Structure.** The governing board of the Roman Inquisition, known as the Holy Office, consisted of a group of cardinals appointed by the pope. This group oversaw local tribunals (courts) located throughout Italy. Each tribunal had a chief official called an inquisitor and several minor figures who assisted him. Most of these inquisitors held degrees in theology*, but not in law. Leading lawyers and theologians from each region aided the court in reaching decisions. The Holy Office in Rome usually reviewed each trial before the final sentence was passed.

The Roman Inquisition took precedence over all other secular and religious courts in Italy that heard heresy charges. It had authority over most parts of the Italian peninsula, but it was not allowed to operate openly in the region ruled by Naples. Other areas of Italy, such as Venice, also placed limits on the activities of the Roman Inquisition.

**Procedures.** The church understood that some accusations of heresy might arise from personal spite. Therefore, it introduced several measures to help protect the accused, such as asking them to name all their enemies before the trial. Prisoners also received a written record of their hearings and had anywhere from several days to a few weeks to prepare a defense and call friendly witnesses. In addition, tribunals appointed defense lawyers for the accused, a legal protection not available in many secular courts at the time. Finally, those convicted by the inquisition could appeal the decision to the highest court in Rome.

Most punishments were fairly mild. For example, the court might humiliate the offenders by requiring them to confess their crimes in public. Fines, community service, and prayers were other common punishments. Even sentences such as imprisonment were not as bad as they might seem. A life sentence might end in parole after a few years, and some prisoners could serve their time under house arrest. The most severe sentence—death by burning at the stake—was very rare. Only those who repeatedly committed heresy, those who showed no regret, and—after the late 1550s—those who denied certain basic Catholic doctrines suffered this penalty. A religious group that comforted the accused during their last hours recorded only about 100 executions between 1542 and 1761.

Many people associate the inquisitions of this period with the use of torture. However, the inquisition did not use torture as a form of punishment, but as a means of persuading people to confess their crimes. In any case, torture was an extreme measure for cases where the evidence of heresy was extremely strong. Local courts could not perform torture without the approval of the local bishop or his vicar.

* **theology** study of the nature of God and of religion

In the late 1400s and early 1500s, individuals accused of heresy in Spain faced trial by the Spanish Inquisition. Those who were found guilty might face execution at the hands of local authorities.

## NATIONAL INQUISITIONS

The rulers of Spain and Portugal established their own inquisitions to try cases of heresy in their kingdoms. These tribunals were bloodier and more ruthless than the one in Rome, executing far more suspects. However, even in Spain and Portugal most cases did not end with the death penalty.

**The Spanish Inquisition.** In 1478 Pope Sixtus IV gave the Spanish rulers FERDINAND OF ARAGON and ISABELLA OF CASTILE approval to establish an inquisition in Spain. The kingdom included many CONVERSOS, Jews who had converted to Christianity—often because they were forced to do so. Accusations that the *conversos* were practicing Judaism in secret led the Spanish tribunal to investigate their loyalty. By targeting converted Jews, the inquisition reinforced anti-Semitic* attitudes in Spain.

* **anti-Semitic** referring to prejudice against Jews

Although this inquisition took its authority from the pope, the Spanish crown controlled it through a central council called the Suprema. Inquisitors did not have to be clergy members, but they did need a law degree. The Spanish Inquisition had power only over baptized Christians, not over Muslims or Jews.

* **Dominican** religious order of brothers and priests founded by St. Dominic

A Dominican* monk named Tomás de Torquemada became the first inquisitor general of the Spanish Inquisition. Local tribunals were set up

throughout Spain and in Spanish territories in Sicily, Sardinia, and the New World. Tribunals in the Americas focused mainly on making sure all Spanish colonists shared the same Catholic beliefs. Their targets included foreigners (especially the French, English, and Portuguese) as well as *conversos*.

The Spanish Inquisition was most active between 1480 and 1530, when it focused on *conversos*. Inquisitors made periodic trips through towns to receive information about possible heretics, and then theologians examined the evidence. If they believed the charges of heresy were true, the court arrested the accused person and seized his or her property to pay for the cost of the trial. In rare cases, the tribunals used torture to extract information in cases of heresy.

The most famous procedure of the inquisition was the auto-da-fé, a public ceremony to sentence those accused of heresy. Many defendants escaped the death penalty through "edicts of grace," which gave them a month to confess and be pardoned. The majority of death sentences issued were against defendants who had been tried and convicted in their absence, and were therefore never carried out. Nonetheless, the court executed around 2,000 *conversos* between 1480 and 1530. Local authorities carried out the death sentence since clergy members were not allowed to shed blood.

In the late 1500s the Spanish Inquisition began to investigate the activities of Muslim converts, known as MORISCOS. It also acted against suspected Protestants. In addition, it began to try other offenses besides heresy. Over time it focused more on such social offenses as swearing and immoral sexual practices. By 1730 the court had became largely inactive, and in 1834 the Spanish closed it down.

**The Portuguese Inquisition.** In 1536 the Portuguese king John III received papal\* approval to set up an inquisition. Its main purpose was to ensure that converted Jews did not go back to practicing Judaism. It also tried cases of witchcraft, sacrilege\*, and bigamy (having more than one spouse). Its procedures were similar to those of the Spanish Inquisition, including the use of torture to gain information. The Portuguese exported their inquisition to their colonies in Asia, Africa, and Brazil.

The Portuguese Inquisition tried only a small percentage of those accused. Death sentences were rare. Out of more than 32,000 people tried between 1536 and 1674, only around 1,600 were condemned to death. This figure included some people who had fled and, therefore, were beyond reach, and some who had already died. Those found guilty might also suffer beating, imprisonment, or exile. In addition, the state could seize their property. The inquisition also played a role in book censorship. Its agents searched foreign ships for works on the INDEX OF PROHIBITED BOOKS, a list of texts banned by the pope. (*See also* **Anti-Semitism; Censorship; Jews.**)

\* **papal** referring to the office and authority of the pope

\* **sacrilege** disrespect of sacred things

**Ireland**

England's involvement in Ireland began several centuries before the Renaissance. The English controlled a small region of the country known as the Pale, which was home to most of Ireland's population. The lords who ruled the Pale, the "Old English," traced their ancestry back to English invaders of the 1100s. They generally supported the policies of the English crown as long as those policies did not conflict with their own interests. During the 1400s and 1500s, Ireland was culturally divided. The Pale was strongly English, but the areas outside the Pale were split between the English and the Gaelic (old Irish) worlds.

## ECONOMY AND POLITICS

The Pale, which consisted of the counties of Dublin, Kildare, Meath, Westmeath, and Louth, was the most fertile and prosperous region of Ireland. The aristocrats and gentry*, who owned most of the land, made money from it in two ways. They collected rents from their tenants, and they employed a system called "coyne and livery" that allowed them to demand food and lodging from tenants to support private armies. Although agriculture was the main source of wealth, a primitive trading economy was emerging in Dublin. Merchants exported farm products such as hides, tallow*, and yarn, and imported wine, salt, coal, and manufactured goods.

Renaissance Ireland lacked any kind of centralized power. Individual lords maintained control over their own lands. England entrusted the responsibilities of government to Old English lords, asking only that they maintain order, collect taxes, and raise troops in case of an emergency. Although this policy was the simplest and least expensive way for the English to handle Ireland, it also posed political risks. Any lord powerful enough to govern effectively might well use his power against the English crown.

The most powerful lords in the Pale were the Fitzgeralds of Kildare, who also had extensive holdings in Gaelic areas. During the late 1400s and early 1500s, the Kildare lords represented the English crown as chief governors of Ireland. Despite outbreaks of local violence, English government under the Kildares was generally effective, and the revenue received by the crown actually increased.

## IRELAND AND ENGLAND

England's relations with Ireland began to change during the Wars of the Roses (1455–1485), a time when two major families in England struggled for control of the throne. Twice during this period, forces based in Ireland attempted to invade England and overthrow its king. One of the invasions was supported by the Irish Parliament and the earl of Kildare. In 1494 England sent a royal deputy to Ireland to punish the lords who had backed the invasion and to place the Irish Parliament under English authority.

**Fears of Rebellion.** In 1533 the English king HENRY VIII broke away from the Roman Catholic Church and established the Protestant

* **gentry** people of high birth or social status

* **tallow** processed animal fat used in candles and soap

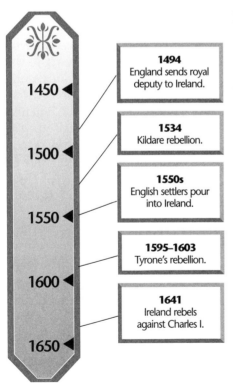

1450 — 
**1494**
England sends royal deputy to Ireland.

1500 — 
**1534**
Kildare rebellion.

1550 — 
**1550s**
English settlers pour into Ireland.

1600 — 
**1595–1603**
Tyrone's rebellion.

1650 — 
**1641**
Ireland rebels against Charles I.

Irish lord Hugh O'Neill led a rebellion against England in 1595. His struggle lasted eight years and proved very costly to the English.

* **guerrilla** type of warfare involving sudden raids by small groups of warriors

Church of England. As a Protestant nation, England faced new complications in its foreign policy. Hostile Catholic powers threatened to invade the country to restore the old religion. Ireland presented a weak point in the English defenses. Its large coastline and rugged terrain made it a perfect base of operations for a foreign power interested in invading England. Moreover, the English had little authority over the regions outside the Pale. A rebellion in Ireland would be difficult and costly to crush.

Henry VIII tried to gain more control over the government in Dublin and to reduce the influence of local lords. His adviser, Thomas CROMWELL, asked the ninth earl of Kildare to end the coyne and livery system and to appoint English officials to Irish government offices. When Kildare protested, the English arrested him. His son Thomas then rose up in rebellion against the English king. It took more than 2,000 troops to crush the uprising. England responded to the Kildare rebellion by appointing an English-born deputy to rule Ireland instead of a lord of the Pale.

**English Domination.** After Henry VIII failed in an attempt to invade France in 1543, the French sent agents to Ireland to stir up trouble. The English responded with more aggressive policies in Ireland. They planned to increase the number of troops in the country, extend English control into Gaelic territories, and seize Irish lands for new English settlers. These policies met with fierce resistance. To carry them out, English agents burned Irish villages and threatened the local population. English writers justified the attacks against the Irish by labeling them as barbarians, naturally inferior to the English.

By the 1550s English settlers were streaming into Ireland. Many of them were courtiers or gentlemen seeking government posts. Unlike the Old English, the newcomers had no ties to the land. They viewed Ireland as a colony and saw no need to share wealth or power with the local population. At the same time, the English imposed a new tax called the cess on the Irish population. This tax was used to maintain the English troops in Ireland, which grew in number from 2,000 men in the 1560s to 6,000 in the 1580s.

Beginning in the 1540s, the English crown took direct control of Irish policy. The old leaders of the Pale, stripped of most of their power, rebelled and sought assistance from Catholic nations in Europe. Three Irish families once loyal to England led uprisings between 1569 and 1579. Tension over Ireland continued throughout the 1580s, and the English continued to seek more control in Gaelic regions. In 1595 another rebellion broke out when England tried to seize the lands of Hugh O'Neill, earl of Tyrone, a previously loyal Gaelic lord. Aided by the Spanish, O'Neill fought a guerrilla* war, avoiding direct clashes with English forces. The English spent huge amounts of money before O'Neill surrendered in 1603.

**Ireland After 1600.** In 1604 England made peace with Spain, and for the next several years Ireland played a smaller role in English politics.

### A Harsh View

Many English writers of the late 1500s argued that England should take control of Ireland by force. They portrayed the Irish as a backward and inferior people. The most famous such argument was Sir Edmund Spenser's *A View of the Present State of Ireland* (1596). Spenser proposed that the English should seize the land and starve the native Irish to death. He argued that the Irish deserved such harsh treatment because they had abused the privileges England had granted them. However, Spenser's work never appeared in print and may not have had any influence on English policy.

* **humanist** referring to a Renaissance cultural movement promoting the study of the humanities (the languages, literature, and history of ancient Greece and Rome) as a guide to living

* **patronage** support or financial sponsorship

English officials focused on building up settlements in the Gaelic areas. Many Scots settled in Ulster, in the north of Ireland. In the 1620s Ireland took on renewed importance during the THIRTY YEARS' WAR (1618–1648), as England considered entering the conflict among several states in central Europe. England feared that if it supported Protestant states in the war, Catholic powers might once again try to attack England through Ireland.

Changes within England also had a negative impact on Ireland. In 1629 the English king CHARLES I dismissed Parliament. He then faced the problem of finding new sources of funds because only Parliament could raise taxes. One possible source was Ireland, where his deputy seized Irish lands—which had minor irregularities in property titles—for the English crown. This policy triggered another rebellion in Ireland in 1641. The king's efforts to end the uprising would eventually cost him the throne.

**The Renaissance in Ireland.** Culture did not blossom in Ireland during the Renaissance as it did in the rest of Europe. Humanist* learning had little impact on the island, where educational opportunities were limited. Until the 1540s the Catholic Church had dominated Irish learning, aided by poets, lawyers, and other educated individuals. In their efforts to control Ireland, English officials frequently clashed with the church, damaging the school system. Education suffered further when Henry VIII closed all the Catholic monasteries in his realm.

In the 1540s English leaders sought to impose English culture on Ireland and establish Protestantism as the official religion. To further this plan, the English crown took control of education in the 1560s and established several Latin grammar schools. In 1594 Ireland gained a Protestant university, known today as Trinity College in Dublin.

Despite English efforts, poets remained important figures in Irish society during the Renaissance. Powerful Irish lords often employed poets to write verses for various occasions. Because the poets depended on the lord's patronage*, their works reflected the lord's point of view. The English saw these poets as a possible threat and tried to reduce their influence. The work of some of the poets reflected a growing sense of national identity. When the earl of Tyrone fled Ireland in 1607, one Irish poet called for him to return and restore Ireland's rightful rulers to power. (*See also* **England; Spenser, Edmund.**)

### Isabella of Castile

**1451–1504**
**Spanish queen**

Isabella of Castile and her husband FERDINAND OF ARAGON had an enormous impact on SPAIN. Their 1469 marriage united two Christian kingdoms, which formed the basis of modern Spain. Known as *los reyes católicos* (the Catholic monarchs), Isabella and Ferdinand ruled jointly. During their reign the international standing of Spain soared, and the nation began a period of exploration and conquest that created a global empire.

Isabella was the daughter of King John II of Castile and Isabella of Portugal. When her father died in 1454, Isabella's half-brother, Henry

IV, became king. However, in the 1460s a group of nobles denounced Henry as a tyrant and declared his younger brother Alfonso the rightful ruler. When Alfonso died suddenly in 1468, Henry again took the throne. The following year Isabella married Ferdinand, prince of Aragon, and on Henry's death in 1474 she inherited the crown of Castile.

Although Isabella had little formal education, she had a good mind, a clear sense of duty, and natural political skills. She realized that a woman could rule only with a strong man at her side. Her husband Ferdinand filled that role superbly. He agreed to live in Castile and gained acceptance by the Castilians. Although Isabella insisted that they rule jointly in Castile, she never gave up her role as the rightful ruler. Remarkably, the couple not only had a good working relationship but also a marriage that included love and trust.

Isabella and Ferdinand accomplished much in uniting Spain and laying the foundation for a global empire. However, this success was not without cost. War dominated much of Isabella's reign, ranging from civil conflicts to a ten-year campaign against the Muslim kingdom of Granada in southern Spain. The Spanish Inquisition* began under Isabella, and her reign is remembered for the expulsion of the Jews in 1492. That same year brought the fall of Granada and the reconquest of Spain from the Moors*. After 1492, Isabella focused primarily on ensuring peace within Spain and on arranging good marriages for her children.

Under Isabella, the Spanish Renaissance leaned toward the humanists* of northern Europe with their emphasis on Christian piety and good works. The queen, an important patron* of the arts, also preferred the art of the northern Renaissance. She collected Flemish* tapestries and paintings by Hans MEMLING and Rogier van der WEYDEN, and she hired German builders and architects.

The queen commanded great respect from her subjects. Although they may have resented the central control and wartime hardships of Spain under Isabella and Ferdinand, they welcomed the monarchs' strong leadership and the safety and security it brought. (*See also* **Inquisition; Moriscos; Queens and Queenship.**)

* **Spanish Inquisition** court established by the Spanish monarchs that investigated Christians accused of straying from the official doctrine of the Roman Catholic Church, particularly during the period 1480–1530

* **Moor** Muslim from North Africa; Moorish invaders conquered much of Spain during the Middle Ages

* **humanist** Renaissance expert in the humanities (the languages, literature, history, and speech and writing techniques of ancient Greece and Rome)

* **patron** supporter or financial sponsor of an artist or writer

* **Flemish** relating to Flanders, a region along the coasts of present-day Belgium, France, and the Netherlands

Islam

Between the 1300s and the 1600s, powerful Islamic rulers controlled much of the Middle East, North Africa, and Spain. While Renaissance culture was spreading across Europe, Islamic civilization thrived in the regions under Muslim rule. Cities such as Cairo in Egypt and Granada in Spain became great cultural centers and attracted distinguished scholars and writers.

**Islamic States.** Egypt fell under Muslim control in the 600s. By 1250, the country was governed by a group of military officers called the Mamluks. The Mamluks had originally been slaves forced to serve in the army, but they used their military power to seize control of the country. The Mamluk capital, Cairo, was the leading city in the Islamic world.

Rulers of other Islamic states sought the approval of the Mamluk leader, or caliph, to confirm their authority. Under the Mamluks, many educated Egyptians became government officials or religious scholars.

Beginning in the early 700s, Islamic rulers had conquered most of central and southern Spain. They set up independent caliphates and built cities featuring splendid palaces and mosques (places of worship). The Muslim kingdom of Granada, in southern Spain, developed a highly sophisticated Islamic culture. Eventually, however, the Christian rulers of northern Spain began to reclaim the territory captured by the Muslims. In 1492 troops from the northern kingdoms of Aragon and Castile took over Granada, the last remaining Muslim stronghold in Spain.

Iran, Iraq, and India also fell under Muslim control during the Middle Ages. In the 1250s, the Mongols* invaded Iran and Iraq. At first the Mongol rulers considered converting to Christianity and forming an alliance with western leaders against the Muslims. However, in 1295 the Mongols decided to adopt Islam. They established Muslim states in Iran and Iraq and became patrons* of Islamic culture and learning. In India, an Islamic state founded in the late 1100s grew into a wealthy empire. From their base at Delhi, in the north, the Muslims gained control of much of India's central plateau.

The most powerful of the Islamic states was the OTTOMAN EMPIRE. Founded by the Ottoman Turks in the 1300s, it eventually included large areas of eastern Europe, the Middle East, and northern Africa. The Ottomans established a capital at Bursa, in western Turkey, and extended their influence into Europe. Although Christian leaders launched attacks and crusades against the empire, they failed to stop the spread of Ottoman power. The only serious threat the Ottomans faced was the Turkish warlord Timur, also known as Tamerlane. Timur established his own kingdom in Iran, Iraq, Anatolia, Syria, and India in the late 1300s. However, his empire fell apart on his death in 1405.

After recovering their power in Turkey, the Ottomans turned their attention to the west. In 1453 the Ottoman sultan MEHMED II conquered CONSTANTINOPLE, the capital of the Byzantine Empire*. He intended to invade Italy, but he died in 1481 before he could carry out his plan. In the 1500s Islamic influence in Europe continued to expand. Muslim troops invaded Hungary and Austria and forced rulers to pay tribute*. The Ottoman Empire remained a significant threat to Europe for some time, but in the late 1600s it fell into a decline.

**Islamic Culture.** During the Renaissance, Muslim culture advanced in several fields, particularly law. In Europe, scholars of this time were reviving classical* ideas, most of which had been lost during the Middle Ages. In the Islamic world, by contrast, the works of ancient Greek philosophers and scientists had been translated into Arabic and had remained part of the culture. However, by the 1100s, some Muslims had begun to oppose the study of philosophy on the grounds that it was contrary to Islamic beliefs. They also objected to the study of science, which was based in part on philosophical ideas.

* **Mongol** member of a central Asian tribe that controlled much of Asia and eastern Europe during the Middle Ages

* **patron** supporter or financial sponsor of an artist or writer

* **Byzantine Empire** Eastern Christian Empire based in Constantinople (A.D. 476–1453)

* **tribute** payment made by a smaller or weaker party to a more powerful one, often under threat of force

* **classical** in the tradition of ancient Greece and Rome

THE RENAISSANCE

The study of Islamic law, which was closely tied to Islamic religious beliefs, flourished under Muslim rule. Legal scholars gathered in academies throughout the Muslim world. They focused on interpreting the Qur'an (the Muslim holy book), the sayings of the prophet Muhammad (founder of Islam), and the teachings of Muslim religious leaders.

Arabic literature made slow progress during the Renaissance due to a decline in the use of the Arabic language. Before 1200 the Muslim kingdoms had used Arabic for all intellectual activities. When the Mongols conquered Iran and Iraq in the 1200s, they adopted the Persian language of Iran because it was easier to learn than Arabic. In Egypt, the Mamluk rulers spoke Turkish and had little interest in promoting the use of Arabic. Eventually, proper Arabic was spoken only in religious schools and legal academies, and secular* learning in Arabic fell into a decline.

* **secular** nonreligious; connected with everyday life

As a result of these developments, Arabic literature focused mostly on religious subjects. Scholars studied poetry and history in an attempt to understand the Qur'an or the history of Islam. Some wrote biographies of great religious scholars who had passed down the sayings of Muhammad. Others produced commentaries about these sayings.

Much of the secular literature in the Muslim world focused on history and geography. The Persian writer Rashid al-Din (1247–1318) wrote about the place of Islam in the history of the world. The North African historian Ibn Khaldun (1332–1406) developed a theory of history and wrote about the forces that drive governments and societies. World traveler Ibn Battuta (1304–1377), who visited the entire Muslim world as well as China, Indonesia, and various parts of Africa, wrote vivid reports of his journeys. Another popular form of literature was storytelling. Tales told at Islamic gatherings during this time became the basis of *The Thousand and One Nights,* the most famous work of Islamic literature. (*See also* **Africa; Moriscos; Religious Thought; Spain.**)

## Italian Language and Literature

* **classical** in the tradition of ancient Greece and Rome

* **vernacular** native language or dialect of a region or country

* **medieval** referring to the Middle Ages, a period that began around A.D. 400 and ended around 1400 in Italy and 1500 in the rest of Europe

The Renaissance was a period of intense literary activity in Italy. The renewed interest in classical* culture that had begun in the late Middle Ages played a major role in this flowering of literature. Italian scholars studied ancient sources and applied the knowledge they gained to their own writing. They also began to translate ancient Greek and Latin works into Italian and to use the vernacular* more widely in serious writing.

**Origins of the Italian Renaissance.** At the outset of the Renaissance, Italian scholars drew on the work of certain medieval* writers, particularly the poet Dante Alighieri of Florence (1265–1321). Dante's great poem *The Divine Comedy,* which describes a journey through the realms of the afterlife, remained popular long after his death. He also influenced later writers through his scholarly works. In *On the Vulgar Tongue,* for instance, he supported the use of the vernacular as more natural than Latin. Dante's argument started a debate on the use of language that continued throughout the Renaissance.

One of the most influential writers of the early Renaissance was the poet and scholar Francesco Petrarca (1304–1374), known as PETRARCH. Petrarch promoted the study of Greek and Latin and praised ancient works as models of clarity and elegance. He worked to create a link between the secular* ideas of the ancient world and Christian religious beliefs. Petrarch also gained fame as a poet. His *Canzoniere* (songbook), a collection of love lyrics* and other poems written in Italian, influenced poets throughout Europe—especially his description of the emotional ups and downs of love.

Like Petrarch, the Florentine writer Giovanni BOCCACCIO (1313–1375) paid a great deal of attention to Greek and Latin sources. He also introduced new literary forms, such as the pastoral*, to Italy. Boccaccio's masterpiece, the *Decameron,* wove together 100 stories told by a group of young men and women. Various Renaissance playwrights, including William SHAKESPEARE, borrowed plots from this work. Boccaccio wrote works in Italian and defended the use of the vernacular as an alternative to Latin.

**The Early Renaissance.** In the early 1400s humanism* began to spread throughout Italy. The works of Petrarch, Boccaccio, and others helped revive interest in classical culture. Humanist writers drew on ancient sources to address social issues. For example, Leon Battista ALBERTI (1404–1472) discussed the civic* duties of the individual in *On the Family.*

Several factors helped promote literary development during the mid-1400s. The discovery of long-lost ancient texts inspired writers with new literary models. Wealthy patrons* among the nobility and the clergy supported authors in their work. Meanwhile, the invention of movable type and the printing press made books available to a growing number of readers.

By the end of the 1400s, four forms had taken center stage in Renaissance literature: lyric poetry, the pastoral, the romance*, and comic theater. Authors followed specific models in each of these genres*. Petrarch's verses influenced the growth of lyric poetry. The works of the ancient Roman writer VIRGIL served as a model for pastoral poems such as *Arcadia* (1502), by Jacopo SANNAZARO. The comedies of the ancient Roman writers Terence and Plautus inspired comic plays. Finally, romance writers drew on medieval tales of chivalry* from France and England.

**The High Renaissance.** Humanist culture reached a peak in Italy between 1490 and 1530. In both literature and art, Italy produced some of its finest talent at this time. Scholars wrote on a variety of subjects, including politics, society, beauty, and the nature of love. The statesman Niccolò MACHIAVELLI (1469–1527), who had a humanist education, applied his talents to the social, political, and military problems of his day. Baldassare CASTIGLIONE focused on princely courts in *The Book of the Courtier,* written between 1508 and 1516. Castiglione's work celebrates the culture of the court while also expressing a sense of longing for the past.

* **secular**  nonreligious; connected with everyday life

* **lyric**  refers to a type of verse that expresses feelings and thoughts rather than telling a story

* **pastoral**  relating to the countryside; often used to draw a contrast between the innocence and serenity of rural life and the corruption and extravagance of court life

* **humanism**  Renaissance cultural movement promoting the study of the humanities (the languages, literature, and history of ancient Greece and Rome) as a guide to living

* **civic**  related to a city, a community, or citizens

* **patron**  supporter or financial sponsor of an artist or writer

* **romance**  adventure story of the Middle Ages, the forerunner of the modern novel

* **genre**  literary form

* **chivalry**  rules and customs of medieval knighthood

The renowned Italian author Petrarch wrote an influential series of poems called *Triumphs* in the mid-1300s. He created his poem *Triumph of Death,* shown here, after the deaths of several of his friends.

---

\* **Counter-Reformation** actions taken by the Roman Catholic Church after 1540 to oppose Protestantism

Poets of the High Renaissance continued to take the works of Petrarch as a model. However, they began to adapt Petrarch's style to suit their own purposes. For example, many female poets, such as Gaspara Stampa (1523–1554), wrote lyrics addressed to men, reversing the usual form in which a male narrator praised a lady.

**The Question of the Language.** In the 1500s a spirited debate broke out about which form of Italian writers should use. In the Middle Ages, the people of Italy had spoken and written in a variety of different forms of Italian. By the Renaissance, the Tuscan dialect spoken in Florence and the surrounding region had become the preferred form. The most respected Italian writers of the 1300s—Dante, Petrarch, and Boccaccio, sometimes called "the Three Crowns"—all wrote in Tuscan.

Throughout the 1500s, most writers and thinkers continued to favor the Tuscan language. Some important writers from other parts of Italy rewrote their works in Tuscan. However, some writers preferred other forms of Italian. The dramatist Angelo Beolco, better known as Ruzzante, wrote comedies in the dialect of Padua, in northeastern Italy. Those who favored the use of Tuscan founded the Accademia della Crusca around 1582. The academy prepared a dictionary of Tuscan Italian that further helped this form of Italian to become the literary language of Italy. Still, some people in other regions continued to use their own local dialects throughout the Renaissance.

**The Late Renaissance.** Toward the end of the Renaissance, two major forces in Italian literature were modern religion and ancient philosophy. The Roman Catholic Church had launched its Counter-Reformation\* in response to the spread of Protestant ideas in Europe. As a result, church leaders in Italy tried to merge Catholic teachings into all aspects of life—including literature. At about the same time, scholars were producing new translations of texts by the ancient Greek philosopher ARISTOTLE, along with commentaries on his work. These texts helped spread Aristotle's ideas, including his rules for writing.

Some Italian writers, such as the poet and playwright Torquato TASSO, combined these two forces in their work. Tasso's poem *Jerusalem Delivered* (1575) followed both Aristotle's guidelines and the teachings of the church. Other writers, such as the scientist Galileo GALILEI, dared to dispute certain views of the church. In works such as *The Assayer* (1623) and *Dialogue on the Two Great World Systems* (1632), Galileo broke with tradition and celebrated human freedom and potential.

By the end of the Renaissance, Italian writers had produced a body of work that made a lasting impression on the field of literature. The writing of Petrarch and other Italian poets influenced the lyric poetry produced in France, England, and Spain. Italian romances from the Renaissance shaped the development of the modern novel. Italian plays provided a basis for the major dramatic writing of the European Renaissance. Lastly, the thought of intellectuals such as Galileo set the stage for the scientific revolution that ushered in the modern era. (*See also* **Art in Italy; Catholic Reformation and Counter-**

Reformation; Chivalry; Classical Scholarship; Drama; Humanism; Individualism; Italy; Literature; Pastoral; Poetry; Translation.)

**\* prince** Renaissance term for the ruler of an independent state

**\* republic** form of Renaissance government dominated by leading merchants with limited participation by others

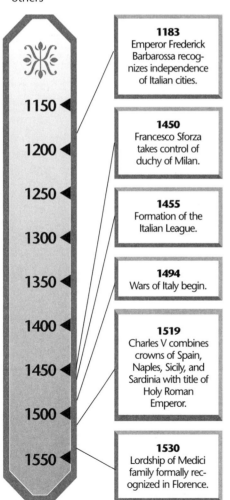

**1150**

**1183**
Emperor Frederick Barbarossa recognizes independence of Italian cities.

**1200**

**1450**
Francesco Sforza takes control of duchy of Milan.

**1250**

**1455**
Formation of the Italian League.

**1300**

**1350**

**1494**
Wars of Italy begin.

**1400**

**1519**
Charles V combines crowns of Spain, Naples, Sicily, and Sardinia with title of Holy Roman Emperor.

**1450**

**1500**

**1530**
Lordship of Medici family formally recognized in Florence.

**1550**

Throughout the Renaissance, Italy was politically divided. Northern Italy included several states ruled by princes\* as well as the Republic of VENICE. FLORENCE was the most important state in north-central Italy, while the popes had authority over large areas of central Italy called the Papal States. The Kingdom of NAPLES dominated the south until 1504, when it was taken over by Spain. Within each region of Italy, people were separated into communities.

**Regional Divisions.** The geography of Italy played a major role in its regional divisions. The Apennine mountains, which extend from north to south, formed a natural barrier. In addition, Italy's location in the midst of the busy Mediterranean Sea brought its coastal cities and towns in contact with people from many other cultures.

Social and economic forces also divided Italy into regions. A commercial revolution that began in the 900s led to the growth of cities across Europe. As Italian cities expanded and prospered, many of them seized power from existing rulers and became self-governing. Some urban communities in northern Italy and elsewhere formed republics\*, and they became thriving industrial, commercial, and financial centers. Business competition led to rivalries between communities.

Political issues were responsible for much of the division within Italy. Disputes over trade routes and resources led to some political clashes. Most important, Italy had no single ruler or dominant state but consisted instead of 15 to 20 small states. This encouraged the five major states—MILAN, Venice, Florence, the papacy, and Naples—to try to gain territory at the expense of smaller states and each other.

Italy also had cultural divisions. People in different regions spoke different dialects. In areas under foreign rule, languages such as French and Spanish came into use. Other customs, such as the style of dress worn in princely courts, also varied from place to place. As a result, people felt a strong association with their city, state, or region rather than with Italy. They expressed their loyalty to a particular area through devotion to local saints and the construction of town halls, law courts, bell towers, commercial centers, and city walls.

**Unity and Identity.** Despite deep divisions, Italy did have an identity that defined the peninsula and its population. People moved freely across local borders to other regions. Merchants and bankers traveled widely throughout the peninsula, setting up agencies in different areas and obtaining multiple citizenships to advance their business interests.

The migration of people within Italy existed on many levels. Workers moved from place to place in search of opportunity, helping Italian cities grow and prosper and increasing communication among regions. Skilled crafts workers and professionals were in great demand everywhere. Some communities hired government officials from other areas, creating a class of well-traveled Italian administrators. Mercenaries* from poorer regions sought military service with wealthier Italian states.

**Italy, 1500**
- Venetian territory
- Papal States
- Territory claimed by the papacy
- Holy Roman Empire
- • City

Swiss Confederation

HOLY ROMAN EMPIRE

Trent

Savoy

Montferrat

Turin

Milan

Milan

Pavia

Mantua

Asti

Saluzzo

Genoa

Genoa

Modena

Bologna

Bologna

RAVENNA

SAN MARINO

REPUBLIC OF VENICE

Venice

OTTOMAN EMPIRE

FRANCE

Massa

Lucca

Florence

Florence

Pisa

Urbino

Pisa

Siena

Ligurian Sea

Piombino

Siena

Piombino

PAPAL STATES

Adriatic Sea

Dubrovnik (Ragusa)

Corsica (to Genoa)

Rome

Pontecorvo

Benevento

Naples

KINGDOM OF NAPLES

KINGDOM OF SARDINIA

Tyrrhenian Sea

Cagliari

N

0   50   100 mi.
0   50   100 km

Mediterranean Sea

Palermo

KINGDOM OF SICILY

Ionian Sea

AFRICA

This wall painting dating from the 1400s shows a view of the city of Rome. The city, part of the Papal States, grew dramatically over the course of the Renaissance and became an important center of the arts.

* **mercenary**   hired soldier

* **patron**   supporter or financial sponsor of an artist or writer

* **federation**   form of government in which power is shared between a central administration and member states

* **duchy**   territory ruled by a duke or duchess

Students from all over Italy enrolled at universities in Padua, BOLOGNA, and other cities. In addition, artists and scholars moved around the country in search of patrons*.

The use of Roman law was another important unifying factor in Renaissance Italy. A legacy of ancient Rome, this body of law not only influenced legal systems but also encouraged a sense of Italian identity, even a feeling of superiority toward other countries. In the 1300s, Renaissance writers such as PETRARCH reinforced this sense of identity.

In spite of these common elements, Italians made few attempts to establish a political union. In 1347 a Roman official proposed forming a federation* of Italian states, but his idea received little support. In 1455 several northern Italian states created an alliance known as the Italian League. However, its purpose was not to unite Italy but to maintain the balance of power between the major states on the peninsula.

**Forms of Government.** During the Renaissance many Italian cities changed from one form of government to another. Between the 1200s and the 1500s, most of the republics were taken over by powerful *signori* (lords). Some of these rulers were foreigners who acquired control by military force, such as Francesco Sforza, who seized the duchy* of Milan in 1450. Most *signori,* however, were local leaders who gained power through networks of alliances. Political conflict, social unrest, and economic weakness contributed to the decline of republican governments and enabled the *signori* to step in.

The process of changing from independent republics to duchies or princedoms did not always go smoothly. In Florence, for example, members of the MEDICI family began to take control of the city in 1434, but a republican government was reestablished in 1494. The lordship of the

## The Papal States

The Papal States—also known as the Lands of St. Peter—were founded during the Middle Ages. In 754 a Frankish king called Pepin the Short gave the papacy the territory he had conquered in Italy. His gift marked the beginning of a period when the popes acted as political as well as spiritual rulers. Over time, the popes received additional land from European monarchs, and the Papal States grew into a swath of territory that extended from coast to coast in central Italy. After the Renaissance, the papacy's spiritual power increased and its worldly power declined. Papal control over the Papal States ended in 1870 when Italy was united politically and Rome became capital of the new Italian nation.

Medici was not formally recognized until 1530. By the end of the Renaissance, only one major Italian city—Venice—had retained its republican government.

**Foreign Invasion.** Italy's location in the central Mediterranean exposed it to the influence of foreign powers and to invasion. The wealth of Italian cities attracted rulers from Spain, France, and northern Europe. Powerful individuals also attempted to seize Italian lands to which they had some claim through family ties.

Beginning in 1494 the Italian peninsula became the battleground for the WARS OF ITALY, a series of invasions by foreign powers. The French monarchs laid claim to Naples and Milan and fought to gain control of Naples and SICILY. In the first half of the 1500s, the HABSBURGS and the kings of France engaged in a power struggle that involved lands and people across Europe. Many of the battles in this conflict took place on Italian soil.

The Italian city-states were not able to defend themselves against the foreign invaders. They failed to join forces to meet the threat, and some cities even tried to take advantage of the situation. The military defeats dealt a blow to the Italians' sense of cultural superiority. As foreign rulers came to dominate the peninsula, some powerful Italian states, such as Milan, ceased to exist. Others, including Venice, survived by remaining politically neutral. Meanwhile, Naples, Sicily, and some of northern Italy became imperial provinces under Spain. In many respects, by the end of the Renaissance, Italy had returned to what it had been in the Middle Ages—a collection of cities and regions controlled by larger states. (*See also* **Art in Italy; Cities and Urban Life; City-States; Dynastic Rivalry; Government, Forms of; Italian Language and Literature; Popes and Papacy; Princes and Princedoms; Representative Institutions.**)

---

| Italy, Art in |
|---|

**See** *Art in Italy.*

---

### 1566–1625
### King of Scotland and England

* **humanist**   referring to a Renaissance cultural movement promoting the study of the humanities (the languages, literature, and history of ancient Greece and Rome) as a guide to living

* **patron**   supporter or financial sponsor of an artist or writer

James I, the first monarch of the STUART DYNASTY of England, ruled the country from 1603 to 1625. Educated in the humanist* tradition, James was a scholar and a generous patron* of the arts. Though he proved to be an able ruler and administrator, he failed to solve the most difficult problems facing England.

**Scottish Upbringing.** James was the son of the Scottish queen MARY STUART and her husband, Lord Darnley. When Darnley was murdered in 1567, suspicion for the crime fell on Mary and her lover James Hepburn. Scotland's Protestant lords rose up and deposed* Mary, crowning the infant James as king. Several regents* ran the kingdom until 1585, when James took control. Four years later he married Anne of Denmark. Their son Charles later succeeded James as king of Scotland and England.

The humanist education James received prepared him well for debates on the leading issues of the day. His studies included Greek and Latin, theology* (with a strong Protestant focus), poetry, mathematics, natural sciences, geography, and political theory. James's Scottish court was a lively place where courtiers competed for the king's ear. He accepted advice from a wide variety of sources, offending some advisers who felt they deserved more influence.

**King of England.** When ELIZABETH I of England died in 1603, James succeeded to the throne peacefully. However, along with the throne he inherited a number of severe problems, including war with Spain, religious tensions at home, corruption in government, and financial difficulties at the court. James made peace with Spain in 1604 and then turned his attention to the troubles in the English church. He held a conference to lay out his plan for creating unity within the church, and throughout his reign he worked to bridge differences between conservatives and reformers in the church. He also sponsored a new English translation of the Bible, still known today as the King James Version.

As a Scotsman, James faced a certain amount of prejudice in England. To attract and reward supporters, he offered many titles of nobility and gifts, which strained the kingdom's finances. His English subjects particularly resented his gifts to Scots and his efforts to unify England and Scotland politically and socially. His original English court and council contained several Scots, but over time the king filled the most important positions with Englishmen.

James's foreign policy, especially toward Spain, caused problems as well. The king believed that Protestant and Catholic rulers could resolve their differences, and he sought alliances with Spain and other Catholic states. He also tried to arrange a marriage between his son Charles and a Spanish princess. His foreign policy became more complicated after the outbreak of the THIRTY YEARS' WAR in 1618. The Austrian HABSBURGS drove his daughter and her husband Frederick, Protestant ruler of the German principality of the Palatinate and king of BOHEMIA, from their homeland. James called for the Spanish branch of the Habsburg family to step in and settle the matter. However, the English people were suspicious of Spanish Catholic influence, and the king's plan to marry Charles into Spain's royal family collapsed in 1623. James died two years later. His son took the throne as CHARLES I.

Although James dealt with the problems he had inherited from Elizabeth, he ultimately failed to solve them. He never achieved his major goals of improving the crown's finances—though the nation's wealth increased during his reign—or of unifying Scotland and England. In addition, while ruling England, the Stuart dynasty lost touch with conditions and sentiments in Scotland. This distancing would later prove disastrous for Charles.

**James and the Renaissance.** James saw himself as a Renaissance ruler. Patronage of the arts played a major role at his court, where material wealth and display were regarded as a sign of England's power and glory. This attitude led to a wave of art collecting after 1604.

James I ruled both Scotland and England in the early 1600s. Although he worked hard to resolve the problems facing England, he never achieved his main goals of improving the crown's finances and uniting England and Scotland.

* **depose**   to remove from high office, often by force

* **regent**   person who acts on behalf of a monarch who is too young or unable to rule

* **theology**   study of the nature of God and of religion

* **Baroque**   artistic style of the 1600s characterized by movement, drama, and grandness of scale

English style reflected a mixture of late Renaissance influences from all over Europe. It blended the designs of the ancient world with those of the Middle Ages and the newly developing Baroque* style. One of the great artists of the period was the architect Inigo JONES, who created magnificent homes that reflected the traditions of ancient Greece and Rome. Jones also composed court masques, a form of entertainment distinct to James's reign. These elaborate spectacles combined music, drama, and dance, and costumed nobles (including royalty) performed for their peers. The celebrated playwright Ben JONSON wrote many masques for James's court.

The king himself contributed to Renaissance culture by writing several books. In his *Trew Law of Free Monarchies* (1598), he supported the principle of the divine right of kings, declaring that the king answers to no one but God. However, James also believed that the king should rule justly and put the welfare of the kingdom before all other considerations. His other works deal with theology, poetry, and political matters,

* **prince**   Renaissance term for the ruler of an independent state

including a book of advice for princes*. (*See also* **Art in Britain; Drama; England; Monarchy; Scotland.**)

## Jeanne d'Albret

### 1528–1572
### Queen of Navarre

* **humanist**   Renaissance expert in the humanities (the languages, literature, history, and speech and writing techniques of ancient Greece and Rome)

* **annul**   to declare legally invalid

As the niece of the French king FRANCIS I and the daughter of the ruler of the kingdom of Navarre in the Pyrenees, Jeanne d'Albret was a key player in the royal politics of France. She worked hard to ensure that her son Henry of Navarre would succeed to the throne. She was also a tireless promoter of the Huguenot (French Protestant) cause.

Jeanne grew up in Normandy, far from the royal court of the VALOIS DYNASTY. Nicholas de Bourbon, a humanist*, supervised her education and may have encouraged an interest in religious reform. After 1537 Jeanne became a pawn in her family's political intrigues. Her father planned a marriage for her with Philip of Spain, while the king arranged that she should wed the duke of Clèves. Jeanne openly objected to marriage with the duke, designed to cement a political alliance, but it took place in 1541. Four years later, however, the marriage was annulled* when the political alliance disintegrated.

In 1548 Jeanne married Antoine de Bourbon, who headed the powerful house of Bourbon-Vendôme. Jeanne became queen of Navarre upon her father's death in 1555. Then, in 1560, she publicly announced her conversion to the Protestantism of John CALVIN. Jeanne devoted much of her energy to the Huguenot cause, becoming involved in religious struggles at the French court and throughout France. Jeanne died before seeing her son secure the throne as HENRY IV through his marriage to Margaret of Valois, the Catholic daughter of Henry II and CATHERINE DE MÉDICIS. (*See also* **France; Wars of Religion.**)

## Jewelry

Jewelry was extremely popular during the Renaissance, reflecting the wealth of the times. Styles of jewelry evolved along with the clothing fashions of the period. Renaissance men wore gold chains and hat

See color plate 1, vol. 2

badges. These large badges—often two to four inches in diameter—stood out against the black velvet headgear of the time. Both men and women favored large rings, often engraved or set with stones. Wealthy Renaissance women also wore earrings and necklaces. As the necklines of dresses became lower, necklaces with dangling ornaments—such as pendants—grew more popular. Pendants might contain diamonds, emeralds, rubies, or pearls.

Wearing jewelry gave people a way to display their social and financial status. In 1362 English law forbade the lower classes to wear gold or silver, preserving these precious metals as a status symbol for the wealthy. In 1530, FRANCIS I of France declared eight precious stones to be "jewels of the crown," making them symbols of the state and banning their distribution during times of financial crisis.

Jewelry could also serve to advertise a person's political or religious beliefs. For example, some hat badges displayed the images of kings or emperors, while others featured saints. Wealthy nobles often had special jewelry made to celebrate family events, such as births, baptisms, or marriages.

The making of jewelry was a job for skilled artisans*, most of whom belonged to the goldsmiths' guild*. Jewelers often took their designs from pattern books that circulated throughout Europe. Once a patron* accepted a design, the jeweler created a three-dimensional model out of plaster, wood, or lead. This model became the basis for a mold into which the jeweler poured liquid gold or silver. The resulting piece was then painted or decorated with precious stones. Renaissance artisans also revived the art of making cameos, gems or hard stones with a portrait or other picture carved in relief*.

As trade routes opened, many precious stones and metals from the New World arrived in Europe, providing a boost to the jewelry-making industry. Gold and emeralds came from South America, pearls from off the coast of Venezuela, diamonds from India, lapis lazuli—a deep blue stone—from Afghanistan, and turquoise from Persia (present-day Iran). New types of jewels quickly spread across Europe, along with different styles of jewelry. (*See also* **Artisans; Clothing; Guilds.**)

* **artisan**   skilled worker or craftsperson

* **guild**   association of craft and trade owners and workers that set standards for and represented the interests of its members

* **patron**   supporter or financial sponsor of an artist or writer

* **relief**   type of sculpture in which figures are raised slightly from a flat surface

## Jewish Languages and Literature

* **Ottoman Empire**   Islamic empire founded by Ottoman Turks in the 1300s that reached the height of its power in the 1500s; it eventually included large areas of eastern Europe, the Middle East, and northern Africa

Jewish authors of the Renaissance wrote in three major languages. The first, Hebrew, was the ancient language of the Jews. In Spain, Jews had developed a tongue called Ladino, a mix of Hebrew and Spanish words. After Spain expelled the Jews in 1492, many of the exiled Jews took Ladino to their new home, the Ottoman Empire*. In Germany, the blend of local words and Hebrew produced a third language, Yiddish, that spread to other areas. Jews in northern Italy, Poland, Lithuania, the Netherlands, and several areas of the Ottoman Empire spoke versions of Yiddish.

### HEBREW

Jews living in many parts of Europe produced works in Hebrew. Italy had a strong tradition of Hebrew literature throughout the Renaissance.

Renaissance scholars considered Hebrew, the ancient language of the Jewish people, a classical language worth studying. This decorated page from the Book of Abraham, a Hebrew text, appeared in a version of the book printed in Lisbon in 1489.

Until the Jews were expelled from Spain and Provence (part of present-day France), Hebrew literature existed in both areas. Later, Hebrew literature flourished in the Ottoman Empire, where many Jews settled. Literature in Hebrew sprang up in Amsterdam around 1600.

In Italy, Jews and humanist* Christian scholars viewed Hebrew, like Latin and Greek, as a classical* language. Some Christian scholars took lessons from Jewish teachers, learning Hebrew grammar, the Old Testament, and sacred Jewish books. They also produced Hebrew dictionaries. Professors taught Hebrew studies in the Italian universities of Rome and Bologna.

* **humanist** referring to a Renaissance cultural movement promoting the study of the humanities (the languages, literature, and history of ancient Greece and Rome) as a guide to living

* **classical** in the tradition of ancient Greece and Rome

**Hebrew Verse.** Hebrew poetry changed dramatically over the course of the Renaissance. Early writers had used the Bible as the sole source for vocabulary. However, later writers gradually began to draw on philosophical and non-Hebrew sources for words. Some poets wrote in more than one language, switching between lines of Hebrew and another language, such as Italian. They also experimented with meter, adapting Hebrew, Spanish, and Italian meters as well as creating new ones.

The writings of Immanuel of Rome (ca. 1260–ca. 1328) helped to make Hebrew poetry a part of Renaissance culture. Immanuel's *Notebooks* (ca. 1300) contains rhymed stories and poems, including 38 sonnets* in Hebrew—the first to be composed in a language other than Italian. To give these poems the musical quality of Italian sonnets, Immanuel combined elements of Italian and Hebrew-Spanish meters. He also adopted the literary styles of his day, practiced by Italian authors such as Dante Alighieri. His sonnets addressed a broad range of subjects, including sexual love, and his characters—both male and female—displayed a variety of traits, desires, and dreams. Immanuel's sonnets fell from favor after his death, but interest in them revived with the publication of his works in 1492. However, Jewish religious leaders banned Immanuel's writings in 1565.

Much Hebrew poetry of the Renaissance focused on religious themes. One common form was liturgical poetry, written for use in religious services. Liturgical poetry thrived in Spain until the banishment of the Jews. In Italy, poets wrote works of this form until after 1500. After the invention of the printing press, however, the patterns of religious services became fixed, and few new liturgical poems were necessary.

Immanuel and other poets of his time wrote personal, nonliturgical Hebrew poems on religious subjects. Later, Italian poets also took up this kind of poetry. The most prominent kind of Hebrew religious verse during the Renaissance came from the Near East. There, Kabbalists* such as Israel Najara wrote poems that gained an enthusiastic following. Their works were most popular in the Near East and in North Africa. Italian poets also wrote Kabbalah-inspired religious poetry. They intended their poems to form a part of mystical* meetings.

Nonreligious Hebrew poetry flourished in Spain during the 1300s and 1400s. The publication of Immanuel's *Notebooks* in 1492 sparked a revival of Hebrew love poetry and sonnets. Other nonreligious poetry of the Renaissance covered a variety of topics. Many Jews wrote verses in praise of their Christian friends, referring to the common beliefs they shared. Others penned lines of grief about the persecution of Jews. In the late 1500s, poems for special occasions—such as weddings and funerals—became popular.

**Other Forms.** Medieval* and Renaissance writers did not consider writing that had rhythm and rhyme, but lacked a verse form, to be poetry. Instead, they called such writing rhymed prose. After the 1300s, Hebrew rhymed prose in Spain and Provence began to reflect the styles of Christian literature. Authors borrowed familiar characters from Christian works, such as foolish husbands, evil doctors, and lustful old

* **sonnet**   poem of 14 lines with a fixed pattern of meter and rhyme

* **Kabbalist**   believer in a mystical Jewish religious system that involves reading encoded messages in the Hebrew Scriptures

* **mystical**   based on a belief in the idea of a direct, personal union with the divine

* **medieval**   referring to the Middle Ages, a period that began around A.D. 400 and ended around 1400 in Italy and 1500 in the rest of Europe

* **satire**  literary or artistic work ridiculing human wickedness and foolishness

* **treatise**  long, detailed essay

men. Jews used rhymed prose for humor, satire*, adventure stories, proverbs, and defenses of Judaism.

Unrhymed Hebrew prose covered a wide range of forms, including letters, treatises*, and sermons. Hebrew scholars of the 1400s wrote extensively about their language, which they saw as the mother tongue. They composed Hebrew grammars and treatises about the language. Hebrew dictionaries appeared in the 1500s. The theory of poetry was also a popular topic for Hebrew writers. The most notable writer on poetic theory was Samuel Archivolti of Italy, who discussed the use of meter in Immanuel's poetry. Archivolti's work became a manual for writing Hebrew poetry.

Although Jewish teachings forbade most forms of drama, they allowed performances for the religious festival of Purim. The oldest surviving Hebrew drama, *A Comedy of Betrothal* (1550), is a Purim play. Judah Sommo, a stage director and writer of Italian drama, composed the comedy in perfect, unrhymed Hebrew. Its plot is a complex love story typical of Renaissance drama. Other Hebrew plays, such as *Foundation of the World,* have religious themes and resemble Spanish *autos*—plays that celebrate the victory of the faith. In *Foundation,* playwright Moses Zacuto used a wide range of verse forms, including sonnets.

## LADINO LITERATURE

Ladino was the spoken and written language of Renaissance Jews in several areas of Spain. Used within the Jewish community, Ladino blended local Spanish dialects with terms from Hebrew and Aramaic, an ancient Jewish tongue. Many of these added words related to religious belief and practice. People usually wrote Ladino in the Hebrew alphabet.

Ladino included old Hispanic words that had disappeared from the Spanish language. After Spain expelled the Jews in 1492, many Ladino speakers settled in the Ottoman Empire. For hundreds of years, their language preserved characteristics of the Spanish tongue as it had been spoken before the Renaissance.

The Spanish burned most literature that was written in the Hebrew alphabet. Only three Ladino works in Hebrew script survive from the 1400s. Some Ladino manuscripts in the Latin alphabet, however, survived the burnings. Because of this, some Ladino translations of the Scriptures, as well as writings on philosophy and ethics*, still exist.

* **ethics**  branch of philosophy concerned with questions of right and wrong

Ladino literature from the mid-1500s through the end of the Renaissance included a variety of forms. Some were religious in nature, such as translations of the Bible, prayer books, and works on Jewish religious practices. In the early 1500s, translations focused on the texts that synagogues and religious schools needed the most. The first complete Ladino translation of the Scriptures did not exist until the 1700s. Other works include adaptations of Hebrew historical accounts and religious legal codes from the Middle Ages. A few poetic works about biblical figures, associated with holidays such as Purim and Passover, also survive.

## YIDDISH LITERATURE

Because people spoke Yiddish in many different countries, foreign words entered the spoken form of the language. Along with the earlier German influences, the Yiddish language included Italian, Slavic, Dutch, Arabic, and Turkish words in different areas. However, Yiddish writers made efforts to keep written Yiddish free of these regional influences. This pure written form of the language connected all Yiddish speakers to the same body of literature, no matter where they lived.

Most Yiddish literature was religious in nature. Most Yiddish writers focused on translating Hebrew works so that Yiddish-speaking Jews could understand them. For example, they produced Yiddish versions of Hebrew prayers and books of the Bible. They also translated Hebrew works on ethics, as well as composing original ethical works in Yiddish. Topics included a person's duties on Jewish holidays or other special occasions, such as weddings and funerals. Fables and tales with religious sources also instructed people in how to live. Many books focused on the roles and religious duties of women, providing special prayers for all events in a woman's life cycle.

Literature in Yiddish also served to spread knowledge. New works and Yiddish translations of Hebrew texts described distant places and the historical past. Because there was no Yiddish newspaper until the 1800s, Yiddish-speaking Jews in the Renaissance used songs to spread news and information. These pieces combined the style of German historical songs with elements of Hebrew tradition.

Yiddish, with its Hebrew alphabet and its mix of Hebrew and German words, gave its speakers footholds in two languages. Those who could read Yiddish could also read Hebrew, although they often did not understand it. At the same time, many Yiddish speakers understood German. However, they did not read it because they disliked using the Roman alphabet, which they associated with Christian priests. Instead, the few Jews who could read the Roman script rewrote German epic* poems in the Hebrew alphabet so that other Jews could read them.

Yiddish-speaking communities in northern Italy were active in literature and printing. During the 1400s and 1500s, Yiddish authors in these areas published both single-story booklets and larger collections. They also introduced the use of illustrations in Yiddish books. Many of their works were adaptations of Italian popular literature. (*See also* **Anti-Semitism; Jews; Ottoman Empire; Religious Thought; Translation.**)

### Dialogues on Love

The Portuguese-born writer Judah Abravanel, better known as Leone Ebreo, helped to shape European views of God and love. In *Dialogues on Love* (composed in Italian around 1502), he explains that love connects all living things to each other and to God. His ideas had little impact on Jewish thinkers, but they spread widely in Christian communities, where they strongly influenced many later philosophers and writers.

* **epic** long poem about the adventures of a hero

---

**Jewish Thought**

**See** *Religious Thought; Philosophy.*

---

**Jews**

European Jews led an uneasy life during the Renaissance. Religious and cultural barriers—and often physical and legal ones as well—stood between them and their Christian neighbors. Authorities in vari-

Many Jewish artworks were religious objects, such as holy books. For example, during the festival of Passover, Jews read from a prayer book called the Haggadah. This illustration of Jews observing Passover appeared in a German Haggadah in the early 1400s.

ous places made Jews live in specific areas, forced them to convert to Christianity, or drove them out of cities and nations. Nevertheless, Jews made significant contributions to Renaissance life and culture.

## JEWISH RELIGIOUS LIFE

Contact with Christians influenced the Jewish religion during the Renaissance. Rabbis, who had traditionally served as experts in Jewish law, began to take on roles like those of priests in the Roman Catholic Church. Similarly, synagogues ceased to be solely places of prayer and developed into centers of social life.

* **laypeople** those who are not members of the clergy

* **mystical** based on a belief in the idea of a direct, personal union with the divine

During the 1500s and 1600s the confraternity movement began to spread among Jews in Italy. Confraternities were groups of laypeople* who gathered together for religious, social, and charitable purposes. The oldest Jewish confraternity in Italy was the burial society known as the Gemilut Hasadim. This group originally served to prepare bodies for the grave and to bury the dead. By the mid-1500s, however, its focus had shifted to preparing the soul before death. If a member was ill for three days, officials of the confraternity would visit him and encourage him to confess his sins to God. This new concern with confession reflects a similar trend among Catholics in the mid-1500s.

Another key influence on Jewish religious life at this time was a messianic movement that began in the late 1400s. The central belief of this movement was that the end of the world was at hand. Messianic Jews believed that a Messiah, a hero sent by God, would soon arrive on earth to punish the Gentiles (non-Jews), restore the dead to life, and establish a perfect kingdom of peace and prosperity, free from evil.

Messianic ideas often grew out of the Kabbalah, a mystical* Jewish religious system that involves reading encoded messages in the Hebrew Scriptures. The ideas of Kabbalah influenced messianic figures such as Shelomo Molcho, a Portuguese New Christian (a descendant of Jews who had become Christians). Although Molcho later converted to Judaism, Christian ideas of the Messiah may have shaped his beliefs. Molcho had several divine visions that he published in a book in 1529. Over the next two years he correctly predicted a flood of the Tiber River in Italy and an earthquake in Portugal. Molcho even met with Pope Clement VII. However, he was eventually burned at the stake after refusing to return to Christianity. Molcho became a legendary religious figure among later generations of Jews.

Renaissance Jews also differed among themselves in religious beliefs and practices. In northern Italy, for example, Jewish women took great care to perform the ritual bath required after their menstrual periods. However, Jews in this region paid little attention to the traditional prohibition against drinking wine made by Gentiles. In southern Italy, by contrast, Jews cared less about the ritual bath but took great pains to avoid Gentile wine. Many factors contributed to local differences of this kind. In eastern regions, for instance, coffee had long made it possible for people to stay up for the midnight ceremony called Tikkun Hazot. The ritual did not become popular in Italy, however, until coffee arrived there in the late 1600s.

## JEWS IN RENAISSANCE SOCIETY

The position of Jews in Renaissance society was full of contradictions. Christian society discriminated against them, yet it could not manage without them, as they filled vital roles in the economy. The church tried to persuade—or force—them to convert to Christianity, yet those who did so were often suspected of being false to their adopted church. Many Jews gained influence at the courts of Christian leaders, but these pow-

erful Jews tended to become targets of resentment. Even within the Jewish community, social roles were often unclear.

**Jewish Communities in Italy.** Jewish communities in medieval* and Renaissance Europe had their own distinct character. Many were very small, containing only one or two families. Even where larger numbers of Jews lived together in one place, they never really controlled their own government. Kings, nobles, popes, and town councils interfered constantly in the affairs of the Jews.

The oldest Jewish community in Europe was in Rome, which had been home to Jews since ancient times. In other Italian cities, Jewish settlements did not form until the mid to late 1500s. By 1600, almost 60 percent of Italy's Jews lived in the Papal States*, mostly in the cities of Rome, Ancona, and Ferrara.

Outside of Italy, Jews faced immense difficulties in establishing their own communities. None existed in France or England. In Germany, Christians frequently attacked Jewish settlements or forced their residents to flee. Jews in the Netherlands lived under cover as Christians until the 1600s, when they began to form openly Jewish communities. Spain, Naples, and Sicily drove all Jews out of their territories in the late 1400s and early 1500s. Portugal forced its Jews to convert to Christianity in 1497.

Jews also had problems forming true communities because they lacked a sense of political organization. Jews conceived of the community as a court of law headed by a scholar. However, from the 1100s on, they debated the question of who had the right to participate in making the law. Some scholars believed the entire community should discuss and decide on laws, while others thought elected representatives should perform this function. Some argued that everyone in the community had to agree to a law, while others claimed the majority should rule. Jewish legal scholars never clearly settled these issues. The decisions of communal councils were often disputed or challenged by members of the community who did not accept the council's right to rule.

Jews also disagreed over whether religious or secular* figures should make the laws. Jewish law, or halakah, did not distinguish between religious and secular realms. It gave rabbis the job of interpreting the law. In Italy, however, the leaders of Jewish communities tended to be secular figures. Few rabbis ever achieved positions of political power. Synagogues, which were places of religion, served as the centers of Jewish social and political life. However, fraternal groups such as the Gemilut Hasadim—which were mostly secular—controlled many social functions and jealously guarded their power in these spheres.

Outsiders had as much difficulty as the Jews themselves in defining the nature of the Jewish community. They did not seem to know for sure whether Jewish communities had any authority over their own affairs or were simply cultural groups. In most places, Jews existed within the legal framework of the larger society. The Jews of Rome, for example, had received a set of legal privileges from the pope that allowed them to collect taxes and to be treated as citizens of Rome. Although

* **medieval** referring to the Middle Ages, a period that began around A.D. 400 and ended around 1400 in Italy and 1500 in the rest of Europe

* **Papal States** lands in central Italy under the authority of the pope

* **secular** nonreligious; connected with everyday life

this status placed Jews under the protection of Roman law, it also required all Jewish institutions to meet the strict legal standards of Christian Rome.

**Jews at Court.** In the late 1500s, Jews began to play an important role in the courts of Europe. As rulers started to form more absolutist* states, they sought to build strong centralized armies and governing bodies. This task required large sums of money, and rulers turned to private business owners to assist them.

Jewish traders were ideally suited to fill this need. Their connections in international trade enabled them to supply food, clothing, and weapons for soldiers. They could also provide luxury items, such as jewels, for the court. In addition, rulers often employed Jews to mint coins, collect taxes, and even conduct secret diplomatic missions. After the THIRTY YEARS' WAR (1618–1648), court Jews played a vital role in most of the small states that made up the Holy Roman Empire*. As outsiders who possessed great political influence, court Jews often faced resentment and anti-Semitism*. Despite this opposition, they remained key figures in European state government until the early 1800s.

**Jews and the Catholic Church.** During the Middle Ages, Catholic authorities had allowed Jews to live among Christians if they accepted some limits on their activities. This approach changed during the Renaissance. Christian leaders and legal scholars adopted policies that separated Jews from Christians physically, or else forced them to abandon Judaism.

The first signs of these new policies appeared just before 1500, as Spain drove all Jews out of its territories and Portugal forced its Jews to convert. However, these forced conversions failed to satisfy government and church officials, who believed that the converts were practicing Judaism in secret. This suspicion led authorities in Spain and Portugal to establish inquisitions, special courts to investigate charges of heresy*— which focused mostly on New Christians.

Another source of friction between Jews and Catholics was usury, the practice of lending money and charging interest. The church banned this practice among Christians but allowed it among Jews. In the 1500s, members of the Franciscan religious order began preaching against usury and other "polluting" activities by Jews. People began to call loudly for the separation of Jews and Christians. Some Christians made wild accusations against Jews, including a charge that Jews in the north Italian city of Trent had killed a Christian child and used his blood in their rituals. This claim led to the destruction of Trent's Jewish community in 1475 and sparked violence in other Italian cities.

Although the Catholic Church wished to convert Jews, church leaders could not agree on the best way to achieve that goal. Some favored a moderate approach that emphasized persuasive preaching. Ignatius Loyola, founder of the Jesuit religious order, adopted this approach and set out ground rules for successful conversions. Others suggested that imposing financial penalties on Jews would force them to convert. Still

* **absolutist** refers to complete control by a single ruler

* **Holy Roman Empire** political body in central Europe composed of several states; existed until 1806

* **anti-Semitism** prejudice against Jews

* **heresy** belief that is contrary to the doctrine of an established church

Visual art was never an important part of Jewish culture, and scholars can only definitely identify a few pieces as the work of Jewish artists. One example is this small silver casket from the 1400s, which illustrates three Jewish women performing rituals of their faith.

others argued for compelling Jews to live in specific neighborhoods, or ghettos, to keep them from "infecting" the Christian community. This separation made it easier to restrict Jewish activities.

One of the most shocking episodes of this time occurred in the Italian city of Ancona, part of the Papal States. The city contained a community of New Christians who had fled Portugal and returned to Judaism. In 1534 Pope Paul III gave them permission to live openly in Ancona as Jews. However, Pope Paul IV reversed this policy, and in 1556 the Roman Inquisition burned 25 Jews at the stake. Many Italian Jews did convert to Christianity as a result of this terror, and many Jews in smaller communities fled to Jewish settlements in larger towns and cities.

In the end, practical considerations prevented Christians from completely excluding Jews from society. As late as the 1570s, cities in northern Italy were offering contracts to Jewish bankers and lenders to encourage them to settle there. In Rome, shutting down Jewish social and cultural life would have bankrupted many Jews and greatly burdened the papal* treasury. The popes gradually reduced the pressure on Jews to convert, and relations between the Catholic Church and Jewish communities returned to their former state.

* **papal** referring to the office and authority of the pope

**The Role of Women.** Like their Christian counterparts, Jewish women lived in a male-centered society that placed heavy restrictions on their lives. However, Jewish law gave Jewish women rights that many Christian women lacked. They could own property, sign contracts, and represent themselves in court. These legal and financial privileges gave them a measure of influence in community affairs.

Some Jewish women in Italy managed to obtain training as scribes* and printers, and a few gained a measure of fame as writers. Others took

* **scribe** person who copies manuscripts

part with rabbis in discussions of Jewish law and participated in healing and birthing practices. One unnamed Jewish woman in Italy expressed pride in her womanhood by saying a prayer of thanks each day that God "had made me a woman and not a man." Her phrasing reversed the traditional words of the blessing in which a man expresses his gratitude for not being born a woman.

Among Jews who had converted (at least outwardly) to Christianity, a few women accumulated considerable wealth and power as the heads of their families. Benvenida Abravanel, a Portuguese New Christian, ran a loan-banking business in Italy and served Florence's powerful MEDICI family. In 1533, when Holy Roman Emperor CHARLES V sought to expel all Jews from Naples, she played a key role in convincing him to put off the plan for eight more years.

Another New Christian, Doña Gracia Nasi, managed her family's extensive financial and cultural affairs after the deaths of her husband and his brother. Fleeing the Portuguese Inquisition, Nasi traveled across Europe to the Ottoman Empire*. There she became one of several Jewish women to gain influence at the court of the Ottoman sultan. She set up her own court and a yeshiva, or Jewish religious school. In 1555, when the pope allowed 25 New Christians to be burned to death in the city of Ancona, Nasi organized a boycott against the city.

Most Jewish women, however, did not hold this kind of power. Rabbis tended to oppose educating women beyond what was necessary to run a household. When a Jewish woman achieved unusual success, it often led to protest from the men in the community. Jewish women were even criticized for being too religious. One rabbi argued that women who devoted themselves excessively to God ignored their chief duty to their husbands and families. Rabbis further supported the power of Jewish men within the home by making it extremely difficult for wives to leave unhappy or even abusive marriages.

* **Ottoman Empire** Islamic empire founded by Ottoman Turks in the 1300s that reached the height of its power in the 1500s; it eventually included large areas of eastern Europe, the Middle East, and northern Africa

## JEWS AND RENAISSANCE CULTURE

Jews made significant contributions to scholarship and the arts during the Renaissance. However, their achievements in these areas clearly reflected the influence of the Christian and secular culture that surrounded them.

**The Visual Arts.** Jewish art in the Renaissance was largely limited to religious objects, such as texts and decorations for the synagogue. Many scholars argue that the Jews never focused on the visual arts because of their strict interpretation of the Second Commandment, which forbade them to make "graven images." The robust visual culture of Renaissance Italy made Italian Jews more inclined to be flexible about this rule. Even so, art never occupied a prominent place in Jewish society, and no individual Jewish artist achieved great fame. Scholars can only positively identify a few pieces as the work of Jewish artists. In addition, some of the most noted Jewish artists converted to Christianity to receive commissions and public recognition.

* **illumination**  hand-painted color decorations and illustrations on the pages of a manuscript

* **treatise**  long, detailed essay

* **patron**  supporter or financial sponsor of an artist or writer

Manuscript illumination* was probably the most popular form of art among Italian Jews in the 1300s and 1400s. The earliest illuminated Hebrew texts are Bibles from the late 1200s, which feature decorations in the margins. In the 1300s scenes of Jewish daily life began to appear in treatises* on Jewish law. These painted scenes, called miniatures, became even more elaborate in the 1400s. One manuscript from around 1470 features two full-page pictures based on the final chapters of the biblical story of Job. The figure of Job himself may have been modeled on the patron* who sponsored the work.

Even after the development of printing, Jewish artists continued to produce illuminated manuscripts. These included new types of documents such as Esther scrolls, used to celebrate the holiday of Purim, and marriage contracts, called *ketubbot.* These large scrolls featured biblical scenes and symbolic images. Jewish families competed to produce elaborate *ketubbot,* hiring the best craftsmen available to create the colorful drawings.

Artistic production thrived in Jewish ghettos. Their physical separation and their status as outcasts from Christian society led Jews to produce art as a way of reinforcing their cultural identity. One major symbol of Jewish culture was the synagogue itself. Most of these buildings were plain on the outside, but their interiors followed the splendid architectural styles of the time. Synagogues typically featured highly decorated ritual objects such as the ark, or cabinet, for the Torah scrolls and the *bimah,* the platform from which the Torah was read. The Torah scrolls themselves often had a "dressing" of expensive cloth, and the ark might feature a curtain embroidered with biblical scenes and symbols.

**Music.** Before the Renaissance, Jews had little music aside from the prayers chanted in synagogues. Many rabbis preached that all Jews should be in perpetual mourning for the destruction of the ancient Temple in Jerusalem. They condemned secular music, musical instruments, and the use of music as a source of entertainment. They did not look on synagogue chants as music, but as a form of recitation. The traditional melodies of these chants, supposedly given to Moses by God on Mount Sinai, were considered sacred and unchangeable. The Hebrew language also made the development of written music difficult because it read from right to left. A workable system of notes for Jewish "art music" for two or more voices did not appear until the 1620s.

One form of traditional Jewish music, the hymn, did exist during the Middle Ages. Unlike prayer chants, hymns were melodic and generally had a fixed rhythm. Composing new melodies for hymns was a common practice. A Jewish text from the 1200s urged readers to "seek for melodies and when you pray employ a melody which will be beautiful and soft in your eyes." Synagogues typically employed a cantor to sing hymns during services. As cantors grew in importance, synagogues introduced new songs to allow them to display their skills. In the 1500s, some synagogues began hiring assistant singers to support the cantor—generally a boy with a high voice and an adult bass. The three-part harmonies these singers produced marked the beginnings of Jewish art music.

### Birth of the Ghetto

The modern word *ghetto* refers to a minority neighborhood within a city. During the Renaissance, it identified the districts in European cities set aside for Jews. The first city to establish a ghetto was Venice, which had been home to Jewish communities during the Middle Ages. In 1516, the city's leaders forced all Jewish residents to live in the section of town known as the Ghetto Nuovo. They could work outside the ghetto during the day, but they had to return to the ghetto at night. The use of the word *ghetto* to refer to a Jewish neighborhood later spread to other parts of Europe.

## As Seen by Christians

Works by Christian artists provide some insight into the way Renaissance Christians viewed their Jewish neighbors. German art often featured anti-Semitic images. Many northern artists portrayed hated biblical figures, such as Cain and Judas, with exaggerated racial features. Italian works, by contrast, seldom showed Jews in any special way. As a result, it is difficult to identify Jewish figures in Italian paintings. However, in the few known Italian portraits of Jews from this period, the subjects often bear the round yellow badges that many Italian states required Jews to wear.

* **theological** relating to theology, the study of the nature of God and of religion

* **humanist** referring to a Renaissance cultural movement promoting the study of the humanities (the languages, literature, and history of ancient Greece and Rome) as a guide to living

During the Renaissance, music became more popular among Jews as a means of celebrating joyous events, such as weddings and certain holidays. At the same time, many Jewish musicians found work in European courts, where they learned the latest styles of Christian music. Although most rabbis tended to discourage the imitation of Christian ways, a few began taking a looser approach to music, introducing multipart singing into the synagogue. Some Jews justified their interest in art music by comparing it to the glorious music performed in the ancient Temple.

The first art music by Jewish composers appeared in Italy in the late 1500s before spreading to Amsterdam and southern France. Few works still remain, and most collections by Jewish composers of the time are incomplete. The best-known early Jewish composer was Salamone Rossi, who is credited with writing the first secular Jewish art music songs. He is the only Jewish Renaissance composer whose complete works have survived. Rossi also composed the only known works of Jewish instrumental music from the period.

**Printing.** The development of printing had a great impact on Jewish life. Printed books led to the appearance of new types of writing, reading, and learning. Printers developed a Hebrew typeface soon after the invention of the printing press, and by 1500 some 200 works had been printed in Hebrew.

Italy was the center of Hebrew publishing in the 1500s. Daniel Bomberg, Italy's leading printer of Hebrew books, set up a press in Venice in 1516. His designs for Hebrew books set the standard that is still in use today. In the 1540s other Jewish printers appeared in Italy, Poland, and the Ottoman Empire. By the 1600s, however, the center of Hebrew printing had moved to Amsterdam.

Christians played a significant role in early Hebrew printing. The Christian printers who invested in Hebrew presses were attracted mainly by profit, but they also had intellectual and theological* interests in Jewish texts. They often employed Jews or Jewish converts as editors and proofreaders, and their workshops became meeting places for humanist* Jews and Christians.

The books published by early Hebrew presses reshaped many aspects of Jewish social life. The most common Hebrew texts in print included prayer books, legal codes, and treatises on the Talmud (the scholarly commentary on Jewish law). Such works helped lay the foundation for a unified legal system in the Jewish world. Books of Jewish customs also helped form a common vision of Jewish life and tradition.

Hebrew presses also printed versions of major Jewish religious texts, such as the Talmud and the *Zohar,* the central work of the Kabbalah. Before printing, knowledge of the Kabbalah had been guarded and limited to a select group of individuals. Printing made this secret knowledge available to a much wider audience. As a result, the Kabbalah assumed a much more important role in the spiritual life of Jewish communities. Printed editions of the Talmud mainly affected scholars, giving them a standard version of the text to study.

* **blasphemy**   act of insulting or failing to show respect for God and for holy things

Christian authorities in many places exercised control over Hebrew printing. Their chief goal was to prevent blasphemy* and anti-Christian statements in Jewish literature. In the 1550s the pope ordered the burning of copies of the Talmud as part of his struggle against heresy in print. The church later changed its policy to checking the content of books before their publication.

**Scholarship.** Like Jewish art and music, Jewish scholarship reflected the influence of the surrounding Christian culture. During the Middle Ages, some Jewish philosophers had engaged in debate with Christian thinkers, while others feared that such discussions would weaken Jewish identity. The humanist movement of the Renaissance increased the contact between Jewish and Christian scholars. Christian humanists sought out Jewish teachers to help them understand the truth of the Hebrew Scriptures. These Jewish scholars not only taught their Christian students Hebrew but also tried to convince them that the Bible contained all forms of human and divine knowledge. They argued for the superiority of the Jewish culture, claiming that even the ancient Greek philosophers would have drawn ideas from the Bible or from discussions with Jewish prophets. This view appealed to humanists, who had a keen interest in discovering the original sources of human wisdom.

Both Jewish and Christian scholars of the Middle Ages had based much of their thinking on the ideas of the Greek philosopher ARISTOTLE. Many Renaissance humanists, however, focused more on the teachings of PLATO. Jewish scholars tried to use Plato's ideas to reinterpret Jewish writings such as the Kabbalah. They aimed to show that the Jewish intellectual tradition was far more ancient than that of the Christian world. Some Jewish scholars, however, condemned these efforts to spread knowledge of the Kabbalah among Christians.

Another strong Jewish intellectual tradition was based on the writings of the Muslim scholar Ibn Rushd, or Averroes (1126–1198). Averroes's comments on the works of Aristotle had influenced thinkers throughout the Middle Ages. Jewish scholar Elijah Delmedigo made Averroes's ideas the focus of a belief system based on reason, as opposed to the mysticism of the Kabbalah. Another follower of Averroes, Judah Messer Leon, attempted to read the Hebrew Scriptures as a literary text, using the rules of rhetoric* laid down by Aristotle. His work reflected an ongoing debate in the Jewish community about the value of rhetoric in teaching.

Yohanan Alemanno of Florence attempted to merge the Hebrew Scriptures and the Kabbalah into a complete system of thought. Studying under Christian humanist Marsilio FICINO, he became convinced that the ideas of Plato could link the Bible and the Kabbalah with the reason of Western thought. His work reflected Ficino's idea of cosmic love as the force that had created all things and that connected all parts of the living world. Jewish scholar Judah Abranavel (also known as Leone Ebreo) picked up on these ideas, suggesting that the Kabbalah carried an ancient wisdom that could shed light even on the pagan* myths of ancient Greece and Rome. Such ideas had little lasting effect

* **rhetoric**   speaking or writing effectively

* **pagan**   referring to ancient religions that worshiped many gods, or more generally, to any non-Christian religion

on the Jewish community, but they did influence later philosophers such as Giordano BRUNO and Benedict de Spinoza. (*See also* **Anti-Semitism; Bible; Books and Manuscripts; Confraternities; Conversos; Ghetto; Illumination; Inquisition; Jewish Languages and Literature; Music, Vocal; Philosophy; Printing and Publishing; Religious Thought.**)

## Jones, Inigo

### 1573–1652
### English architect and designer

\* **classical** in the tradition of ancient Greece and Rome

\* **masque** dramatic entertainment performed by masked actors

One of the most important designers of Renaissance England, Inigo Jones served as court architect to the Stuart kings. He developed a unique building style based on the classical\* principles of the Italian Renaissance architect Andrea PALLADIO. Jones's work paved the way for the ARCHITECTURE of the late English Renaissance.

After early training as a painter, Jones worked at St. Paul's Cathedral as an apprentice woodworker. In the summer of 1603, he went to Denmark and prepared designs for the Danish king Christian IV. After returning to England in 1604, Jones worked for Queen Anne, the wife of JAMES I, creating stage settings for court masques\*.

In 1610 Henry, the Prince of Wales, hired Jones to redesign the royal garden at Richmond based on Renaissance principles. Three years later, Jones traveled to Heidelberg, Germany, to attend the wedding of James I's daughter, Elizabeth. He then went to Italy, where he studied Roman ruins and the works of Palladio. When Jones returned to England, he received a commission from Thomas Howard, earl of Arundel, to remodel the earl's home and to create a gallery to house his collection of ancient statues.

In 1615 James I employed Jones to redesign London, to make it an ideal city and a fitting capital for the STUART DYNASTY. In his plans for London, Jones followed *all'antica* (in the antique manner) principles to create a grand Renaissance style. He planned to place buildings in this style at significant points in the city, echoing the renovation of Rome undertaken by Pope Sixtus V in the 1580s. A few years later, the king instructed Jones to survey the ancient ruins of Stonehenge, looking for links to Britain's heroic past. The architect later claimed that the underlying harmony of the design of Stonehenge was proof of England's Roman ancestry.

Jones designed a number of important buildings for the Stuarts, including the queen's house at Greenwich and a new Star Chamber and Banqueting House at Whitehall Palace. The Banqueting House, one of Jones's most famous buildings, included movable scenery for performances of court masques. In the design for Whitehall, Jones tried to show the power and magnificence of the Stuarts and to create a structure that would rival the great palaces of France and Spain. The full project remained a fantasy, however, as most of what Jones planned for Whitehall was never built.

In 1633 Jones began renovating St. Paul's Cathedral in London. He resurfaced the interior walls with *all'antica* ornamentation and added a giant classical portico\* to the west front of the building. However, with the outbreak of the English Civil War in 1642, work on the cathedral

\* **portico** porch or walkway supported by regularly spaced columns

was abandoned just as Jones's career was drawing to a close. (*See also* **Art in Britain; London; Palaces and Townhouses; Theaters.**)

**Jonson, Ben**

**1572–1637**
**English poet and playwright**

* **classical** in the tradition of ancient Greece and Rome

* **satire** literary or artistic work ridiculing human wickedness and foolishness

Ben Jonson, one of Elizabethan England's greatest writers, led a life filled with social, political, and religious reversals. Jonson was the close and friendly rival of playwright William SHAKESPEARE, a friend of the English poet John DONNE, and the unofficial national poet of England. He was also an accomplished writer and one of the finest Greek scholars of his day. Many people of his own time considered him to be as good a writer as Shakespeare or better.

**Early Life and Works.** Jonson was probably born in or near London. As an adult, Jonson reported that his father, a Protestant minister, had died just a month before Ben was born. Young Ben went to a small private school before attending Westminster School. He probably did not go on to a university, although some rumors hold that he briefly stayed at St. John's College at Cambridge University. After completing his schooling, he worked with his stepfather as a bricklayer, an occupation he hated. Around 1591 he enlisted as a soldier in the Netherlands, where the English were fighting the Spanish.

After returning to England, Jonson began working as a writer and an actor. By 1594 he had married, and in 1597 he joined the acting company Pembroke's Men. His earliest surviving play, *The Case Is Altered*, was first performed the same year. Like many Renaissance writers, Jonson based his play on classical* examples—in this case, ancient Roman comedy. Pembroke's Men also produced Jonson's satire* *Isle of Dogs* in 1597. It painted an unflattering portrait of recent events at the royal palace. The queen's advisers found the play so offensive that they shut down all of London's theaters. They also jailed its main actors, including Jonson.

Jonson scored his first major success as a playwright in 1598, with *Every Man in His Humor*. This urban comedy—a popular dramatic form of the time that focused on city life—featured exaggerated character types. Although Jonson originally set the play in Florence, he later shifted the setting to London. Shakespeare and his company, the Lord Chamberlain's Men, performed the play at the Curtain Theater.

At the same time, Jonson found himself in serious trouble. In 1598, while *Every Man in His Humor* was still in performance, Jonson killed a fellow actor. He was arrested and tried for manslaughter. During his time in prison, Jonson became a Catholic. In some of the poems that he wrote during this period, he spoke directly to other Catholics and discussed his newfound faith. Jonson narrowly escaped the death penalty, but the court had him branded on the thumb with a hot iron as a convicted criminal.

Jonson's career thrived in spite of his personal difficulties. In 1599, Lord Chamberlain's Men presented Jonson's *Every Man out of His Humor*, another comedy that featured broad character types. Some of his other comedies of this time satirized the royal court, politics, and popular poetry. Jonson's words stung—one of the writers he targeted later wrote a play portraying him as hostile, rude, and disrespectful.

**Jonson in the Royal Court.** In 1603, Jonson welcomed the reign of the new king, JAMES I, with flattering writings. He made a name for himself at court with his masques—elaborate dramatic entertainments that marked important events. During the following years Jonson served as the court's semi-official poet.

Despite his position as the court's favored writer, Jonson continued to experience trouble with the law. As a Catholic in James's Protestant court, he attracted suspicion. In 1604, after the production of his tragedy *Sejanus,* officials charged Jonson with "popery" (that is, practicing Catholicism, which was illegal at the time) and treason. The printed versions of *Sejanus* do not support these charges. However, Jonson admitted that the version of the play that the actors had performed on stage differed from these printed versions.

*Eastward Ho!,* a play that Jonson cowrote, landed him in jail again. The printed version of the play made gentle fun of King James's favoritism toward his fellow Scots. Like *Sejanus,* this play may have been harsher in its original version. Jonson and the other authors feared that their punishment would be severe, but powerful members of the court had them released.

Later in 1605 Jonson found himself caught up in the events surrounding the Gunpowder Plot—a conspiracy* by several Catholics to blow up the houses of parliament. Shortly before authorities discovered the plot, Jonson attended a dinner party with many of the men involved. However, he also helped the authorities obtain information to stop the plot. Later, he wrote a poem to congratulate the man who discovered the conspiracy.

**Mature Works.** *Volpone,* Jonson's greatest and fiercest comedy, first appeared on stage in 1606. This dark play includes fraud, seduction, and corruption. Unlike popular comedies of the day, *Volpone* did not have a happy ending. Instead the play ends with two characters awaiting whipping and imprisonment as punishments for their crimes.

Jonson's next plays relied on complex plots. The surprises that unfolded in *Epicene, or The Silent Woman* (first performed in 1609 or early 1610) kept audiences guessing up until the play's final moments. The complicated plot of *The Alchemist* (1610) followed three con men claiming to be able to give people whatever they want. Jonson set the play in the same district of London where the play was first performed in 1610.

That same year, England's anti-Catholic laws became more severe. People who still refused to attend services in the Protestant Church of England faced stiff penalties and restrictions. Perhaps as a result, Jonson chose to return to the Church of England.

The year 1616 was an eventful one for Jonson. A London printer published Jonson's *Workes,* a collection of his literary achievements up until his middle years. Jonson supervised the book's publication carefully. The

Ben Jonson was one of the most famous playwrights in Renaissance England and the country's unofficial national poet. Although his talent won him the favor of the king, James I, Jonson experienced trouble with the law throughout his life and wound up in jail on several occasions.

---

* **conspiracy** plotting with others to commit a crime

---

**Uplifting Theater**

Before the publication of Jonson's *Workes* in 1616, many people did not consider the text of a play a serious type of literary work. However, Jonson included plays in his *Workes* because he wanted his dramatic writing to receive the same kind of scholarly attention as classical literature. By doing this, he presented himself not as a "playwright"—a term he disliked—but as a true Renaissance scholar.

*Workes* included two large collections of poems, eight plays, and other pieces. In the same year, the king granted Jonson a pension for life—an act that made Jonson the unofficial national poet. After Shakespeare's death in April 1616, Jonson was clearly the greatest living poet in Britain.

**Later Years.** From 1618 to 1623, Jonson visited Scotland, received an honorary degree from the University of Oxford, and continued to write masques and royal entertainments. Some scholars also believe that he taught rhetoric* at Gresham College in London. He wrote the fullest surviving record of his life and opinions—*Conversations with Drummond*—during this period.

In spite of his successes, Jonson felt less welcome at court during the final years of James's reign, and even less so after CHARLES I took the throne in 1625. When Charles courted a Spanish princess in 1623, Jonson played almost no role in the plans for receiving the prince's intended bride. Instead that honor fell to his rival, Inigo JONES. In response, Jonson wrote "An Epistle* Answering to One That Asked to Be Sealed of the Tribe of Ben." In it, he describes his own social group—the "tribe of Ben"—as superior to the court. Jonson also addressed Charles's rise to power in his next play, *The Staple of News* (1626). Jonson's satire discussed sons who scheme to manage their fathers' fortunes.

The last decade of Jonson's life was filled with difficulties. In 1628, he suffered a stroke, which weakened him and kept him from working. Many of his poems from this time concerned his disabilities and his financial needs. His last comedies, which focused on rural and romantic themes, were not theatrical successes.

Ben Jonson died in 1637. He was buried at Westminster Abbey, the resting place of London's leading poets. His death attracted more attention than Shakespeare's, and most of London's nobles attended his funeral. The following year, one of Jonson's friends edited a collection of poems in his memory. A two-volume edition of Jonson's own writings appeared in 1640–1641. (*See also* **Drama; Drama, English; English Language and Literature.**)

* **rhetoric**   art of speaking or writing effectively

* **epistle**   formal letter

**Josquin des Prez**

ca. 1450–1521
**French composer**

* **secular**   nonreligious; connected with everyday life

Josquin des Prez was one of the greatest composers of the Renaissance. He created many religious and secular* pieces and developed a new style that influenced composers for a century after his death. Josquin's unique musical style led the German religious reformer Martin LUTHER to pronounce him "the master of the notes."

Josquin was born in northern France, where he received training as a choirboy. Later, he had an active musical career in France and Italy, performing and writing music for church officials and royalty, including the French king Louis XII. Over the course of his career, Josquin wrote 18 masses, 70 secular pieces, and 50 motets (sacred musical works for several voices without instruments). Many of Josquin's motets feature lyrics in honor of the Virgin Mary. Others are musical settings for the Bible's psalms.

Josquin also gained recognition for his original musical style. Earlier composers of vocal music had emphasized musical structure while downplaying the lyrics. Josquin crafted melody lines that brought out the meaning of the words. He also showed great talent for expressing emotion through music. His love song "A Thousand Regrets" weaves together several voice parts to create a powerful sense of sorrow. (*See also* **Music; Music, Vocal.**)

## Julius II

### ca. 1445–1513
### Pope

* **papacy**    office and authority of the pope

* **patron**    supporter or financial sponsor of an artist or writer

* **Papal States**    lands in central Italy under the authority of the pope

* **Holy Roman Empire**    political body in central Europe composed of several states; existed until 1806

* **fresco**    mural painted on a plaster wal

Pope Julius II, known as the warrior pope, involved himself in several wars in defense of the church and its land. Although his military actions damaged the holy reputation of the papacy*, he successfully protected its interests. In addition, Julius was one of the leading patrons* of the arts in the Renaissance.

Julius was born Giuliano della Rovere in Albissola, a town in northwestern Italy. He owed his career to a wealthy uncle who financed his education. In 1471 this uncle became Pope Sixtus IV, and shortly after that Giuliano became a cardinal. This new position led him to France and other countries to serve as an official representative of the pope.

In 1474 Giuliano went to war-torn Umbria, part of the Papal States*, to end the fighting there. In Umbria he gained a taste for battle, which suited his energy and strength. He remained in Rome until his enemy ALEXANDER VI became pope. Feeling unsafe, Giuliano went to France and later to northwestern Italy, where he lived until Alexander's death.

In 1503 Giuliano returned to Rome and was elected pope. His strong character and his reputation as a defender of the church helped him win the position. As Julius II he struggled to recover some lands that Venice had taken in the Romagna, a part of the Papal States. In order to defeat the Venetians, Julius joined the League of Cambrai in 1509. This alliance combined the forces of the French king Louis XII, Spain's FERDINAND OF ARAGON, and the emperor-elect of the Holy Roman Empire*, MAXIMILIAN I. The group effectively pressured the Venetians into returning the land. However, Julius continued his battle to protect papal interests. Wanting to ensure Italy's safety from the mounting French threat, he turned against his former ally and joined the anti-French Holy League. The League, which consisted of leaders from Spain, England, and other countries, fought to drive French troops from Italy. Julius was finally victorious in 1512.

In addition to his military actions, Julius II was one of the most important artistic patrons of the Renaissance. He commissioned one of the most famous works of the Renaissance, the Sistine Chapel ceiling, painted by MICHELANGELO BUONARROTI. Julius also employed RAPHAEL to paint several frescoes*, including the famous *School of Athens* for his Vatican apartment. Raphael's portrait of Julius influenced the way artists portrayed popes for centuries. (*See also* **Popes and Papacy.**)

# Index

*Note: Volume numbers precede each page number, separated by a colon. Page numbers in boldface type refer to main discussions of a topic.*